D0915370

 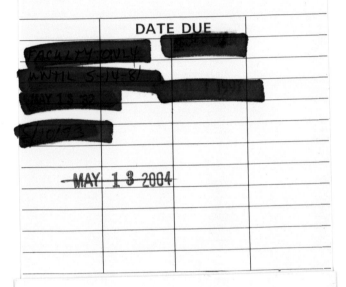

Cognitive Science Series, 3

Cognitive Science Series

1. Frank C. Keil, *Semantic and Conceptual Development: An Ontological Perspective*
2. Edwin Hutchins, *Culture and Inference: A Trobriand Case Study*
3. William E. Cooper and Jeanne Paccia-Cooper, *Syntax and Speech*

Syntax and Speech

William E. Cooper
Jeanne Paccia-Cooper

Harvard University Press
Cambridge, Massachusetts
London, England
1980

Library of Congress Cataloging in Publication Data

Cooper, William E.
　Syntax and speech.

　(Cognitive science series; 3)
　Bibliography: p.
　Includes index.
　1. Psycholinguistics. 2. Grammar, Comparative and
general—Syntax. 3. Speech—Physiological aspects.
I. Paccia-Cooper, Jeanne, 1955–　joint author.
II. Title. III. Series.
P37.C63　　　401'.9　　　　　80-16614
ISBN 0-674-86075-6

To our parents
William and Mildred
Joseph and Marguerite

Preface

Like many other human behaviors, speech production is so commonplace an activity that we seldom notice that it involves a very elaborate system of mental operations, still largely unexplored. Intuition tells us that a speaker first formulates an idea or set of ideas and then somehow translates these into a linguistic code. The code itself contains a number of identifiable components, bearing the labels *semantic, syntactic, lexical,* and *phonological.* The semantic component deals with the specification of meaning; the syntactic, with the structure of clauses and phrases; the lexical, with the choice of individual words; and the phonological, with the selection of a sequence of speech sounds, executed ultimately as part of a motor program. One would like to know how linguistic units are represented within each component and also how this information is processed in real time. We shall endeavor to show that the effort is worthwhile despite the complexity of the task, both for what can be learned about the nature of mental activity and for the way in which this knowledge can be applied to problems of practical interest.

The starting point for this book is the assumption that speakers typically formulate some type of syntactic representation of clause and phrase units at a stage of processing carried out *before* the stage at which they formulate a phonological representation. This direction of information flow—from syntactic to phonological—suggests that the form of the speaker's acoustic output may be influenced by the nature of the syntactic code. If so, it should be possible to infer aspects of the syntactic code, involved in ongoing speech activity, by measuring observable properties of the speech wave.

Throughout this book we shall be concerned with three major factors in speech production—the mental representation of syntactic structures, the processing operations performed on these structures, and acoustic attributes of the speech wave that seem to be influenced by such structures and processes. Accordingly, our research effort draws on three academic disciplines: linguistics, because it provides clues about the kinds of syntactic units that are likely to be mentally represented during speech production; psychology, because it is aimed at the discovery of these mental representations and the processing operations that manipulate them; and communications engineering, because it provides the tools for measuring the speaker's acoustic output in a highly precise and efficient manner. In large part, the disciplines of linguistics and communications engineering may be regarded as the "givens" of this study, while psychology represents the unknown that we are trying to unveil. Although this study is primarily oriented toward psychological issues, certain findings may be of more interest to linguists and engineers. In particular, chapter 3 is recommended for engineers, chapters 4–5 for linguists, and chapter 7 for both groups.

Concepts from each discipline are introduced as needed in the text, so that most of the discussion can be understood by readers with little specialized background. For instructors who might wish to use the book as supplementary material in courses, chapters 1, 2, 6, 7, and 8 are recommended.

The book represents the culmination of a five-year period of theory and experimentation on the relation between syntax and speech coding. The project was launched in 1975, when William Cooper conducted research as part of a doctoral dissertation in the Department of Psychology at the Massachusetts Institute of Technology. Professor Merrill Garrett, Dr. Dennis Klatt, and Dr. A. W. F. Huggins played a key role in the early phase of the study. Garrett offered advice on syntax, Klatt discussed phonetics, and Huggins provided the AUDITS computer program for acoustic analysis, to be described in chapter 1. The project also benefited from suggestions made by Professors Noam Chomsky, Jerry Fodor, Richard Held, John Robert Ross, and Kenneth Stevens. Dumont Billings helped by running some of the early experiments.

The dissertation provided a number of useful pointers but very little in the way of solid answers. Jeanne Paccia-Cooper joined the enterprise during the summer of 1976, and during the next four years we designed and conducted most of the experiments and formal analyses reported in this book. Many people helped us at various stages, including Merle Blumer, Kittredge Cary, Martha

Danly, Carmen Egido, Trude Huber, Steven Lapointe, Julie Meister, D. Keith North, John Sorensen, and Kazuhiko Yorifuji.

Parts of this book have been adapted from the following publications: W. E. Cooper, "Syntactic Control of Timing in Speech Production: A Study of Complement Clauses" (*Journal of Phonetics* 4:151–171, 1976; copyright by Academic Press Ltd.); W. E. Cooper, "Syntactic-to-Phonetic Coding" (in B. Butterworth, ed., *Language Production*, vol. 1, *Speech and Talk*, New York: Academic Press, 1980); W. E. Cooper, C. Egido, and J. M. Paccia, "Grammatical Control of a Phonological Rule: Palatalization" (*Journal of Experimental Psychology: Human Perception and Performance* 4:264–272; copyright 1978 by the American Psychological Association; reprinted by permission); W. E. Cooper, S. G. Lapointe, and J. M. Paccia, "Syntactic Blocking of Phonological Rules in Speech Production" (*Journal of the Acoustical Society of America* 61:1314–20, 1977); W. E. Cooper, J. M. Paccia, and S. G. Lapointe, "Hierarchical Coding in Speech Timing" (*Cognitive Psychology* 10:154–177, 1978); C. Egido and W. E. Cooper, "Blocking of Alveolar Flapping in Speech Production: The Role of Syntactic Boundaries and Deletion Sites" (*Journal of Phonetics*, in press; copyright by Academic Press Ltd.); J. M. Sorensen, W. E. Cooper, and J. M. Paccia, "Speech Timing of Grammatical Categories" (*Cognition* 6:135–153, 1978). We thank the publishers and coauthors Carmen Egido, Steven G. Lapointe, and John M. Sorensen for permission to make use of this material.

Aspects of this study have been presented in courses given at M.I.T. during 1977 and 1978 and at Harvard University during 1979 and 1980. Thanks go to Professors Jonathan Allen, George N. Clements, François Grosjean, and students who participated in these courses. At Harvard, the comments of Robin Barr, Cheryl Clark, Brian Doherty, Susan Ehrlich, James Gregory, Elanah Kutik, Steven Pinker, Carlos Soares, and Rachelle Waksler were particularly helpful. Finally, we thank Drs. Ronald Cole and Victor Zue for valuable discussions of phonological rules, as well as Eric Wanner of Harvard University Press and Professor Merrill Garrett of M.I.T. for comments and suggestions on the manuscript.

This work was generously supported by the National Institutes of Health in the form of grants NS-13028 and NS-15059 and a postdoctoral fellowship.

Cambridge, Massachusetts

Contents

1. Introduction   1
2. Hierarchical Coding of
   Major Phrases   24
3. Phrase Structures and
   Grammatical Categories   53
4. Deletion Rules   69
5. Movement Rules   90
6. Blocking of Phonological Rules   128
7. Theory and Further Experimentation   161
8. Ramifications   210
   Notes   241
   References   251
   Index   267

1 | Introduction

BECAUSE of its pervasive role in human activity, speech occupies a favored position among topics typically studied in cognitive psychology. Yet we know very little about the mental operations that accompany speaking, and this lack of understanding is especially acute for normal conversation. Following in the tradition of the physical sciences, the study of speech processing was dominated in its early stages by an atomistic strategy of research, in which an understanding of very small units of speech was pursued before dealing with larger units (for example, Lehiste, 1967). These small units consist of syllables as well as individual consonant and vowel phonemes. The outcome of such research has greatly improved our understanding of the building blocks of speech, and much work still remains to be done within this framework. However, increasing emphasis is being placed on larger units, including phrases, sentences, and entire discourses.

Research on these larger domains can sometimes make use of methods and findings that have emerged from studying smaller ones. For example, this study draws on methods and results of acoustic analyses that were originally employed in the investigation of inherent properties of individual syllables and phonemes. Not surprisingly, however, many new challenges present themselves for which previous atomistic work cannot serve as a guide. As a research environment, this situation is ideal. On one hand, there is satisfaction in the ability to utilize old methods and findings in designing new studies, giving one the feeling that science is indeed cumulative. On the other hand, there is considerable opportunity for addressing novel issues.

Information Flow in Speech Production

We will refer to the entire set of operations by which a speaker transforms ideas into an acoustic output as *speech coding*. An act of speech coding is enormously complex, and we cannot hope to cover it all here. Let us focus primarily on aspects of the speaker's syntactic representation of an utterance and the way in which this representation influences properties of the speech wave. As a way of introducing this topic, it is helpful to consider a possible model of information flow during speech production, shown in figure 1.1. As noted below, some characteristics of this model play a central role in our research endeavor; a few features are orthogonal to the study, but are included here nonetheless because of their intuitive appeal and the prospect of stimulating further work. Although far from being a detailed schematization of the speech coding process, this model will suffice to introduce the key concepts involved in the line of research.

According to the model, information is processed at a number of different levels when a speaker plans and executes a meaningful utterance. These processing operations are so automatic that,

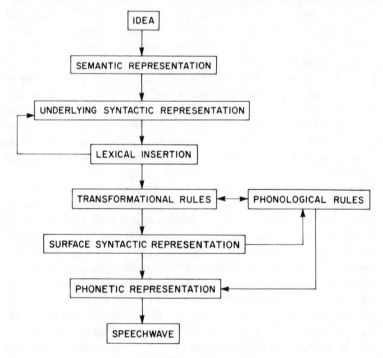

Figure 1.1　*Possible model of information flow during speech production. This model will be reevaluated in chapter 7.*

in everyday conversation, we are no more aware of most of them than of the component operations that comprise such activities as our heartbeat or our eye movements.

At the first assumed stage of coding, the speaker generates an idea, which is then translated into linguistic form as a semantic representation.[1] At the next level, the speaker formulates a partial grammatical representation of the utterance. This representation may include a decision about whether the mode of the utterance is declarative, imperative, or interrogative, as well as some decisions about the identity and linear ordering of some high-level phrase structure nodes.

The speaker is then believed to choose one or more major lexical items, typically including the head noun of the subject noun phrase. Following this selection, the grammatical representation is presumably further elaborated to include modifiers of the subject. In turn, lexical items are chosen to represent these newly elaborated categories, and the grammar-lexical processing recycles until a full terminal string is computed. The computation of the grammatical structure itself is believed to proceed from the top down, and, within each hierarchical level, from left to right.[2]

Aside from the method of lexical insertion, the system of grammatical coding postulated here for speech production is analogous to the system of phrase structure rules in a generative grammar (Chomsky, 1957; Jackendoff, 1977). The phrase structure rules derived by linguists are written in the form "$X \rightarrow Y$" (rewrite constituent X as constituent(s) Y) and are applied in a fixed order. For example, the structural representation of the simple sentence "Harry rode the new pony" involves the application of the rewrite rule in (1) below, according to the top-down, left-to-right order specified in (2).

(1)

    (i) $S \rightarrow NP + VP$
    (ii) $NP \rightarrow N$
    (iii) $VP \rightarrow V + NP$
    (iv) $NP \rightarrow$ determiner (DET) + ADJ + N

(2)

    (i)   S
    (ii) NP + VP
    (iii) N + VP
    (iv) N + V + NP
    (v) N + V + DET + ADJ + N

The derived phrase structure can be schematized by the tree diagram in figure 1.2.

Referring back to the model of speech production, when a fully elaborated underlying structure has been formulated, it is assumed that the structure may undergo transformations that move, add, or delete constituents, analogous to transformational rules in a generative grammar (see, for example, Chomsky, 1965; Akmajian and Heny, 1975). The existence of this level in actual speech coding is highly controversial at present, chiefly because there is little empirical evidence that can be brought to bear on this issue (for a review, see Fodor, Bever, and Garrett, 1974, chap. 7). We shall assume a transformational framework here for purposes of exposition. In chapters 4 and 5, this assumption will be investigated empirically.

The output of the transformational level comprises the surface structure. The question of the precise form of surface structure, which remains controversial in both linguistic and psycholinguistic research, will be considered throughout this book.

Phonological rules of stress assignment may apply to the output of the surface structure and possibly earlier, during the transformational stage (Bresnan, 1971). Phonetic segments are selected

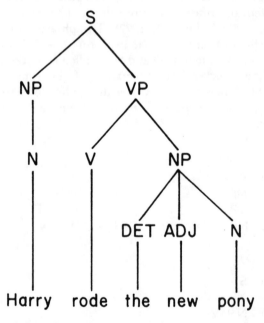

Figure 1.2 *Structural representation of the sentence "Harry rode the new pony" according to Chomsky's phrase structure rule, S → NP + VP.*

based on the output of the surface structure. Finally, the phonetic representation is transferred to a motor program that generates the articulatory configurations of speech, yielding an acoustic output. The acoustic signal itself includes quasi-continuous variations in time, frequency, and amplitude. For our purposes, the durations of speech segments and pauses are of chief concern in the time domain, since these durations seem to be influenced by the speaker's syntactic representations. Another feature of the speech output that bears this influence involves the voice fundamental frequency (F_0), corresponding to the rate of the speaker's vocal fold vibrations and closely related to the perceived attribute of voice pitch. Variations in speech amplitude also seem to be influenced by syntactic coding, and, together with variations in duration and fundamental frequency, are correlated with differences in stress (see Lehiste, 1970, for a review). In this book, however, we shall focus primarily on the timing of speech segments and pauses.

The choice of duration as a dependent variable, as opposed to, say, voice fundamental frequency—both seem to be heavily influenced by syntactic structures—was based on the fact that duration is a simpler variable to measure from the acoustic stream of speech. Fundamental frequency contours contain information varying in both time and frequency, whereas duration is unidimensional. By studying timing first, we believed that we would be in a better position later to tackle the more complex variable of fundamental frequency, and this strategy has proven helpful (Sorensen and Cooper, 1979; Cooper and Sorensen, 1980).

Let us return now to consider some very general aspects of the information flow model in figure 1.1. According to this model, speech output should not begin until all higher-level computations have been completed. In order to render the model applicable to typical spontaneous speech, however, it is necessary to allow for a large measure of flexibility in terms of the major unit of linguistic information that is selected for initial processing. As implied thus far, this major unit often consists of an entire sentence or a main clause, but intuition and evidence from false starts in spontaneous speech suggest that speakers sometimes begin articulating a smaller unit before the processing of a superordinate unit has been completed. In order to incorporate this feature into the present model, it is necessary to allow for flexibility in the size of the speaker's choice of a processing unit (for related discussion, see McNeill, 1979).

For present purposes, the important feature of the model in figure 1.1 is the direction of information flow between the speaker's syntactic and phonetic representations. Since, as assumed here, the speaker formulates at least a partial syntactic representation prior to a phonetic representation, then it follows that the precise nature of the syntactic code can influence the phonetic form, and hence the acoustic output, of the utterance. If this line of reasoning is correct, it should be possible to utilize measurable acoustic properties of speech to infer aspects of the speaker's syntactic representation. We attempt here to test this possibility using a wide range of sentence contexts.

Previous work on speech timing has shown that the durations of speech segments and pauses are influenced by a number of factors (for reviews, see Lehiste, 1970; Klatt, 1976). In particular, the timing of *segments* is influenced by speaking rate, by the phonetic structure of the segment, and by conditioning effects of neighboring segments. Additionally, the timing of speech segments is influenced by stress rhythms (for example, Kozhevnikov and Chistovich, 1965; Martin, 1972; Allen, 1973; Ohala, 1975; Fowler, 1977).

The duration and location of *pauses* also depend on a variety of factors. For example, pauses may reflect word-finding difficulty, general hesitation, or drastic changes in the planning of the semantic content of an utterance (cf. Boomer, 1965; Goldman-Eisler, 1968; Martin, 1971). Pausing is also influenced by such factors as overall speaking rate and length of the constituent (Bierwisch, 1966; Grosjean, Grosjean, and Lane. 1979).

In addition to these extragrammatical factors, empirical work has confirmed that temporal phenomena in speech may be syntactically determined. In the case of pausing, it is important to distinguish between pauses that are typically due to word-finding difficulties and those that are syntactically determined. The former type of pause occurs most frequently just prior to major content words (for example, MacClay and Osgood, 1959), whereas the latter occurs most frequently at major syntactic boundaries (for example, Boomer and Laver, 1968). Here, we will focus on syntactic influences on speech timing, with less interest in extragrammatical factors until chapter 7. Concern with the latter in chapters 2–6 will chiefly involve attempts to control any possible influences they might have in the experimental studies.

Syntactic Influences on Temporal Properties of Speech

Before delving into experimentation, it is useful to consider some syntactic influences on speech timing that can be ascertained by intuitive listening. Many of our experiments were stimulated by such observations. Perhaps the most readily perceptible speech timing effects occur at major constituent boundaries. For example, the duration of the verb "leaves" is typically lengthened when it occurs in clause-final position, as in (3b) below. In addition, we can easily observe that "leaves" may be optionally followed by a pause when this verb occurs at the boundary between two major syntactic constituents, as in (3b), but not when it occurs within a constituent, as in (3a) (disregarding hesitation pauses that reflect word-finding difficulty).

(3)   (a)   When John leaves Kathy, we'll be upset.
      (b)   When John leaves, Kathy will be upset.

Empirical support for these intuitions exists regarding both segmental lengthening (Martin, 1970; Lindblom and Rapp, 1973; Klatt, 1975; Kloker, 1975; Cooper, 1976a) and pausing (Martin, 1967, 1970; Goldman-Eisler, 1968, 1973; Grosjean and Deschamps, 1975).

While both segmental lengthening and pausing can be observed in the above sentences, pausing is typically the more perceptible of the two (cf. Martin, 1970), and so we shall restrict the remainder of this discussion to cases of intuitive observations of pausing. It should be emphasized at the outset, however, that these observations must be supplanted by acoustic measurements, a task undertaken in subsequent chapters.

We shall rely primarily on acoustic measurements because such data provide a more direct reflection of the speaker's internal code than do perceptual judgments, not because individual acoustic measurements are in any way less idiosyncratic. Perceptual judgments of pausing are determined by a complex interaction between acoustic factors and the listener's linguistic knowledge and expectations. As such, these judgments provide an excellent source of evidence bearing on theories of speech perception (see chapter 8). However, since perceptual judgments reflect speech production quite indirectly, they are not as valuable as acoustic measurements in testing hypotheses about the speaker's code, our main topic.

In previous work, Lieberman (1963) showed that linguists' perception of juncture is influenced by independent structural considerations, casting circularity on an earlier proposal by Trager and Smith (1951) that constituent structure could be determined by perceptual judgments of juncture in speech. Lieberman found, in effect, that linguists tend to "hear" junctures at major constituent boundaries even when no acoustic pause is present. In addition, Martin (1970) found that subjective listening also yields perceived pauses in cases where segmental lengthening is present in the acoustic stream without pausing. The studies of Lieberman and Martin converge to indicate that there is no simple correspondence between the occurrence of an acoustic pause and the perception of pausing.

Nonetheless, simple observations about perception of pausing do provide preliminary clues about the form of the speaker's syntactic code, and such observations also serve to illustrate some of the issues that will occupy the focus of experimentation and acoustic measurements in subsequent chapters.

A well-known example involves the location of pauses in sentences such as (4). Although this particular kind of sentence seldom occurs in everyday conversation, it is helpful in providing information about the cognitive capabilities of the speaker.

(4)   This is the cat that caught the rat that stole the cheese.

In general, it has been assumed that syntactic pauses occur at the ends of major constituents. Chomsky (1965, p. 13) pointed out, however, that the locations of pauses in (4) occur typically after "cat" and "rat," and that these locations do not correspond to the ends of major constituents. The phrase structure for (4), illustrated by the bracketing in (4'), would predict, according to the constituent-final assumption, that no pauses should occur until after the sentence-final word, "cheese."

(4') $[_S$ this is$[_{NP}$ the cat$[_S$ that caught$[_{NP}$ the rat$[_S$ that stole the cheese$]_S]_{NP}]_S]_{NP}]_S$

Either the assumption regarding constituent-final pausing is incorrect, or the grammatical coding of (4) differs from (4') at the stage of the speaker's processing at which pauses are programmed. The latter alternative has been advocated by Lieberman (1967), Chomsky and Halle (1968), and Langendoen (1976), who suggest that a readjustment rule applies to (4') to derive (4''), such that the embedded clauses become sister-adjoined to the main clause, as shown in figure 1.3.

(4'') $[[_S$ this is $[_{NP}$ the cat$]_{NP}]_S[_S$ that caught$[_{NP}$ the rat$]_{NP}]_S[_S$ that stole the cheese$]_S]_S$

It will be helpful at this point to examine closely the tree diagrams in figure 1.3 and their correspondence with the bracketed versions of (4') and (4'') shown in the text. The readjustment rule serves to

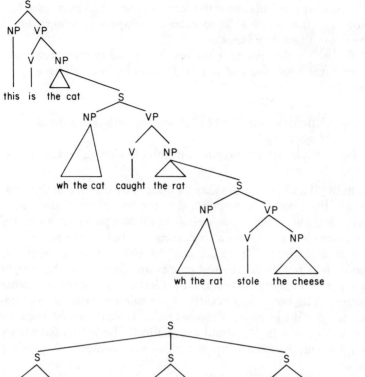

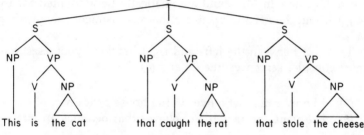

Figure 1.3 *Underlying (top) and readjusted (bottom) tree structures for sentence (4).*

"flatten" the tree structure, so that, instead of containing multiple right-branching clauses, the sentence contains multiple conjoined clauses of equal hierarchical status. Given this structure, pauses are inserted appropriately after "cat" and "rat."

This example illustrates a common problem confronting us in wishing to make use of temporal phenomena in arriving at the form of a speaker's grammatical code. First, a general assumption is made—in this case, that syntactic pauses occur at the ends of major constituents. Then, we find an apparent exception—(4), which can be accounted for either by altering the presumed structure of the exception or by abandoning the general assumption. In this particular case the former course has been adopted. However, it is worthwhile to examine where a consideration of the latter alternative leads.

To review the evidence on which the assumption regarding constituent-final pausing is based, consider the following sentences:

(5) Although John went to the movies with Sue, I decided not to go along.

(6) I am leaving tomorrow, but John is leaving Friday.

In both (5) and (6), pauses may be optionally inserted at the location of the comma, corresponding to the end of the clause. However, in these sentences, as well as in (3), the pause location may alternatively be specified as occurring just before the *beginning* of the second clause. Therefore, on the basis of these sentences alone, it is not clear whether pauses are determined by a right bracket terminating one clause, by a left bracket starting another clause, or by both. Significantly, if the rule for pausing were determined at the *beginning* of clauses rather than at the end, then the pause locations in (4) would automatically be accounted for by (4'), without the need to postulate the readjustment rule yielding (4'').

To select between the left- and right-bracket hypotheses, one must consider sentences like (7) and (8).

(7) I know a man who lives in the house next door.

(8) Everyone in the garden believes that petunias are pretty.

In these sentences the second clause is structurally embedded within the main clause, so that the beginning of the embedded clause does not coincide with the end of the main clause. In such cases, the end of the main clause occurs at the end of the entire sentence string. In (7) an embedded relative clause begins with the relative pronoun "who," and in (8) an embedded complement clause starts with the complementizer "that." In both cases, no pause typically occurs at the beginning of the embedded clause, suggesting that syntactic pausing is in fact primarily determined by the endings of clauses rather than by their beginnings. If this is so, then the approach taken by Langendoen (1976) and others is well founded.

But problems remain, and their resolution leads to a more general rule of pausing. If the principle of constituent-final pausing is to be retained, we must provide an account for pausing in nonrestrictive relative clauses, as in (9).

(9) John, who is believed to be sick, was seen outdoors yesterday.

In this sentence, pauses typically accompany both the beginning and the end of the relative clause. The pause at the end of the relative clause can be accounted for by constituent-final pausing; however, a problem arises in accounting for the additional pause that occurs at the *beginning* of the nonrestrictive relative. This problem extends to parenthetical expressions, as in (10), where a pause may occur just prior to the beginning of the parenthetical.

(10) (a) John, I think, is sick.
      (b) John, by the way, should not leave Chicago before dawn.
      (c) John should, I guess, take out the garbage.

An account of the pauses in (9) and (10) may be based on the notion that nonrestrictive relatives and parentheticals are conjoined with the main clause (for example, Thompson, 1968). Given this assumption, the pauses for (9) and (10), as well as the data in (4)–(8), can be accounted for by a single principle, given in (11).

(11) *Pause Rule for Conjoined Clauses.* Insert pauses at the beginning and end of a clause that is immediately dominated by the highest S node in the phrase structure.

With (11), all the pause data reviewed thus far can be accounted for, assuming the structure (4″) for (4), including the pauses that occur at the beginning and end of each string. Further support for a rule like (11) has been provided by Downing (1970, 1973) and Emonds (1976).[3]

Principle (11) also applies to pausing that accompanies sentences in which the canonical word order has been violated by root transformations—transformations that move a constituent and attach it to the highest S node in the tree (Emonds, 1976). An example of a sentence in which a root transformation (in this case, Left Dislocation) has moved a constituent to the front appears in (12b).

(12) (a) The owner of the park scolded the children.
      (b) The owner of the park, she scolded the children.

An experiment to be presented in chapter 5 shows that speakers typically pause at the end of the preposed constituent, just after "park" in (12b).[4] If it is assumed, with Emonds (1976), that the preposed constituents are attached to the highest S node in the tree, and furthermore that the rule for pausing applies after the preposing transformation, then the pausing in (12b) can be accounted for as a case of constituent-initial pausing under (11). According to this view, the pause is determined not at the end of the preposed constituent, but at the *beginning* of the main clause. In a converse manner, (11) (or a similar rule such as Downing's) provides an account of pausing before a constituent that has been moved to the end of a string by a root transformation such as Right Dislocation (Ross, 1967), as in (13).

(13)   I like it, this hammer.

Any other attempt to provide a unified account for pausing in the variety of cases reviewed thus far becomes very unwieldy. The pause rule in (11) thus represents an improvement over the constituent-final rule assumed previously.

But the story for pausing is still not complete. Consider another class of syntactic pause, illustrated in (14).

(14)   The tall, handsome man left without saying a word.

Here a pause may be inserted between two adjectives that both modify the head noun, "man." Clearly, this pause cannot be handled by (11). It is not at the boundary between conjoined clauses nor at the boundary of any major grammatical constituent.

Now note that pausing is eliminated between the two adjectives if they are separated by a conjunction, as in (15).

(15)   The tall and handsome man left without saying a word.

Since the presence of a conjunction typically eliminates the pause, it may be speculated that the conjunction and pause each serve the same purpose—to separate the two conjoined constituents in the processing of both the speaker and listener. The pause in (14) may be viewed as a *replacement* for the missing conjunction. The pauses described for sentences (3)–(10) and (12)–(13), however, cannot be accounted for in this manner, so (14) demonstrates a different kind of syntactic pause from that subsumed under (11).

Now consider sentence (16), in which the verb of the second

clause has been deleted under identity with the first verb by Gapping (Ross, 1970; Jackendoff, 1971; Stillings, 1975).

(16) John ate the rice, and Harry, the beans.

The pause optionally inserted after "Harry" in (16) may be viewed like the pause in (14). Here, in (16), the pause in some sense replaces the deleted verb. We may thus propose that, in addition to (11), a second general rule of syntactic pausing exists to account for examples like (14) and (16). This additional rule permits pausing as a replacement for a deleted constituent.

This rule covering pauses at deletion sites may be too general, since pauses do not typically occur just before the parenthetical words in (17)–(19) when these are deleted.

(17) I know the man (that) Harry shot.
(18) Bob finished his homework and (he) went outside.
(19) Bob (finished work) and Harry finished work.

It appears, rather, that the rule for pausing which accounts for (14) and (16) is restricted to deletions that do not involve daughters of S (daughters of S include categories like complementizer, noun phrase, and verb phrase immediately dominated by S). An alternative formulation would retain an unrestricted pause rule for all deletion sites, but would eliminate (17)–(19) on the basis that these sentences have virtually identical underlying and surface structures and do not contain true deletions. At present, this possibility has some independent motivation for (18) and (19) (Dougherty, 1970; Hudson, 1976).

Finally, consider (20), in which the parenthetical words may undergo deletion.

(20) John cooked (the beans) and Harry ate the beans.

It is debatable whether a true deletion occurs here (Ross, 1967; Koutsoudas, 1971; Hudson, 1976). Chomsky (1957) originally noted that sentences like (20) are typically accompanied by contrastive stress on the two verbs, as well as by a pause at the deletion site. The optional pause here can be handled either by the rule for pausing at deletions noted above, or by the pause rule for conjoined clauses in (11).

A rule for pausing at deletion sites implies the existence of a coding level analogous to transformations, and hence implies that there exists a distinction between levels of underlying and surface structure (see figure 1.1). In effect, by accounting for pauses in terms of the notion of *deletion*, we are naturally led to postulate the existence of a level of underlying structure from which deletion could have occurred. This line of reasoning thus yields a claim about the existence of more than a single level of coding in speech, although it is by no means clear that both of the levels indicated here are purely syntactic. We shall consider this issue at length in chapter 4.

This detailed look at pausing has shown how informal observations can provide preliminary information about the form of the speaker's syntactic code. In subsequent chapters, we shall present experimental studies of acoustically defined pausing as well as segmental lengthening to provide a more substantial basis for inferring structural properties of this code. As suggested by this discussion of informal pausing, however, the route to inference making is typically fraught with difficulties even when the data themselves are transparent.

In addition to exploring the structures represented in the speaker's syntactic code, we would like to know something about the manner in which these structures are processed in real time. Since segment and pause durations are inherent properties of the speech wave, they may provide direct information about on-line speech activity.

To this end, in chapter 7 we examine the psychological underpinnings of pausing and segmental lengthening, asking such questions as whether either or both of these phenomena are attributed to the speaker's planning of upcoming material and/or to the speaker's relaxation upon the completion of processing a major constituent.

Syntactic Boundaries and the Application of Cross-Word Phonetic Rules

In addition to segmental lengthening and pausing, syntactic boundaries appear to influence speech in another way, by regulating the application of phonetic rules that normally operate across word boundaries. We assume that, at some processing level, a speaker applies phonetic rules over a specified syntactic domain, such that phonetic information lying outside this domain cannot be taken into consideration in the application of the rules. Thus, for a given syntactic domain X including phonetic segments $s_1, s_2, \ldots, s_{nx}$, phonetic rules applied to any segment s_1 can utilize information contained only in segments (typically adjacent to s_1)

contained within X. By determining which cross-word phonetic rules apply across a range of different syntactic boundaries, it is possible to obtain information about the scope of syntactic domains that constrain speech coding. We shall deal extensively with this notion in chapter 6.

The concept of syntactic blocking has already been studied from a linguistic standpoint (for example, King, 1970; Zwicky, 1970; Baker, 1971; Baker and Brame, 1972; Selkirk, 1974). Selkirk (1974), for example, has proposed that French liaison contexts are sensitive to syntactic categories in a manner that provides support for the $\bar{X}$ theory of categories (Chomsky, 1970; Jackendoff, 1974). In French, a word-final obstruent is typically deleted in the environment of a following consonant, as in "dans la salle," in which the /s/ of "dans" is deleted. Liaison contexts are those contexts in which the deletion rule fails to operate, as in "dans une salle," where the /s/ of "dans" is pronounced. If liaison contexts were determined on a purely phonological basis, one would expect liaison to occur *whenever* a word-final obstruent is followed by a vowel. Yet Selkirk observed that liaison is blocked in the environment of all but the weakest of syntactic boundaries. Selkirk noted that liaison contexts in elevated speech are extended somewhat, operating at boundaries between an inflected member of grammatical category X and its complement, both of which are dominated by $\bar{X}$ (Chomsky, 1970); Rotenberg (1975), however, questioned the validity of the elevated style assumed by Selkirk. It is possible that the blocking of liaison is determined more by stress pattern than by syntactic boundaries per se. As we shall see at various points throughout this study, the question of whether particular effects in speech are attributed to syntax or stress is often difficult to resolve.

Problematic Distinctions

Up to this point we have mentioned some distinctions that may seem clear-cut upon first glance but that are in fact blurred under certain circumstances. Here we discuss the difficulties associated with some of these distinctions as they relate to the present study.

STRUCTURE VERSUS PROCESS

Individual findings from the acoustic output permit inferences about the workings of the speaker's internal code, but in many cases it is unclear whether results should be assigned to the components of the code that involve structural representation or to the processing operations that manipulate such structures. In these cases, our choice of assignment is guided largely by intuition and by whatever previous findings can be mustered to bear on the issue at hand.

This difficulty in distinguishing between structure and process is by no means foreign to researchers in cognitive psychology (for example, Anderson, 1978). In virtually any detailed study of an unknown cognitive system, one must make assumptions about processing operations to make inferences about structural representations, and vice versa, knowing full well that these assumptions may turn out to be wrong in some cases.

Syntax versus Semantics

The distinction between syntax and semantics has been the focus of much controversy in theoretical linguistics (for example, McCawley, 1968; Jackendoff, 1972), and this difficulty leads to problems of assigning psychological findings to one or the other type of mental representation. The problem of distinguishing syntax from semantics was heightened in linguistics when generative semanticists (for example, Lakoff, 1965; McCawley, 1968; Ross, 1969) proposed increasingly more abstract underlying syntactic structures for sentences, so that the role of semantic interpretation was minimized. For example, Ross (1969) proposed that auxiliary verbs in surface structure were derived from main verbs that take sentential complements in underlying structure. According to this treatment, the close relationship between (a) and (b) in (21) below, for example, would be captured by the similarities of their deep structures rather than by rules of semantic interpretation.

(21) (a) Smoking may be hazardous to your health.
      (b) It is possible that smoking is hazardous to your health.

Chomsky (1970, 1976) and others maintained, however, that constructions bearing identical underlying structures in a generative semantics schema actually exhibit syntactic differences that can best be captured at the level of underlying syntactic structure (for a review, see J. D. Fodor, 1977). In the present study, we generally adopt the linguistic framework of interpretative semantics proposed by Chomsky, Jackendoff, and others, but we have also tried to choose structures for study that typically engage issues lying squarely within the realm of syntax rather than near the borders of the syntax-semantics dispute. It is possible, however, that certain of the syntactic interpretations that will be assigned to the results may ultimately be reworked in semantic terms.

UNDERLYING VERSUS SURFACE STRUCTURE

The related distinction between underlying and surface structure is marked by controversy in theoretical linguistics; we simply have too little information on which to anchor a definition of one or the other syntactic component. As Chomsky (1970) has observed, simplification of one component inevitably leads to complications of the other, and linguists have yet to arrive at a metatheoretical formula to help them decide when an equitable trading relationship has been proposed.

The distinction between underlying and surface structures becomes problematic in sentences like (22a) below, for example. Here the surface structure contains two conjoined direct object NPs; the question arises whether these NPs are also simply conjoined in underlying structure or whether they are derived from two separate clauses, as in (22b) below (for discussion, see Dougherty, 1970). According to this latter view, the surface structure in (22a) would then be derived via a deletion transformation that deletes the subject and verb of the second underlying clause under identity.

(22) (a) John likes baseball and basketball.
     (b) John likes baseball and John likes basketball.

In this study we favor the view that the underlying and surface structures for (22a) are equivalent, simplifying the transformational component of the grammar. We attempt to neutralize this distinction in many instances by examining structures whose underlying and surface representations are isomorphic in relevant respects. In other tests we examine the distinction directly, as in chapters 4 and 5.

The terms *underlying* and *surface* may mislead some readers into thinking that issues surrounding the precise form of underlying structure are altogether more profound than issues surrounding the precise form of surface structure. In fact, the general and detailed characteristics of both types of structure are quite important and highly controversial, from the standpoints of both linguistic theory and psycholinguistics (see Chomsky, 1970; Fodor, Bever, and Garrett, 1974; Jackendoff, 1977). We shall endeavor to show here that both underlying and surface types of representation are of major interest in formulating hypotheses about the speaker's mental code and in interpreting the results of experimental studies on this topic.

EXPLANATION VERSUS DESCRIPTION

Given a set of experimental findings, we need to know what distinguishes a mere description of these findings from a true explanation. Explanation, for our purposes, involves an understanding of the acoustic data in terms of the speaker's mental structures and processes. Ideally, the explanation should handle the findings uniquely, but in most cases more than one possible explanation is consistent with even a large array of findings. While the aim of our investigation is to arrive at explanation, the role of mere description should not be neglected. A quantitative description of results, including their magnitude and location, can have implications for interests in communications engineering, such as speech synthesis or speech recognition by machine (see chapter 8). In addition to their practical importance, the descriptive results provide a useful starting point on which further theoretical studies can be based. For these reasons, measurement details are included throughout the text as reference material.

Experimental Methods

In order to study a speaker's computational processes, it would be most desirable to examine a corpus of spontaneous speech. While certain general effects can be studied in this manner (see Kloker, 1975), work on specific hypotheses cannot be conducted with proper control or efficiency using such data. This same drawback applies to analyses of errors committed during spontaneous speech (for example, Fromkin, 1971; Garrett, 1975; Fay, 1977; Shattuck-Hufnagel, 1979), although, as we shall see in chapters 5 and 6, such analyses sometimes bear implications for issues examined here from an experimental standpoint.

As noted earlier, a number of syntactic and extrasyntactic factors combine to influence phonetic attributes in normal speaking (Klatt, 1976). An experimental method is needed to study each of these factors in isolation, providing a basis for subsequent study of interaction. Accordingly, a sentence-reading procedure (Cooper, 1976a) was devised in which the phonetic form of the utterances could be tightly controlled. In each test a short list of sentences (or paragraphs) is read by a speaker after a period of practice during which he is familiarized with the task and the particular materials. Each sentence contains one or more key words, placed at the location(s) of syntactic boundaries or other locations of interest. The choice of key words is influenced by the degree to which their phonetic representation facilitates acoustic analysis. In studies of speech timing, for example, key words must be readily segmentable from a digitized oscillographic trace of the speech waveform.

The sentences of each group typically contain the same key words and share as many words and syllables as possible, compatible with signaling the structural distinction under study. The stress pattern of the sentences is matched as closely as possible so that any effects may be attributed to a direct syntactic influence rather than to an intermediary influence of stress.

By using normal English sentences in our studies, we hope to combine a routine yet complex task with a high degree of experimental control. Such testing should allow us to build a data base that will be useful in guiding the study of interactions between syntactic effects and other influences on speech timing. The construction of appropriate natural sentences offers some advantage over procedures that involve nonsense mimicry of natural speech (Lindblom and Rapp, 1973; Liberman and Streeter, 1976). The latter procedures provide an adequate and highly efficient means of studying stress effects, but the use of meaningful sentences allows one to study the effect of syntax and its interaction with other variables in a setting that approximates natural speaking. In addition, the results of experiments with meaningful speech can be applied more directly to practical problems such as speech synthesis.

In most of these studies, ten to twenty paid volunteers, with little or no formal training in linguistics or speech science, are tested individually in a large sound-insulated chamber for approximately forty to fifty minutes per session. The participants are native English speakers from area universities, mostly undergraduates. No speaker has any history of speech or hearing impairment. During the session, the speaker is presented from seven to ten sentence lists, each list representing a separate experiment. At the beginning of a session, the speaker is told that the general purpose of the experiments is to study aspects of speech production. The speaker is then told that he will be given practice in reading lists of sentences in order to train him to utter each sentence "as a unitary whole, as if it were spoken spontaneously," rather than "word by word," as in unpracticed reading. The speaker is encouraged to speak as naturally as possible but to avoid placing contrastive or emphatic stress on any word or syllable in a sentence, unless specifically instructed otherwise for the purpose of experiments designed to test stress effects.

Following these preliminary instructions, the speaker is given the first of a series of typewritten lists of sentences. Each sentence is presented on a single line with no punctuation except for a sentence-final period. The speaker is told to consider each sentence in the list independently of the others. (The order in which sentences and lists are presented to speakers is pseudorandomized and counterbalanced.) During practice, the speaker is asked to utter a given sentence aloud once, providing the experimenter with a final opportunity to check for contrastive or emphatic stress and to check recording levels. The speaker then utters the given sentence twice for recording.

Since the sentence pairs by design resemble each other so closely, "filler" sentences are inserted throughout the sentence lists. These fillers are appropriately matched with the "real" experimental sentences in terms of length and semantic relatedness so that the subject is not aware of their filler status. The fillers serve to camouflage the nature of the experimental sentences. To minimize start-up and end effects in the reading of the sentence lists, additional fillers are always used as the first and last sentence of each experiment.

The speaker is told to expect to produce a few mispronunciations during the test. For mispronunciations or for any changes from the speaker's nonemphatic normal prosody, the speaker is instructed to pause, utter the word "repeat," and then say the sentence token again. After reading a given list, the speaker is provided a short rest period, encouraged to take a drink of water, and then asked to begin the practice procedure with a new list.

Acoustic analysis of segment durations is performed using an oscillographic display of speech, digitized at a sampling rate of 10 kHz on a PDP-9 computer. The analysis is performed on the first of the two recorded exemplars, except for rare occasions when this exemplar contains contrastive or emphatic stress that went unnoticed by the experimenter during recording. The segment durations are measured from this display with the aid of a computer-controlled cursor (Huggins, 1969). The cursor is maneuvered by velocity and position dials to mark the onset and offset of each key segment. The time difference between the segment onset and offset is displayed on the oscilloscope screen to the nearest 100 μsec. An example of the oscilloscope display is shown in figure 1.4. For key word segments beginning with a word-initial voiceless stop consonant and ending with a vowel preceding a voiceless stop (for example, /e/ of "Jake"), the reliability of each measurement has been determined to be within ±3 msec, based on a duplicate set of measurements made without the experimenter's remembrance of, or reference to, the original measure-

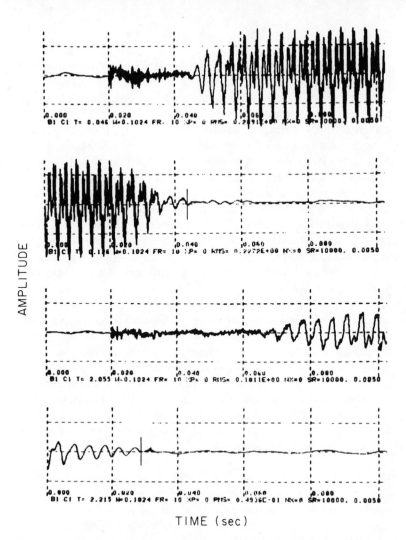

AMPLITUDE

TIME (sec)

Figure 1.4 *Sample digitized oscillograms showing segment boundaries for "Dick" and "take" in the same utterance by a female speaker. The top trace shows the initial 80 msec of /dı/, with the onset of the segment aligned with a dotted vertical line at 0.020 sec on the display. In the second trace, the end of /dı/ is marked by a solid vertical bar after 0.040 sec of the display window. Note that irregular pulses of very small amplitude are excluded from the /dı/ segment, in order to maximize measurement reliability. In the third trace, the beginning of /te/ is aligned with a dotted vertical line at 0.020 sec. The bottom trace shows the segment ending for /te/, marked by a solid vertical bar after 0.020 sec. The last few glottal cycles probably occurred after the beginning of oral closure for the word-final voiceless stop in this word. In such cases, the segment duration included these glottal cycles to maximize measurement reliability (from Cooper, Sorensen, and Paccia, 1977).*

ments for the same utterances. Further details of the measurement procedure are discussed in chapter 2, experiment 1.

After the acoustic measurements are obtained, statistics are applied to the data to test certain hypotheses formulated during the design of the experiment. In most cases, the appropriate statistic consists of a two-tailed *t* test for matched pairs (Harnett, 1975). This test is designed to determine whether the means of two sets of measurements are significantly different from one another when both sets of measurements have been obtained for the same subjects. The statistic may be applied when it is reasonable to assume that each set of measurements is normally distributed. This assumption holds well for the present data, with the few exceptions noted in later chapters.

While the experiments utilize an adequate number of speakers to perform statistical tests across subjects, the experiments do not employ a sufficiently large number of sentence materials to perform statistical tests across items or across both subjects and items (cf. Clark, 1973). This limitation on items was imposed because of the difficulty of constructing properly matched sentence materials as well as the overall expense of the experimentation. Throughout the discussion, we shall assume that consistent results obtained with two or more representative sentence pairs generalize to a larger class, but it should be borne in mind that this assumption must ultimately be put to critical testing with experimentation that involves more sentence items.

Conclusion

In this chapter we reviewed some of the main issues of speech production and presented a model of information flow indicating that aspects of the speaker's syntactic representation might be coded in acoustic properties of the speech wave. Three acoustic properties—segment durations, pause durations, and the blocking of cross-word phonetic conditioning effects—were discussed as candidates that might be particularly revealing of the speaker's syntactic representation. In order to examine possible syntactic influences on these acoustic properties in more detail, we devised a sentence-reading procedure to disentangle syntactic influences from the many extrasyntactic influences that normally accompany spontaneous conversation.

Still, the proposed experiments with sentence reading will not be of much lasting value if they do not reflect processes that accompany normal speaking. Let us compare, then, the act of practiced reading, as described in this chapter, with the act of spontaneous speaking. First, as shown by Kloker (1975), it is known that clause-final lengthening—one of the major phenomena on which this study is based—accompanies spontaneous speech as well as practiced reading. It is thus reasonable to assume that the kinds of inferences made on the basis of reading experiments with this phenomenon generalize to spontaneous speech.

A chief difference between practiced reading and spontaneous speech, however, is the extent to which the speaker is actively engaged in formulating new information. In spontaneous speech, the formulation of ideas, as well as much of their translation into a linguistic code, represent choices completely absent from practiced reading. The results for reading reflect processing stages that in spontaneous speech presumably operate subsequent to these major decisions. Another difference between spontaneous speech and practiced reading involves the typical domain of phonological planning engaged in by the speaker. With practiced reading of the sort used here, our results might show a consistent bias toward greater planning. If so, our results will be more indicative of the speaker's planning *capabilities* than of the planning that routinely accompanies a conversation. Nonetheless, the study of such capabilities should provide useful guidelines for any theory that attempts to account for the characteristics of spontaneous speech. In addition, the practiced reading task can be used to explore a number of issues and applications in speech coding that involve topics other than planning, as indicated in later chapters.[5]

With this background we are ready to present the main body of empirical and theoretical work. Studies of pausing and segmental lengthening are discussed in chapters 2 through 5. In chapter 6 we present studies on the blocking of cross-word phonetic rules. Chapter 7 contains a theory to account for the main findings of previous chapters, and, finally, applications are discussed in chapter 8.

2 | Hierarchical Coding of Major Phrases

HOW DO SPEAKERS code phrasal constituents? As discussed in chapter 1, the phrase structure system of a language includes a set of rules defining syntactic constituents and their hierarchical interrelationships. Recall, for example, that the structural representation schematized in figure 1.2, repeated here for convenience, may be derived by applying the rewrite rules in (1) below, according to the top-down, left-to-right order specified in (2).

(1)
    (i)   S → NP + VP
    (ii) NP → N
    (iii) VP → V + NP
    (iv) NP → determiner (DET) + ADJ + N

(2)
    (i)   S
    (ii) NP + VP
    (iii) N + VP
    (iv) N + V + NP
    (v) N + V + DET + ADJ + N

Given this kind of linguistic description, we may ask whether the speaker computes such a representation during speech coding. The question can be subdivided into two parts: (a) Are syntactic constituents such as noun phrase and verb phrase processed as units? (b) Are constituents related to one another hierarchically in the manner specified by linguistic theory? (For example, does the constituent verb phrase dominate the constituents verb and noun phrase?)

In linguistics, the representation of phrase structure in formal

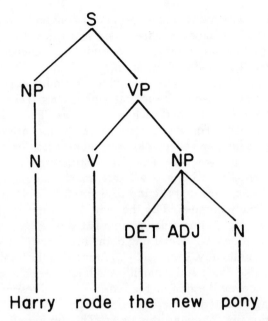

Figure 1.2 *Structural representation of the sentence "Harry rode the new pony" according to Chomsky's phrase structure rule, S → NP + VP.*

grammar is as important as the representation of transformational rules. The importance of providing a correct description of phrase structure rules has recently been underscored by attempts to diminish the scope and power of the transformational component of the grammar (Chomsky, 1973; Jackendoff, 1977). In psycholinguistics, the description of the speaker's phrase structure code would represent an advance in our understanding of the internal representations that accompany speech production.

In this chapter we attempt to infer properties of the speaker's code by examining speech timing for a number of related sentence structures. As noted in chapter 1, both segmental lengthening and pausing accompany major constituent boundaries in speech; we reasoned that a closer look at syntactically determined timing effects might provide answers to the kinds of questions about phrase structure coding that are posed above.

As discussed in chapter 1, in order to study the influence of syntax on speech timing one must control for extragrammatical influences on speech timing that might otherwise account for systematic durational effects. Because such influences often involve the phonetic structure of material neighboring the key word segments, it was advantageous to begin our study by considering structurally ambiguous sentences, which contain identical word strings, but which have differing phrase structures. Ambiguities of this type provide an opportunity to study the influence of grammatical structure in virtual isolation.

Previous work has already demonstrated timing effects for different readings of some structural ambiguities (Lehiste, 1973). These ambiguities included such sentences as "The old men and women left early." For this sentence, an ambiguity arises because the left-branching adjective "old" can modify just "men" or else both "men" and "women." The phrase structures corresponding to these alternative readings are diagrammed in figure 2.1. For the former reading, shown at the top of figure 2.1, "old" and "men" are immediately dominated by the same NP, whereas for the latter reading, "old" is immediately dominated by an NP that dominates an additional NP containing both "men" and "women." For this type of ambiguity, Lehiste (1973) found that the total duration of phrases like "men and women" was longer when speakers intended to convey the first of the two readings. Presumably, this lengthening occurred primarily for the segment "men" and for a pause optionally following this word. This timing effect can be accounted for in terms of the differing phrase structures for the two readings (later in this chapter we will consider and rule out alternative accounts). As noted at the outset of this study, it has been found that lengthening accompanies the ends of major phrases, accounting for the present effect. The structures of the reading in which "old" modifies just "men," reveals that, for this reading, "men" marks the end of an NP, whereas for the reading in which "old" modifies both "men" and "women," "men" occurs in non-phrase-final position. This interpretation suggests that the phrase structures coded during speech production are quite elaborate. In addition to processing major constituents—such as clauses—as units, it also appears that speakers compute representations of relatively minor phrase nodes, such as that corresponding to "old men" in figure 2.1.

There exist a variety of other structural ambiguities, not tested previously, which appear to involve an influence of phrase structure on speech timing that is even more revealing of the speaker's syntactic code. Like the structural ambiguity discussed above, each of these ambiguities involves a dominance relation between a constituent and either of two possible additional constituents.

The ambiguities studied here differ, however, in that they each involve a right-branching, as opposed to a left-branching, modifying constituent. Figure 2.2 schematizes the phrase structure difference that distinguishes the two readings of each ambiguity. As

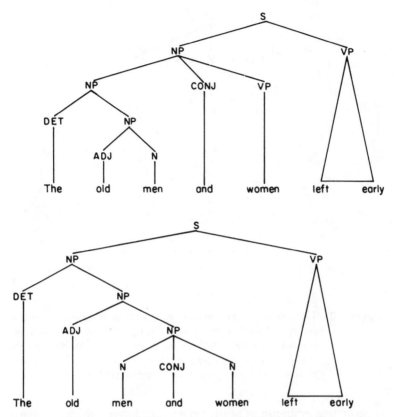

Figure 2.1 *Two structural representations of the ambiguous sentence "The old men and women left early." The upper tree represents the reading in which "old" modifies just "men," while the lower tree represents the reading in which "old" modifies both "men" and "women."*

shown in figure 2.2, each ambiguity studied here involves a right-branching constituent z, which is immediately dominated by either of two possible constituent nodes, w and x in the structural representations. A direct consequence of these differing phrase structure relations is that in the former case constituent z is immediately preceded by the end of two constituents, x and y, whereas in the latter case only one constituent, y, ends just before z. Hence, if speakers compute representations analogous to linguistic phrase structures, then we would predict that the material immediately preceding z would be longer for the version of an ambiguity corresponding to the top diagram in figure 2.2, assuming that phrase-final timing effects are cumulative for different coinciding phrase nodes.

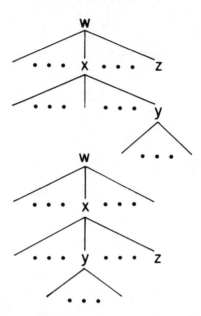

Figure 2.2　*Two structural representations of an ambiguous sentence of the general type studied in this chapter. The upper tree corresponds to the (a) readings of sentences discussed in experiments 1–6. Note that the end of* y *coincides with the end of* x *in (a) but not (b). This figure is revised from Cooper, Paccia, and Lapointe (1978).*

Structural ambiguities of the type studied here, which involve a right-branching modifying constituent, permit us to investigate the speaker's coding of a wide variety of syntactic constituents, including S, NP, VP, PP, and ADV. Because English is primarily a right-branching language, ambiguities with left-branching modifiers, such as that containing the phrase "old men and women," are typically limited to the ambiguous assignment of a modifying adjective. The study of ambiguities with right-branching modifiers is additionally advantageous because, since these ambiguities include phrases with the simultaneous ending of a varying number of constituents, one can investigate whether the constituents represented during speech production are hierarchically interrelated.

Let us begin by examining the timing effects produced for ambiguities in which the modifying constituent is immediately dominated by either the main S node or a lower node in the phrase structure representation (experiments 1 and 2). In experiments 3–5, we look at a variety of ambiguities involving constituent relations of dominance at a level in the syntactic structure lower than the main S. Experiments 5 and 6 involve ambiguities in which the modifying constituents are themselves clauses. Finally, in experiment 7, we consider whether the effects obtained for the ambiguities studied in experiments 1–6 generalize to paragraph contexts.

EXPERIMENT 1: ADVERB MODIFICATION

Sentence Materials and Procedure

Two ambiguous sentences were used in experiment 1.

(3)   My Uncle Abraham presented his talk naturally.
(4)   Lieutenant Baker instructed the troop naturally.

In each of these ambiguities, the adverb "naturally" can modify either the entire sentence or the VP, as illustrated in figure 2.3. The linguistic rationale for this structural analysis is presented in Jackendoff (1972). When the adverb modifies the entire sentence, the meaning of sentence (3), for example, can be paraphrased by (3′); when the adverb modifies the VP, the meaning can be paraphrased by (3″):

(3′)   Of course my Uncle Abraham presented his talk.
(3″)   My Uncle Abraham presented his talk in a natural manner.

Ten speakers were tested in accordance with the procedures for sentence reading described in chapter 1. Each test sentence appeared with its intended meaning following in parentheses, as shown below. None of the subjects reported any difficulty in comprehending these intended meanings.

(3)   (a)   My Uncle Abraham presented his talk naturally.
              (Of course Abraham presented his talk.)
       (b)   My Uncle Abraham presented his talk naturally.
              (Abraham presented his talk in a natural way.)
(4)   (a)   Lieutenant Baker instructed the troop naturally.
              (Of course Lieutenant Baker instructed the troop.)
       (b)   Lieutenant Baker instructed the troop naturally.
              (Lieutenant Baker instructed in a natural way.)

Acoustic measurements were obtained for the durations of the key segment / taᵂ / of "talk" in sentence (3) and /tru/ of "troop" in sentence (4). In each case, the key segment was measured from the onset of the /t/ release burst to the beginning of the silent in-

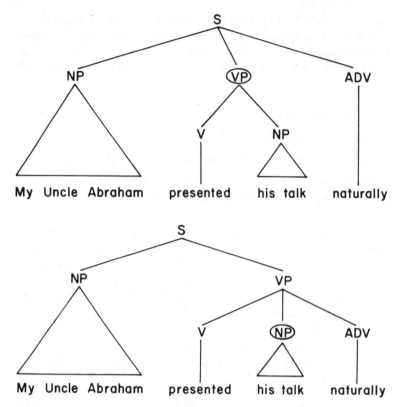

Figure 2.3   *Two structural representations of an ambiguous sentence in experiment 1. A circle appears around the maximal constituent to the immediate left of the measured pause location. The upper tree represents the (a) reading of the sentence; the lower tree represents the (b) reading. In this figure and all others in this chapter, the structural representations correspond to a surface (as opposed to an underlying) level of syntactic description.*

terval for the word-final voiceless stop /k/ or /p/. The error in measuring segment durations was minimized by using key words that included voiceless stops in both the word-initial and the word-final positions.

In addition to these segments, the duration of the "silent" interval beginning with the word-final voiceless stop was measured to provide an index of pause duration. This interval included the silent interval for the stop consonant, a release burst if any(most utterances did not exhibit this feature), and an optional pause preceding the word-initial nasal of the adverb "naturally."

By deciding to estimate the word and pause durations in this manner, it was possible to adopt criteria for demarcating the beginning and end of each interval such that these criteria could be applied to all utterances in a uniform and precise fashion. At the same time, it must be understood here and throughout subsequent studies that our "word segments" do not include the silent interval or release burst of word-final stop consonants, whereas our "pauses" do. Despite the fact that these intervals include more than a single type of acoustic information, it is still possible to interpret the nature of any lengthening effects obtained in the experiments. In particular, it seems that any significant lengthening of a word segment is due primarily to elongation of the vowel and any other sonorant or continuant phonemes within the measured word, while any substantial lengthening of the pause interval can be attributed primarily to pausing between words rather than to lengthening of the word-final stop consonant closure.

Results

As predicted, the duration of the key segment in both ambiguous sentences was significantly longer for the (a) reading, in which the adverb "naturally" modified the entire sentence (sentence (3): $p < 0.001$, $t = 6.42$, $df = 9$; sentence (4): $p < 0.01$, $t = 3.34$, $df = 9$; two-tailed t tests for matched pairs). In sentence (3), the duration of the segment $/ta^w/$ averaged 241.9 msec for the (a) reading and 209.7 msec for the (b) reading. In sentence (4), the duration of the segment /tru/ averaged 242.9 msec for the (a) reading and 216.7 msec for the (b) reading. The lengthening for these segments thus averaged 15 percent in sentence (3) and 12 percent in sentence (4).

The duration of the following silent intervals was also longer for the (a) readings of both sentences. In sentence (3), this interval averaged 183.1 msec for the (a) reading and 130.4 msec for the (b) reading (40 percent lengthening). In sentence (4), the interval averaged 228.9 msec for the (a) reading and 94.1 msec for the (b) reading (143 percent lengthening). Despite these very large mean effects, statistical significance was reached only for the silent interval in sentence (4) (sentence (3): $p > 0.20$, $t = 0.98$, $df = 9$; sentence (4): $p < 0.02$, $t = 3.18$, $df = 9$; two-tailed t tests for matched pairs).

The finding that the effects of segmental lengthening are smaller but more consistent than those for pausing is in agreement with other studies to be presented throughout this book. Because pausing is an optional feature of speech, its variability both within and across speakers is considerable. In this experiment, the standard deviations for each reading across speakers were 106.5 and 168.3 msec for the (a) and (b) readings of sentence

(3) and 126.4 and 46.4 msec for the (a) and (b) readings of sentence (4), respectively.[1] In contrast, the standard deviations for the segment durations averaged about 25 msec for the two sentences. The particularly large standard deviations for the pauses in sentence (3) may partially account for why the pause difference between the two readings of this sentence fell so far short of statistical significance despite the large mean effect.

EXPERIMENT 2: VOCATIVE VERSUS HEAD NOUN

Sentence materials and Procedure

Two ambiguous sentences were used in experiment 2.

(5)   Here is the famous Duke James.
(6)   Here is the famous Pope Carl.

In each sentence, the proper noun "James" or "Carl" can serve either as a vocative, designating the person to which the speech is directed, or as a head noun in the NP "the famous Duke James."[2] In structural terms, the ambiguities can be represented as in figure 2.4. It can be seen from this figure that the proper noun is attached to a higher constituent in the reading in which it functions as a vocative.

The testing procedure was similar to that of the previous experiment. The test sentences were presented to the same ten subjects with the following interpretations:

(5)   (a)   Here is the famous Duke James.
            (James meets the Duke.)
      (b)   Here is the famous Duke James.
            (The name of the Duke is James.)
(6)   (a)   Here is the famous Pope Carl.
            (Carl meets the Pope.)
      (b)   Here is the famous Pope Carl.
            (The name of the Pope is Carl.)

Acoustic measurements of duration were obtained for the key segments /du/ in "Duke" and /po/ in "Pope," as well as for the following pauses.

Results

For both sentences the duration of the key segment was significantly longer in the (a) reading when the proper noun served as a vocative (sentence (5): $p < 0.02$, $t = 3.06$, $df = 9$; sentence (6):

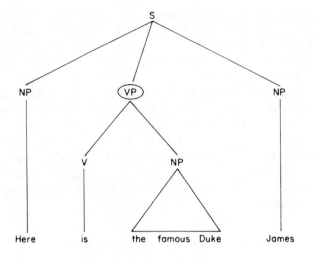

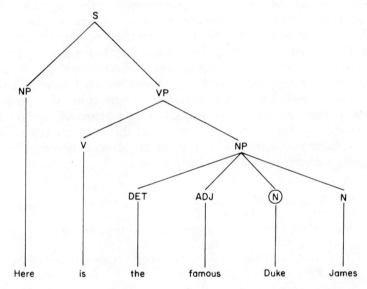

Figure 2.4 *Two structural representations of an ambiguous sentence in experiment 2. The upper tree represents the (a) reading of the sentence.*

$p < 0.001$, $t = 5.88$, $df = 9$). For sentence (5), the duration of /du/ averaged 164.7 msec in the (a) reading and 138.3 msec in the (b) reading (19 percent lengthening). For sentence (6), the duration of /po/ averaged 199.1 msec for the (a) reading and 164.1 msec for the (b) reading (22 percent lengthening).

The duration of the following pause was also longer in the (a) version of each sentence (sentence (5): $0.06 > p > 0.05$, $t = 2.24$, $df = 9$; sentence (6): $p < 0.05$, $t = 2.56$, $df = 9$). For sentence (5), the pause duration averaged 134.0 msec for the (a) reading and 34.4 msec for the (b) reading (290 percent lengthening). For sentence (6), the pause duration averaged 90.2 msec for the (a) version and 24.4 msec for the (b) version (270 percent lengthening). As in experiment 1, the results for both segment and pause durations show that lengthening occurs when the key material marks the end of a relatively greater number of constituents. In both experiments, the lengthening effects for the segment durations were smaller in magnitude but more consistent than the lengthening effects for the pauses.

EXPERIMENT 3: PREPOSITIONAL PHRASE MODIFICATION I

In each of the preceding experiments, lengthening was observed when the most inclusive constituent containing the key material was immediately dominated by the S node in the structural representation (see figures 2.3 and 2.4). In the third experiment we tested whether the lengthening effects would generalize to a type of ambiguity involving constituent relations of dominance at a lower level in the syntactic structure. It was thus possible to determine whether an account of the previous effect should be formulated in terms of the notion of the relative number of constituent boundaries or in terms of the absolute notion of immediate dominance by the S node.

Sentence Materials and Procedure

Two ambiguous sentences were used in experiment 3.

(7)   Lieutenant Baker instructed the troop with a handicap.
(8)   Jeffrey hit the cop with a stick.

In each sentence an ambiguity arises because the prepositional phrase beginning with "with" can modify either the verb phrase or the noun phrase dominated by the verb phrase, as shown in figure 2.5. For example, the prepositional phrase "with a handicap" can designate the manner in which the troop was instructed (VP modification), or it can designate the handicapped condition of the troop (NP modification). The structural analysis provided here is in agreement with Akmajian and Heny (1975).

The testing procedure was similar to previous experiments. The

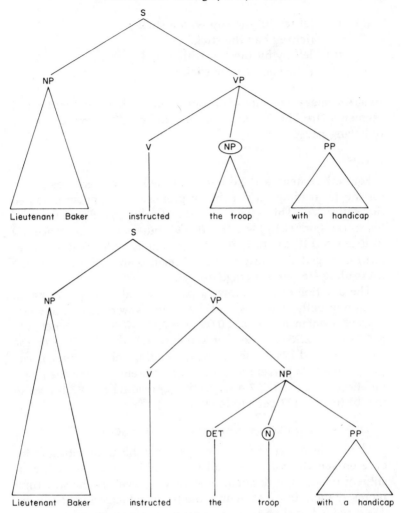

Figure 2.5 *Two structural representations of an ambiguous sentence in experiment 3. The upper tree represents the (a) reading of the sentence.*

test sentences were presented to the same ten subjects in pseudorandom order with the following interpretations:

(7)   (a)   Lieutenant Baker instructed the troop with a handicap.
            (The lieutenant was handicapped.)

       (b)   Lieutenant Baker instructed the troop with a handicap.
            (The troop was handicapped.)

(8) (a) Jeffrey hit the cop with a stick.
        (Jeffrey had the stick.)
    (b) Jeffrey hit the cop with a stick.
        (The cop had the stick.)

Acoustic measurements of duration were obtained for the key segments /tru/ in "troop" and /ka/ in "cop," as well as for the following pauses.

Results

For both sentences, the duration of the key segment was longer for the (a) reading, in which the prepositional phrase modified the entire VP. This effect was statistically significant for sentence (7) ($p < 0.01$, $t = 4.16$, $df = 9$) but not for sentence (8) ($0.20 > p > 0.10$, $t = 1.67$, $df = 9$). For sentence (7), the duration of /tru/ averaged 238.1 msec in the (a) reading and 205.1 msec in the (b) reading (16 percent lengthening).

The duration of the following pause was also longer in the (a) version of both sentences, and these effects were statistically significant (sentence (7): $p < 0.05$, $t = 2.42$, $df = 9$; sentence (8): $p < 0.02$, $t = 2.95$, $df = 9$). For sentence (7), the duration of the pause averaged 174.6 msec in the (a) reading and 78.6 msec in the (b) reading (122 percent lengthening). For sentence (8), the pause duration averaged 127.7 msec in the (a) reading and 97.1 msec in the (b) reading (32 percent lengthening).

EXPERIMENT 4: PREPOSITIONAL PHRASE MODIFICATION II

The results of experiment 3 suggest that the grammatical influence on speech timing generalizes to ambiguities involving constituent relations of dominance at varying levels in the structural representation. In experiment 4 the test conducted in experiment 3 is extended to slightly more complex sentence structures.

Sentence Materials and Procedure

Two ambiguous sentences were used in this experiment.

(9) I left Chuck with a better understanding of his problem.
(10) I saw Chuck looking through the window.

In both sentences, the phrase beginning after "Chuck" can modify either the VP or the NP that the VP dominates, as in experiment 3. The structural relations are shown in figure 2.6. In sentence (9), the prepositional phrase beginning with "with" can designate either the manner in which Chuck was left (I had a better under-

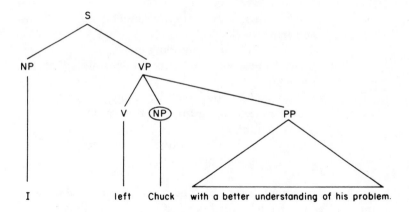

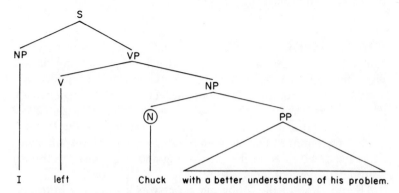

Figure 2.6 *Two structural representations of an ambiguous sentence in experiment 4. The upper tree represents the (a) reading of the sentence. It is possible that the PP is immediately dominated by S in the upper tree and by VP in the lower tree, rather than as shown here (Williams, 1975). This revision would still preserve the height relation, however.*

standing) or Chuck's condition (Chuck had a better understanding). In sentence (10), the adverbial phrase beginning with "looking" can similarly designate either the manner in which I saw Chuck (I was looking through the window) or Chuck's condition (Chuck was looking through the window). These sentences thus represent somewhat more complex sentence structures than those in experiment 3, but they involve the same type of ambiguity.

The testing procedure was similar to that of previous experiments. The test sentences were presented to fifteen subjects in pseudorandom order with the following parenthesized interpretations:

(9) (a) I left Chuck with a better understanding of his
          problem.
          (I had a better understanding.)
     (b) I left Chuck with a better understanding of his
          problem.
          (Chuck had a better understanding.)
(10) (a) I saw Chuck looking through the window.
          (I was looking.)
     (b) I saw Chuck looking through the window.
          (Chuck was looking.)

Acoustic measurements were obtained for the duration of the key
segment /čʌ/ in "Chuck" for both sentences, as well as for the
duration of the following pause.

Results

For both sentences, the duration of the key segment was significantly longer in the (a) reading, in which the modifying phrase
was attached to the VP rather than to the NP (sentence (9):
$p < 0.01$, $t = 3.80$, $df = 14$; sentence (10): $p < 0.001$, $t = 5.73$,
$df = 14$). For sentence (9), the duration of /čʌ/ averaged 225.7
msec in the (a) reading and 202.1 msec in the (b) reading (12 percent lengthening). For sentence (10), the duration of /čʌ/
averaged 224.0 msec in the (a) reading and 192.2 msec in the (b)
reading (17 percent lengthening).

The duration of the following pause was also longer in the (a)
reading of both sentences. This effect was statistically significant
for sentence (10) but not for sentence (9) (sentence (9): $p > 0.20$,
$t = 0.75$, $df = 14$; sentence (10): $p < 0.01$, $t = 3.98$, $df = 14$). For
sentence (9), the pause duration averaged 139.1 msec in the (a)
reading and 69.5 msec in the (b) reading (100 percent lengthening). For sentence (10), the pause duration averaged 66.5 msec in
(a) and 26.2 msec in (b) (154 percent lengthening).

The lengthening effects obtained in this experiment provide
further support for the notion that constituent relations influence
speech timing in structurally ambiguous sentences.

EXPERIMENT 5: INDIRECT QUESTION VERSUS RELATIVE CLAUSE

In experiment 5 the analysis of structural ambiguities is extended to another type, involving clauses that may be considered
either indirect questions or relative clauses. As in experiments 3
and 4, this type of ambiguity involves a structural representation
in which the modifying constituent is attached to a VP or to the
NP in which the VP dominates. This experiment thus provides a

further test of generality for the account in terms of cumulative phrase-final lengthening.

Sentence Materials and Procedure

A single ambiguous sentence was used for this experiment.

(11)   Pam asked the cop who Jake confronted.

In this sentence, the clause "who Jake confronted" can act as either an indirect question (modifying the VP) or a relative clause (modifying the NP), as shown in figure 2.7. On the first reading the sentence takes the meaning "Pam asked the cop which person Jake confronted"; on the second reading the sentence takes the meaning "Pat asked which cop? The cop that Jake confronted."

The test procedure was similar to that for previous experiments. The fifteen subjects who participated in experiment 4 were presented with the sentence as follows.

(11)   (a)   Pam asked the cop who Jake confronted.
               (Who did Jake confront?)
       (b)   Pam asked the cop who Jake confronted.
               (Which cop? The cop that Jake confronted.)

Acoustic measurements were obtained for the duration of the key segment /ka/ in "cop" and of the following pause.

Results

The duration of the key segment /ka/ was significantly longer when the WH clause functioned as an indirect question, attached directly to the entire VP ($p < 0.001$, $t = 5.04$, $df = 14$). The duration of the segment averaged 227.5 msec for this reading, compared with 204.3 msec for the reading in which the WH clause functioned as a relative clause (11 percent lengthening).

The following pause was also significantly longer when the WH clause functioned as an indirect question ($p < 0.01$, $t = 3.46$, $df = 14$). The duration of the pause averaged 204.3 msec for this reading, compared with 119.1 msec for the relative clause reading (72 percent lengthening). The lengthening results for the segment and pause indicate that the influence of constituent relations on speech timing extends to complex structures containing a main and an embedded clause.

EXPERIMENT 6: SCOPE OF NEGATION

In experiment 6 we extend the analysis of structural ambiguities to a case involving the scope of negation (Lasnik, 1972).

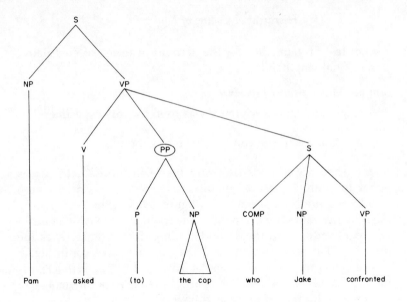

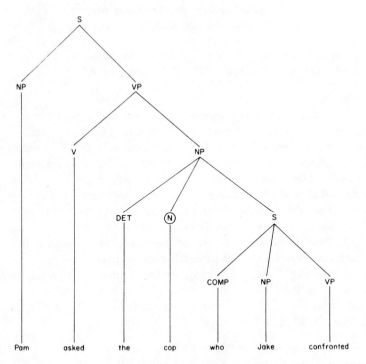

Figure 2.7 *Two structural representations of an ambiguous sentence in experiment 5. The upper tree represents the (a) reading of the sentence.*

Sentence Materials and Procedure

Two ambiguous sentences were used.

(12) Dick didn't fly the kite because it was a beautiful day.
(13) John didn't date Pat because of her body.

In each sentence the negative can serve to negate the proposition of the entire sentence or of the subordinate clause only. In sentence (12), for example, negation of the entire sentence yields the reading "Dick did not fly the kite, for the reason that it was a beautiful day." Negation of only the subordinate clause yields the reading "Dick did fly the kite, but not for the reason that it was a beautiful day." This distinction involving the scope of negation can be represented in the structural configurations of figure 2.8. Similar to the other ambiguities considered thus far, the subordinate clause beginning with "because" is directly dominated by one of two possible constituents of different heights in the structural representation. It is thus predicted that lengthening will be observed just prior to this clause on the reading in which the clause is directly dominated by the higher of the two constituents (in this case, corresponding to the reading in which the proposition of the entire sentence is negated).

The testing procedure was similar to that of previous experiments. The test sentences were presented to seventeen subjects in pseudorandom order with the following parenthesized interpretations:

(12) (a) Dick didn't fly the kite because it was a beautiful day.
           (Dick did not fly the kite.)
      (b) Dick didn't fly the kite because it was a beautiful day.
           (Dick did fly the kite.)
(13) (a) John didn't date Pat because of her body.
           (John did not date Pat.)
      (b) John didn't date Pat because of her body.
           (John did date Pat.)

Acoustic measurements were obtained for the key segments /ka^i/ of "kite" in sentence (12) and /pæ/ of "Pat" in sentence (13), as well as for the following pauses. A few speakers uttered a word-final glottal stop instead of /t/ in "kite" and "Pat," continuing vocal fold vibration during the interval of oral closure for the stop.

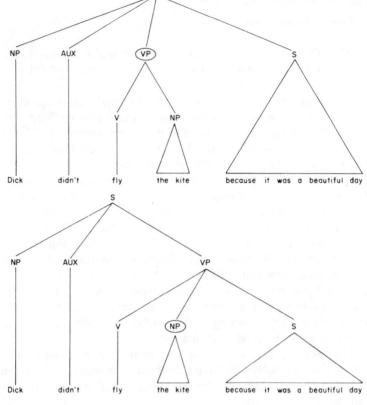

Figure 2.8   *Two structural representations of an ambiguous sentence in experiment 6. The upper tree represents the (a) reading of the sentence.*

In such instances, the glottal stop interval was included in the
pause measurement.

Results

The duration of the key segment was significantly longer in the
(a) reading of both sentences, as predicted (sentence (12):
$p < 0.001$, $t = 4.82$, $df = 16$; sentence (13): $p < 0.001$, $t = 4.03$,
$df = 16$). For sentence (12), the duration of /kaⁱ/ averaged 236.7
msec in the (a) reading and 202.9 msec in the (b) reading (16 percent lengthening). For sentence (13), the duration of /pæ/
averaged 238.4 msec in the (a) reading and 207.7 msec in the (b)
reading (16 percent lengthening).

The duration of the following pause was also significantly
longer in the (a) reading of both sentences (sentence (12): $p < 0.05$,

$t = 2.49$, $df = 16$; sentence (13): $p < 0.01$, $t = 3.24$, $df = 16$). For sentence (12), the pause duration averaged 73.6 msec in the (a) reading and 32.4 msec in the (b) reading (127 percent lengthening). For sentence (13), the pause duration averaged 120.1 msec in the (a) reading and 78.0 msec in the (b) reading (54 percent lengthening).

EXPERIMENT 7: PARAGRAPH CONTEXTS

The striking consistency of the results for experiments 1–6 suggests that speakers compute a hierarchical grammatical representation analogous to the tree structures in figures 2.2–2.7 and that this representation exerts a systematic influence on speech timing. But while the results suggest that this form of grammatical representation is included in the speaker's cognitive repertoire, it is possible that this representation would not influence speech timing in the context of a situation that more closely approximates natural speaking. In particular, the previous results, while indicative of the speaker's cognitive ability, may reflect a conscious strategy by which speakers attempt to provide cues to aid a listener in disambiguating the sentence.

In normal speaking situations, syntactic ambiguities are normally resolved by the context of a discourse. Experiment 7 was conducted to determine whether some of the effects observed previously for isolated sentences would generalize to paragraph contexts in which speakers were not aware of the presence of a structural ambiguity.

Paragraph Materials and Procedure

Disambiguating paragraphs were constructed containing one sentence each from experiments 2, 3, 4, and 6. The selected sentences included (5), (7), (10), and (12), repeated below for convenience.

(5) Here is the famous Duke James.
(7) Lieutenant Baker instructed the troop with a handicap.
(10) I saw Chuck looking through the window.
(12) Dick didn't fly the kite because it was a beautiful day.

Two disambiguating paragraphs were prepared for each of these sentences in order to force each of the two possible readings. An example of a pair of disambiguating paragraphs used in the experiment appears below, involving sentence (12).

(12) (a) Dick was an eccentric in many ways. For example, on Saturday he told me how much he liked to fly

kites. It was a beautiful sunny day, with a strong breeze, so I asked him whether he wanted to go outside to fly his kite. But then he said he only liked to fly the kite on cloudy days. I was hoping he would agree to fly the kite anyway. But Dick didn't fly the kite because it was a beautiful day. I can never understand him.

(b)   Saturday we woke up very early. We were surprised to see that it was a really nice day, since the weatherman had predicted that it would rain. After breakfast we talked about our plans for the day. Since it was such a nice day, we decided to go to the beach to fly our kites. When we arrived Dick was already flying his kite. But Dick didn't fly the kite because it was a beautiful day. He was practicing for the kite-flying contest.

In paragraph (12a), the context forces the reading in which the scope of negation includes the entire sentence ("Dick did not fly the kite, for the reason that it was a beautiful day"); in paragraph (12b), on the other hand, the context forces the reading in which the scope of negation includes the subordinate clause only ("Dick did fly the kite, but not for the reason that it was a beautiful day"). If the results with isolated sentences extend to paragraph contexts, then lengthening should be observed just prior to the subordinate clause in paragraph (12a) versus (12b).

Paragraphs (5) and (7) were presented to each of ten subjects in pseudorandom order on typewritten pages such that the key material appeared at about the middle of a line. Ten different subjects read paragraphs (10) and (12). The speakers were unaware of the ambiguous nature of the key sentences embedded in the paragraph contexts. The ten speakers who read paragraphs (5) and (7) also participated in experiments 1–3 later in the same session, with the paragraphs presented first to avoid calling attention to the ambiguous nature of the key material.

Each speaker first became familiarized with a given paragraph by reading it silently one or more times. The speaker then read the paragraph once aloud for recording. Other experimental details were similar to those described in chapter 1.

Results

The mean duration of the key segments and following pauses for each paragraph are presented in table 2.1. These results show that the key word segment was longer in the (a) reading of each of

Table 2.1 *Mean duration (msec) of key word segments and pauses for each paragraph in experiment 7*

Test sentence	Key word segment		Pause	
	Reading (a)	Reading (b)	Reading (a)	Reading (b)
(5)	168.1	143.1	199.8	90.2
(7)	222.6	218.2	91.8	120.3
(10)	190.2	159.6	113.8	99.2
(12)	211.8	194.6	79.3	76.6

the four sentences, in agreement with the previous results when the sentences were presented in isolation. The lengthening was statistically significant in one of the four cases (sentence (5): $p < 0.01$, $t = 3.42$, $df = 9$). The duration of the pause was longer in the (a) reading of three of the four sentences, and this effect was statistically significant in two of the sentences (sentence (5): $p < 0.001$, $t = 6.28$, $df = 9$; sentence (10): $p < 0.05$, $t = 2.71$, $df = 9$). The results for the duration of both segments and pauses are consistent with the results obtained for the same sentences presented in isolation, although the magnitude and consistency of the effects for paragraphs were less pronounced.[3]

The greater magnitude of lengthening observed for isolated sentences in experiments 1–6 may be attributed to the speaker's awareness of the ambiguity in these sentences and, hence, a conscious attempt to disambiguate the strings via prosodic information. In the context of full paragraphs, the semantic environment provides sufficient clues to disambiguation, eliminating the need to disambiguate via prosody.

The fact that lengthening still occurs to some extent in paragraph contexts suggests, however, that one component of the lengthening effect is an automatic feature of speech not dependent on the speaker's awareness of a potential ambiguity. Consequently, it appears that the inferences about hierarchical coding based on the results of these experiments with ambiguities are probably applicable to the processing of nonambiguous strings as well (see chapter 7), although a good deal of further testing with paragraph contexts is still needed before we can clarify this issue.

General Discussion

The results of these experiments show that a variety of superficially distinct ambiguities exert the same systematic effect on speech timing. This finding provides evidence for viewing the ambiguities studied here as members of the same structural type, formalized earlier in figure 2.2. Previous treatments of these ambiguities did not uncover this unifying relation (see Lieberman, 1967; Kooij, 1971; Liberman, 1975; Williams, 1975; O'Shaughnessy, 1976). Additional confirmation that these ambiguities are of the same general type derives from the disambiguating effect of syntactic movement transformations. As noted by Emonds (1976) and Williams (1975), the preposing of constituent z in most dialects forces the reading in which z is immediately dominated by the higher of the two nodes (w of w,x), as shown for versions of the sentences used in this study.

(14)   Naturally, Uncle Abraham presented his talk.
(15)   James, here is the famous Duke.
(16)   With a handicap, Lieutenant Baker instructed the troop.
(17)   With a better understanding of his problem, I left Chuck.
(18)   "Who did Jake confront?" Pam asked the cop.
(19)   Because it was a beautiful day, Dick didn't fly the kite.

The influence of structural ambiguities on speech timing obtained in this study may be explained in terms of the notion of cumulative phrase-final lengthening. This account implies that speakers are capable of computing a hierarchical representation of grammatical structure analogous to that shown in figures 2.3–2.8 and that, furthermore, this representation exerts a systematic influence on speech timing.

A cumulative lengthening account is plausible in view of the general top-down model of speech production proposed in chapter 1. According to this model, which is intended to apply to ambiguous and nonambiguous sentences alike, lengthening is applied at a number of successively narrower domains of grammatical coding, including clauses and major phrases. The greater durations obtained at the ends of more major constituents in the (a) readings of sentences in this study can thus be viewed as arising from the application of an additional amount of lengthening associated with the end of the node x that dominates the node y (see figure 2.2).

To illustrate this principle we present an account of why the duration of the key word "talk" in sentence (3) was longer for the (a) reading. The structure of the (a) reading, shown at the top of figure 2.3, reveals that the key word "talk" marks the end of the entire VP phrase as well as the end of the dominated NP phrase. According to the top-down model of speech coding, phrase-final lengthening will thus be applied to "talk" during two separate stages of the speaker's computation, first when computations are applied to the VP phrase and second when they are applied to the NP phrase. For the (b) reading, whose structure appears at the bottom of figure 2.3, the key word "talk" marks the end of only a single phrase—namely, the direct object NP. We can now provide a natural account of why the total duration of "talk" was longer in the (a) reading, based on two reasonable assumptions: (i) a detectable amount of phrase-final lengthening applies to the last word of a VP phrase, and (ii) the amount of phrase-final lengthening that applies to the last word of the two identical NP phrases is the same. Under these assumptions, lengthening at the end of the VP will be applied to "talk" in the (a) but not the (b) reading, and an additional amount of lengthening at the end of the NP will be applied to "talk" in both readings. Since the latter amount of lengthening is the same for both readings, the overall duration is longer in the (a) reading. This account applies systematically to each of the structurally ambiguous sentences considered in experiments 1–6.

A hierarchically based account of the present results may also be formulated in terms of the structural relations existing for the constituent *following* the key material. This formulation, referred to previously as the Node Height Principle (Cooper, Paccia, and Lapointe, 1978), states that speech timing effects will border the modifying constituent z, when z is immediately dominated by the higher of two constituent nodes, w, of w,x (see figure 2.2). A hierarchical account stated in terms of the Node Height Principle can handle each of the right-branching ambiguities studied here, but proves to be inadequate upon consideration of left-branching ambiguities of the type discussed earlier in this chapter. For left-branching ambiguities, the modifying constituent is bounded by lengthening when it is immediately dominated by the *lower* of two possible constituent nodes (see figure 2.1 and corresponding discussion in the text). Thus, a hierarchically based account formulated in terms of cumulative phrase-final lengthening appears superior to one formulated in terms of node height relations.

Although the implications of an account based on cumulative lengthening are in full accord with the results of related work to be presented in later chapters, we should also consider an alternative account that relies on simple linear coding.

According to a plausible linear account, lengthening is applied when constituent z modifies or is associated with one of two possible constituents (w of w,x) when the first segment contained in w occurs earlier in the linear string than the first segment contained in x. Note that this account can handle all the results of the previous experiments. When the account is applied to experiment 1, for example, lengthening is produced in the key region for the (a) reading because, as shown in figure 2.3, the adverb "naturally" (constituent z) modifies constituent w, beginning with the first word of the sentence, "my." In the (b) reading, on the other hand, constituent z modifies constituent x, beginning with the fourth word of the string, "presented." The linear account can handle the results of experiments 2–7 in a similar fashion.[4] This hypothesis could handle each of the ambiguities considered so far. However, this account falters when one considers question-answer situations like the one below.[5]

(20)   Question: What is my Uncle Abraham doing?
       Answer: Presenting his talk naturally.

In the answer portion of (20), we have an ambiguity similar to (3) and (4). It is apparent that lengthening borders "naturally" when it modifies the entire sentence rather than the verb phrase, as in the related strings considered previously. A cumulative lengthening account can readily handle the effect in (20). However, the linear hypothesis stated above cannot account for this effect, since in the surface linear string the S and the VP begin with the same word, "presenting."

Yet another alternative to the present account would attempt to explain the timing effects in terms of semantics rather than syntax. According to this sort of account, lengthening and pausing would border a modifier z when it modifies the semantically more global of two constituents (w of w,x). Each of the ambiguities considered here could be described in terms of this semantic globality or in terms of structural dominance. While the structural dominance account is consistent with other data on speech timing for nonambiguous sentences, the account in terms of semantic globality cannot be generalized to nonambiguous sentences, largely because relations of semantic inclusion are barred from occurring within the same sentence (Postal, 1974; Cooper, 1976b). In addition, when we consider cases where a relation of semantic globality obtains between sentences having the same structural relations, we see no apparent effect on speech timing. Consider, for example, the strings below.

(21)   (a)   This bird is yellow.
       (b)   This canary is yellow.

If the semantic globality hypothesis is generalized, then the modifier "yellow" should be bordered by lengthening of the previous word, "is," in (21a) versus (21b), since the modified constituent in (21a) is "this bird," semantically more global than the modified constituent in (21b), "this canary." Our intuition about this comparison is consistent with other experimental studies in which we have found no systematic relation between similar semantic variables and speech timing (Cooper and Paccia-Cooper, 1978). It thus seems that the timing effects presented here are best captured by a structural account, in which lengthening is attributable to the presence of a relatively greater number of constituent boundaries.

The question of *why* speech is elongated at phrase boundaries remains unsolved. We speculate that lengthening in this case represents a relaxation response of the speech system upon completion of processing a phrasal constituent, whereby the internal clock for computing durations is slowed down. This relaxation account is in accord with the structural account proposed above in terms of the notion of cumulative phrase-*final* lengthening. It is conceivable that the results are attributed to an alternative factor of the speaker's planning for an upcoming constituent, although, as we shall see in chapter 7, planning is not typically accompanied by lengthening for structural variables of the type studied here.

Conclusion

The results of this study provide support for a hierarchical representation of syntactic structure in speech production, incorporating a variety of specific dominance relations among constituents. The major phrasal constituents coded in speech appear to include NP and VP.

In the case of the VP constituent, this conclusion is particularly important, since the existence of such a constituent has been called into question on linguistic grounds. Throughout the foregoing analysis, we have assumed the existence of the VP node in accord with Chomsky's (1965) phrase structure grammar. While Chomsky and many of his colleagues have maintained that the VP is essential for capturing certain regularities of the grammar, Keyser and Postal (1976), among others, have argued that a clause is directly elaborated in terms of three constituents—noun phrase, verb, and noun phrase, as shown in figure 2.9. Since the initial breakdown of the clause into smaller constituents is a property that must be specified for all sentences generated by the grammar, the dispute over the existence of a VP node is pivotal for both theories of linguistics and psycholinguistics.

Experiment 1 of this study, in conjunction with the notion of cumulative phrase-final lengthening, appears to provide critical

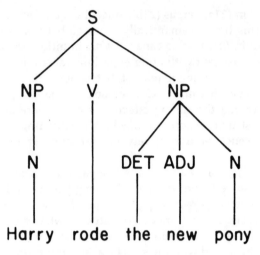

Figure 2.9   *Structural representation of the sentence "Harry rode the new pony" according to Keyser and Postal's phrase structure rule, S → NP + V + NP.*

information on this issue. According to the analysis proposed by Keyser and Postal (1976), in which no VP node is employed, there should be no difference in the duration of the key word in the two readings of the structural ambiguities studied in this experiment, since the key word occurs at the end of the NP direct object in both readings, as shown in figure 2.10.

However, the results of the experiment showed significant lengthening of the key word in the (a) reading of this type of structural ambiguity. By postulating a VP node in speech production, this effect was readily accounted for in terms of cumulative phrase-final lengthening, as demonstrated in the preceding discussion. Generally, the experiment provides support for the notion that NP and VP are the major phrasal constituents coded during speech production, and the same line of argumentation can be applied to other experiments (for example, experiment 3) to infer hierarchical relationships between constituents within the VP, including NP and PP.

The results of this study should also be considered in light of the possible distinction between underlying and surface representations of syntactic structure, discussed in chapter 1. We chose to adopt a *surface* representation for each of the ambiguities described in this study (see figure 2.3) under the assumption that speech timing effects are more likely to be influenced by this type of structural representation because such a representation is com-

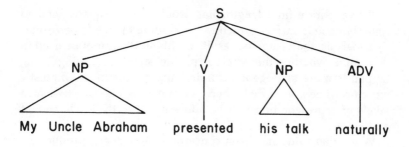

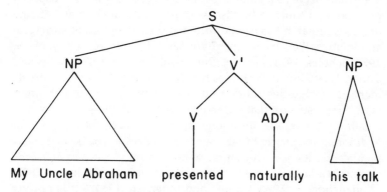

Figure 2.10   *Two structural representations of the ambiguous sentence (3), according to Keyser and Postal's linguistic analysis, S → NP + V + NP. The upper tree corresponds to the (3') reading; the lower tree represents the (3'') reading.*

puted at a level of coding that transmits information directly to the phonological component (see figure 1.1). However, for each of the sentences studied here, it is quite possible that the underlying and surface structures are isomorphic in all relevant respects, since current formulations of transformational grammar have enriched surface structures considerably (see, for example, Jackendoff, 1972; Akmajian and Heny, 1975; Emonds, 1976). According to this view, the present study would not speak to the issue of whether speech timing effects are computed at one or the other of these two possible levels of representation. On the other hand, some linguists have argued that the underlying and surface structures are not isomorphic for each of the sentences considered here. For example, Ross (1970) has proposed an underlying performative analysis for vocatives of the type studied in experiment 2, although Anderson (1968) and Fraser (1970) have argued that the performative nature of vocatives should not be represented at a syntactic level of coding at all. In any event, the notion of cumulative phrase-final lengthening would apply equally well to underlying and surface structures, according to Ross's performative analysis; therefore, the results of this study cannot be used to determine whether the level of phrase structure coding being tapped is more analogous to underlying or to surface linguistic structure. The issue of whether speech coding involves two such levels of representation will be addressed directly in chapters 4 and 5.

While this study has been concerned with speech production, the results serve as a guide for conducting related work on speech perception, a topic to be discussed primarily in chapter 8. Some previous research has been directed at the perception of structural ambiguities (Levelt, Zwanenburg, and Ouweneel, 1970; Nash, 1970; Scholes, 1971; Lehiste, Olive, and Streeter, 1976; Wales and Toner, 1979), but such studies have not included systematic treatment of ambiguities considered here. Some of the present large-scale effects suggest that differences in speech timing may provide a sufficient cue for disambiguation in speech perception. In addition, it is apparent that major differences in speakers' fundamental frequency contours also typically accompany the distinct readings of these structural ambiguities (Atkinson, 1973; O'Shaughnessy, 1976; Cooper and Sorensen, 1980).[6] It is not yet known whether these additional differences are required to permit perceptual disambiguation.

3 | Phrase Structures and Grammatical Categories

I S SEGMENTAL TIMING influenced by the type of grammatical category to which a word belongs? By *grammatical category* we refer to the traditional classification of words into categories such as noun, verb, and adjective; these terms are the fundamental units on which the phrase structure rules of a grammar are typically based. In chapter 2 it was found that phrase units such as noun phrase and verb phrase influence speech timing, lending some credence to the notion that these units are coded as such during speech production. Here we ask whether the smaller units, involving grammatical categories such as noun and verb, exert an influence on timing that is independent of the superordinate phrase structures to which these categories belong.

As a starting point for examining this possibility, let us consider a well-known fact—that words of different grammatical categories have varying probabilities of receiving primary stress in an utterance. In particular, so-called content words, belonging to categories such as noun and verb, are more likely to receive primary stress than so-called function words, belonging to categories such as determiner and conjunction. Since primary stress is typically accompanied by the acoustic correlate of longer duration, in addition to higher fundamental frequency and intensity (Fry, 1957), it is reasonable to suppose that segmental timing is influenced by the grammatical category to which a word belongs. In a program designed to synthesize speech by rule, Coker, Umeda, and Browman (1973) have incorporated this principle in their rules for segmental duration, assigning nine different stress levels to lexical items.

The influence of grammatical categories on speech timing is accepted as self-evident for major versus minor grammatical categories. By major categories, we mean categories such as noun, verb, adjective, and adverb; by minor categories, we mean categories such as determiner and conjunction. But it has also been claimed that durational differences exist *within* the class of major categories. For example, it has been informally reported that nouns are typically longer than verbs (Lightfoot, 1970; Scholes, 1971; Coker, Umeda, and Browman, 1973). Unlike the durational effect for major versus minor categories, the differences observed within the class of major categories cannot be accepted as self-evident and have not been documented in controlled experiments. Accordingly, we conduct tests in this study to determine the effects of category type in sentences matched for phonetic environment in the region surrounding the measured segment. We seek to determine whether timing effects traditionally ascribed to the influence of category types were in fact attributed to this source or to independent influences of constituent boundaries.

As just noted, it has been observed informally that the duration of nouns is typically longer than that of verbs. This difference is usually attributed to the fact that nouns form a larger lexical class than verbs, such that the information load carried by a given noun is larger than that carried by a verb, under the assumption that word duration is a positive correlate of information load (Coker, Umeda, and Browman, 1973). However, another interpretation may be advanced, relying on the notion of phrase-final lengthening. As shown in chapter 2, phrase boundaries are often accompanied by segmental lengthening. In English, nouns typically occur in phrase-final position at the ends of NPs; verbs, on the other hand, usually occur at the beginning of VPs. Thus the influence of grammatical category type on segment duration is typically confounded with the influence of phrase position.

EXPERIMENT 1

In experiment 1 we attempted to document the durational difference between nouns and verbs in matched sentence materials. The duration of the same word segment was measured in its occurrence as either noun or verb in sentence pairs matched for phonetic environment and stress contour. Structurally, the nouns occurred in phrase-final position and the verbs occurred in phrase-initial position. As such, the present experiment is aimed at simply determining the validity of the noun-verb durational difference that has been traditionally claimed.

Sentence Materials and Procedure

Eight test sentences were devised for this experiment, following the method of sentence construction described in chapter 1. The test materials included four pairs of sentences, with each pair containing a key word as either noun or verb. The test sentences appear below. The key word in each pair is in italics.

(1) (a) I showed Marie a *coach* that Eve will like.
     (b) I helped Maria *coach* the team last night.
(2) (a) John gave Marie a *tape* that Christopher made.
     (b) John helped Maria *tape* the Christmas parade.
(3) (a) Thomas gave Eve a *coat* that was covered with paint.
     (b) Thomas helped Eva *coat* the old ceiling with paint.
(4) (a) Tom told Eve a *joke* about Harry.
     (b) Tom and Eva *joke* about Harry.

In each case the key word began and ended with an obstruent to facilitate segmentation of the waveform. The key word was always preceded by an unstressed schwa.

Ten speakers were tested following the procedure described in chapter 1. For each sentence, the measured segment started at the release burst of the word-initial obstruent and ended at the termination of glottal pulsing just prior to the word-final voiceless obstruent in the key word. For example, in pair (1) the measured segment of the key word "coach" included the consonant /k/ and the following vowel.

Results and Discussion

The mean durations and standard deviations of the key segments for each sentence type appear in table 3.1. It can be seen that the mean duration of the key segment was longer in each sentence pair when this segment was a noun rather than a verb. In sentence pairs (1)–(3), this difference was statistically significant (pair (1): $p < 0.001$, $t = 6.16$, $df = 9$; pair (2): $p < 0.01$, $t = 3.56$, $df = 9$; pair (3): $p < 0.01$, $t = 4.37$, $df = 9$; two-tailed t tests for matched pairs). In pair (4), a nonsignificant difference was observed in the same direction ($0.10 > p > 0.05$, $t = 2.03$, $df = 9$; two-tailed t test for matched pair).

The results support the notion that nouns are of longer duration than corresponding verbs. However, the results do not permit us to determine whether this difference in duration is attributable to grammatical category type or to phrase position. An account based on phrase position is attractive, because specification of a word's position in a constituent is already required to account for the results obtained in chapter 2.

Table 3.1 *Mean durations (msec) and standard deviations of the key segment portion of the italicized key words in experiment 1*

	$\bar{X}$	S_x
(1) (a) I showed Marie a *coach* that Eve will like.	208.8	30.9
(b) I helped Maria *coach* the team last night.	161.7	14.2
(2) (a) John gave Marie a *tape* that Christopher made.	189.2	38.1
(b) John helped Maria *tape* the Christmas parade.	165.2	27.0
(3) (a) Thomas gave Eve a *coat* that was covered with paint.	202.5	27.2
(b) Thomas helped Eva *coat* the old ceiling with paint.	172.4	25.9
(4) (a) Tom told Eve a *joke* about Harry.	184.8	28.2
(b) Tom and Eva *joke* about Harry.	171.9	15.4

EXPERIMENT 2

In the normal contexts in which nouns and verbs occur in English (see experiment 1), it is not possible to quantify separately the effects of grammatical category type and phrase position. The sentence pairs in experiment 2 contain noun-verb pairs placed in constituent-final position. In this way, the position of the key word in the constituent would be held constant within a pair, and any remaining effect could be attributed to grammatical category type.[1]

Sentence Materials and Procedure

Eight test sentences were constructed for this experiment. The test sentences appear below, with the key words italicized.

(5) (a) John will find Eve a *coach* if she ever decides to sing professionally.

(b) John will help Eva *coach* if she ever decides to start a basketball team.

(6) (a) At the swimming meet Paul found Marie a *coach* and hoped her team would win the diving contest.

(b) At the swimming meet Paul watched Maria *coach* and hoped her team would win the diving contest.

(7) (a) During class Beth told Marie a *joke* but Renée read the syllabus.

(b) Usually Beth and Maria *joke* but today they were serious.

(8) (a) Whenever Professor Jones is late for class Jeff tells Eve a *joke*.

(b)   Whenever Professor Jones is late for class Jeff and Eva *joke.*

The procedures were similar to those described previously, involving ten speakers. The key segment of the first appropriate token of each sentence was measured for duration.

Results and Discussion

Sentence pairs (5) and (6) showed essentially no difference in the length of the key segment, "coach": the duration of the noun in (5a) averaged 2.4 msec or 1.1 percent longer than the verb form in (5b), and the noun in (6a) was 3.1 msec or 1.3 percent longer than the verb in (6b), with $p > 0.5$ for both pairs (two-tailed *t* tests for matched pairs.)

An effect in the opposite direction accompanied pairs (7) and (8).[2] The duration of "joke" as a verb in (7b) was significantly longer than as a noun in (7a); ($p < 0.05$, $t = 2.76$, $df = 9$; two-tailed *t* test for matched pairs), and in sentence pair (8), a nonsignificant effect occurred in the same direction ($0.20 > p > 0.10$, $t = 1.59$, $df = 9$; two-tailed *t* test for matched pairs). The mean segment durations and standard deviations for all four pairs are shown in table 3.2.

By placing noun-verb homophones of the type found in experiment 1 in constituent-final position, we hoped to document the independent influence of grammatical category type on segment duration. Given the results of experiment 1, it was expected that the nouns might exhibit longer durations than the verbs. The absence of systematic effects across the four sentence pairs in this experiment suggests that nouns might not be inherently longer than verbs after all. In order to account for the results, two additional influences can be considered. First, the assumption that there is no interaction effect between grammatical category type and constituent position may be incorrect. In particular, verbs may show more clause-final lengthening than nouns. Verbs in clause-final position violate the normal canonical word order (subject-verb-object) of English. The speaker may lengthen a verb in constituent-final position to allow the listener more time to process this unusual word order. This possibility will not be tested here.

A second possible influence, to be tested in experiment 3, involves the debatable deletion of a direct object (Chomsky, 1965; Grinder, 1971; but see Sampson, 1972). As noted in chapter 1, one class of deletions, exemplified by Verb Gapping, acts to lengthen the word prior to the deletion site. It could be argued that deletion

Table 3.2 *Mean durations (msec) and standard deviations of the key segment portion of the italicized key words in experiment 2*

	$\bar{X}$	S_x
(5) (a) John will find Eve a *coach* if she ever decides to sing professionally.	226.2	20.1
(b) John will help Eva *coach* if she ever decides to start a basketball team.	223.8	25.3
(6) (a) At the swimming meet Paul found Marie a *coach* and hoped her team would win the diving contest.	239.5	20.7
(b) At the swimming meet Paul watched Maria *coach* and hoped her team would win the diving contest.	236.4	19.8
(7) (a) During class Beth told Marie a *joke* but Renée read the syllabus.	219.8	24.9
(b) Usually Beth and Maria *joke* but today they were serious.	241.4	24.4
(8) (a) Whenever Professor Jones is late for class Jeff tells Eve a *joke*.	247.4	18.8
(b) Whenever Professor Jones is late for class Jeff and Eva *joke*.	260.0	27.2

Note that the durations of the key words are longer in experiment 2 than for matched words in experiment 1. The longer durations obtained in this experiment may be attributed to the fact that the key words occurred at either the boundary separating two main clauses, as in sentences (4)-(7), or at the end of the utterance, as in sentence (8). It appears that segmental lengthening is greater in these locations than at the less major boundaries tested in experiment 1.

of the direct object occurs in each of the (b) versions of sentences (5)-(8). For example, if the deleted material is reinserted in sentence (5b), the result is the following:

(5) (c) John will help Eva coach *a basketball team* if she ever decides to start a basketball team.

It is conceivable that the deletion of the italicized words above may act to lengthen the verb "coach." If so, it is possible that the generally null results obtained in experiment 2 may be attributed to the combination of two opposing effects: (1) the supposed inherently longer duration of nouns than verbs, and (2) lengthening of the verb just prior to the deletion site produced by Object Deletion.

Alternatively, the present results suggest that the durational difference between nouns and verbs observed in experiment 1, traditionally ascribed to their status as different grammatical categories, may rather be attributed solely to differences in position within a constituent. If so, there would be no need to specify individual category types in a theory of speech timing.

EXPERIMENT 3

Experiment 3 was designed to test whether the debatable rule of Object Deletion acts to lengthen the duration of a verb in constituent-final position. Sentences were constructed using verb homophones, some of which take objects (transitive) and some of which do not (intransitive). Lengthening of an intransitive verb in constituent-final position cannot be due to an influence of Object Deletion, since by definition such a verb takes no direct or indirect object. Examples of such verbs are "sleep," "shiver," and "die." For purposes of constructing matched sentence pairs, we will also consider verbs that take objects optionally, depending on the subject. One such verb is "fly": compare "The pilot *flew* the plane" with "The bird *flew*."

Sentence Materials and Procedure

Ten test sentences and three fillers were constructed for this experiment. The test materials consisted of four groups of sentences matched for key word position and stress contour. Following each sentence below, a description is given of the key verb's position and object relation.

(9) (a) If the pilot *flies* the plane we'll surely crash.
   (PIP = phrase-initial position, TR = transitive)

   (b) If the pilot *flies* the plane will surely crash.
   (PFP = phrase-final position, TR)

   (c) If the parrot *flies* the boy will feed him cake.
   (PFP, IN = intransitive)

(10) (a) If the baby parakeet *flies* to Lisa we'll be happy.
   (PIP, IN)

   (b) If the baby parakeet *flies* Teresa will be happy.
   (PFP, IN)

(11) (a) If the tailor *dyes* the cloth we'll refuse to buy the suit.
   (PIP, TR)

   (b) If the tailor *dyes* the cloth will no longer hold a crease.
   (PFP, TR)

   (c) If the tailor *dies* the cloth in his shop will all be sold.
   (PFP, IN)

(12) (a) If the tailor *dies* in the summer his shop will be sold.[3]
           (PIP, IN)
      (b) If the tailor *dies* in the summer his shop will be sold.
           (PFP, IN)

The procedure, involving ten new speakers, was identical to that of the previous experiments. The duration of the key segment of the verb was measured for the first appropriate token of each sentence. For "flies," the measured segment began with the onset of voicing for the /l/ and ended with the offset of regular voicing of the vowel. The offset sometimes overlapped with the onset of frication noise of the /s/. In such instances, the offset was marked where the /s/ noise was no longer modulated in a semiperiodic manner characteristic of regular voicing. The key word "dies" or "dyes" was measured from the beginning of the burst of the /d/ to the offset of voicing as described for "flies." The fact that the key words did not begin with clear release bursts nor end with voiceless obstruents was necessitated by the limited number of verbs in English that fulfill the other criteria for this experiment.[4] The estimated measurement error for the key segments was about ±10 msec.

Results and Discussion

Comparing transitive verbs in phrase-initial and phrase-final position, significant lengthening occurred for the phrase-final cases: (9b) versus (9a), $p < 0.001$, $t = 8.34$, $df = 9$; (11b) versus (11a), $p < 0.01$, $t = 4.64$, $df = 9$; two-tailed t tests for matched pairs. Intransitive verbs in phrase-final position were also significantly longer than the phrase-initial transitive verbs: (9c) versus (9a), $p < 0.001$, $t = 8.35$, $df = 9$; (11c) versus (11a), $p < 0.001$, $t = 4.82$, $df = 9$; two-tailed t tests for matched pairs. The mean segment durations and standard deviations are shown in table 3.3

The percent lengthening of (9b) and (9c) versus (9a) averaged 49 and 51 percent, respectively; for (11b) and (11c) versus (11a), the percent lengthening averaged 40 and 46 percent. These effects must be attributed to constituent-final lengthening. The close similarity of the magnitudes of lengthening in the transitive (b) and intransitive (c) sentences of groups (9) and (11) indicates no significant effect of Object Deletion on word duration. In addition, grammatical category effects were neutralized, since all the key words were verbs. The only account consistent with the data from experiments 1–3 is one based on constituent-final lengthening.

Further evidence against a lengthening account based on Object Deletion can be obtained by comparison of the sentences in pairs

Table 3.3 *Mean durations (msec) and standard deviations of the key segment portion of the italicized key words in experiment 3*

	$\bar{X}$	S_x
(9) (a) If the pilot *flies* the plane we'll surely crash. (PIP, TR)	219.7	38.0
(b) If the pilot *flies* the plane will surely crash. (PFP, TR)	326.3	32.3
(c) If the parrot *flies* the boy will feed him cake. (PFP, IN)	330.7	41.7
(10) (a) If the baby parakeet *flies* to Lisa we'll be happy. (PIP, IN)	210.0	46.5
(b) If the baby parakeet *flies* Teresa will be happy. (PFP, IN)	297.4	40.8
(11) (a) If the tailor *dyes* the cloth we'll refuse to buy the suit. (PIP, TR)	231.7	44.9
(b) If the tailor *dyes* the cloth will no longer hold a crease. (PFP, TR)	323.9	57.6
(c) If the tailor *dies* the cloth in his shop will all be sold. (PFP, IN)	338.6	39.5
(12) (a) If the tailor *dies* in the summer his shop will be sold. (PIP, IN)[3]	234.3	34.1
(b) If the tailor *dies* in the summer his shop will be sold. (PFP, IN)	369.9	34.9

(10) and (12). Recall that, in these sentences, intransitive verbs appear in phrase-initial versus phrase-final position. Significant lengthening was found for "flies" in (10b) versus (10a) ($p < 0.01$, $t = 4.13$, $df = 9$) and for "dies" in (12b) versus (12a) ($p < 0.001$, $t = 10.6$, $df = 9$; two-tailed t tests for matched pairs). Again, this lengthening must be attributed to the influence of constituent position, since any effects produced by grammatical category type and Object Deletion are neutralized. The magnitude of the lengthening in pair (10) was 42 percent, and in pair (12) it was 58 percent.

Two additional experiments have been conducted to extend the results of experiment 3. One study involved five test sentence pairs. The verbs were placed in constituent-final and non-constituent-final positions. Two of the sentence pairs appear below with the key words italicized.

(13) (a) If graduate students *teach* the class we'll complain to the chairman.

(b) If graduate students *teach* the class will complain to the chairman.

(14) (a) After we *talked* to Rita we went to class.
      (b) After we *talked* Teresa went to class.

All five sentence pairs showed significant lengthening of the verb
in constituent-final position ($p < 0.001$ for all pairs, t values ranging from 4.98 to 10.5, $df = 9$; two-tailed t tests for matched pairs).
The average percent lengthening for key segments ranged from 21
to 49 percent, with a mean lengthening of 35 percent. A second
study involved an additional four sentence pairs and ten speakers.
Two of the pairs were ambiguous sentences, one of which is
shown below.

(15) (a) If you can *coach* naturally you can join our team.
           (If you can coach in a natural way.)
      (b) If you can *coach* naturally you can join our team.
           (Of course you can join if you can coach.)

All pairs showed lengthening of the verb in constituent-final position (from 16 to 50 percent) that was significant ($p < 0.001$ for all
pairs, t values ranging from 4.81 to 7.63, $df = 9$; two-tailed t tests
for matched pairs). Taken together, the results of experiments 1–3
support the notion that words are lengthened in constituent-final
position. Furthermore, this lengthening can be predicted on the
basis of constituent position, without considering possible effects
of (1) the inherent length of a word based on its membership in a
certain major grammatical category, or (2) the deletion of an object following a verb, leaving the verb in constituent-final position. The findings of experiment 2 also suggest that a single rule of
lengthening is appropriate for constituent-final lengthening with
both nouns and verbs. Therefore, the distinction between nouns
and verbs need not be specified in a first-order theory of speech
timing or in durational rules for speech synthesis.

EXPERIMENT 4

In experiment 4 we extended our study to the major categories
of adjective and adverb. The durations of adjectives and adverbs
were compared by measuring /tu/, the phonemic form of the English homophone pair "two," adjective, and "too," adverb. On the
basis of the results of experiments 1–3, we suggest that no difference exists in the inherent duration of adjectives and adverbs.
Since typical English sentences contain "two" as an NP-initial adjective and "too" as a constituent-final adverb, lengthening of the
adverb can probably be accounted for by constituent-final position, without resorting to accounts of inherent length based on

category type. If constituent-final position acts to lengthen segments, "too" should exhibit longer segment durations than "two." This prediction is in full accord with intuition.

Sentence Materials and Procedure

Two pairs of test sentences were constructed. In pair (16) the key segment was bounded on the left by a word-final obstruent /k/ and on the right by a word-initial /s/. In pair (17) the key segment was bounded on the left by a word-final vowel /o/ and on the right by a word-initial /p/. The test sentences appear below, with the key word italicized.

(16) (a) Joey signed the check *too* seemingly nervous.
     (b) Joey gave Monique *two* slippers for Christmas.
(17) (a) John should make Kathy go *too* peacefully if possible.
     (b) Mrs. Scott offered Joe *two* pieces of her homemade pie.

The testing and data analysis procedure, involving ten subjects, was identical to that in previous experiments. The phonetic environment in pair (16) occasionally led to an overlapping of the vowel portion of /tu/ and the following word-initial /s/. In such cases, the offset of /tu/ was marked at a point where the /s/ frication no longer appeared to be modulated in a semiperiodic manner (see the discussion of "flies" in experiment 3). The error estimate for these cases was ±10 msec.

Results and Discussion

The mean segment durations for the key segment for each sentence are presented in table 3.4. It can be seen that the duration of /tu/ as an adverb was longer than as an adjective. This difference was statistically significant for both pairs: (16a) versus (16b), $p < 0.001$, $t = 10.1$, $df = 9$; (17a) versus (17b), $p < 0.001$, $t = 8.86$, $df = 9$; two-tailed t tests for matched pairs.

It seems likely that this effect, like that obtained in experiment 1 for nouns versus verbs, is attributable to constituent-final position rather than to any inherent durational differences based on category membership. To test this claim directly, it would be interesting to compare adjectives and adverbs when both appear in phrase-final position, analogous to the test for nouns and verbs conducted in experiment 2. For example, in the ambiguous string "John has /tu/," the adjective and adverb forms of /tu/ both appear in phrase-final position. If phrase position is the sole syntac-

Table 3.4 *Mean durations (msec) and standard deviations of the italicized key words in experiment 4*

	$\bar{X}$	S_x
(16) (a) Joey signed the check *too* seemingly nervous.	248.0	43.7
(b) Joey gave Monique *two* slippers for Christmas.	156.3	20.9
(17) (a) John should make Kathy go *too* peacefully if possible.	258.0	41.4
(b) Mrs. Scott offered Joe *two* pieces of her homemade pie.	137.3	26.8

tic determinant of segmental timing differences between adverbs and adjectives, then the duration of /tu/ should be the same when this is used as either the adjective "two" or the adverb "too." According to our intuition this indeed seems to be the case.

However, because of the structure of the English language this comparison represents only an imperfect test of the above claim. The adjective form of /tu/, the only adjective-adverb homophone known to us, is a left-branching structure in English, and so by definition cannot occur in constituent-final position in underlying syntactic structure. Thus, for the adjective reading of the above ambiguity, "two" marks the site of a deleted noun phrase. As we will see in chapter 4, deletions of this type may influence speech timing. Hence our observation regarding the string "John has /tu/" may be confounded: any lengthening for the adverb reading due to category membership may be counteracted by lengthening for the adjective reading due to the presence of a deletion site. Thus, while it appears that phrase position is the sole determinant of timing differences between adjectives and adverbs, this cannot be demonstrated conclusively using the present paradigm.

It would be interesting also to conduct a more general test of the claim that phrase position is the only aspect of syntactic structure that influences the segmental timing of words belonging to different major grammatical categories. Such a test would involve comparing the durations of words *across* the two subgroups of major grammatical categories already studied. Nouns and verbs typically carry more information in a sentence than do their modifiers, adjectives and adverbs. Thus, while no inherent durational differences appear to exist between adjectives and adverbs, nor between nouns and verbs, it is possible that nouns and verbs as a group have longer durations than adjectives and adverbs, independent of phrase position. To test this possibility, an experiment was conducted comparing the duration of a word serving alternatively as a noun and as an adjective, such as "black," while controlling for phrase position, as in (18) below.

(18) (a) My favorite colors are *black* and purple.
      (b) My uncle purchased a *black* umbrella.

"Black" functions as a noun in (18a) and as an adjective in (18b). In both sentences this homonym occurs in non-phrase-final position. If the timing differences between words belonging to different major grammatical categories are attributable solely to differences in phrase position, then we would expect "black" to be of the same duration in (18a) and (18b). The results for three sentence pairs with eight speakers revealed a slightly longer duration for the noun, averaging about 10 msec for each of the three pairs. This effect was statistically significant for only one sentence pair, however. It appears that a small difference in inherent duration may exist for the major categories of noun and adjective, although this difference is quite small in comparison to the difference in word duration attributed to phrase-final and non-phrase-final positions.

EXPERIMENT 5

Thus far we have studied segmental lengthening of words in major grammatical categories. In experiment 5 we extend our focus to the distinction between major and minor grammatical categories. While the previous experiments suggest that major categories bear the same inherent duration, there is every reason to suspect that very different inherent durations exist for major versus minor categories. Unlike major categories, phonological reduction is a distinguishing property of minor grammatical categories (prepositions,[5] determiners, and conjunctions). In particular, a word belonging to any of these categories may undergo vowel reduction in casual speech.

In this experiment the major category of adjective was compared with the minor category of preposition by placing the homophone pair "two" and "to" in sentences matched for phrase position of the key word. It was expected that "to" would be much shorter than "two," since the former is phonologically reducible (Chomsky and Halle, 1968).

Sentence Materials and Procedure

The four pairs of sentences constructed for this experiment are shown below, with the key segment italicized.

(19) (a) We heard Janice read *two* poems at the literary convention.

      (b) We heard Janice read *to* poets at the literary convention.

(20) (a) I saw John run *two* kilometers last night.

      (b) I saw John run *to* Canaveral last night.

(21) (a) Alice said she must write *two* pages this afternoon.

      (b) Alice said she must write *to* Patty this afternoon.

(22) (a) Ted watched the couple walk *two* blocks down the street.

      (b) Ted watched the couple walk *to* Bob's down the street.

The procedure, involving ten speakers, was identical to that in the previous experiments.

Results and Discussion

The mean segment durations for all key segments are shown in table 3.5. The duration of *to* was significantly shorter in every case: $p < 0.001$ for all pairs, $t = 9.70$ in pair (19), $t = 12.6$ in pair (20), $t = 8.83$ in pair (21), and $t = 9.72$ in pair (22), $df = 9$; two-tailed t tests for matched pairs. The percent of shortening was approximately 50 percent in all pairs, as shown in table 3.5. The results thus confirm our intuition that words belonging to minor grammatical categories are shorter in duration than words of major categories. The large difference in duration noted here indicates that at least a binary distinction between major and minor categories must be included in a theory of speech timing and in rules for speech synthesis.

General Discussion

The results of these experiments indicate that segmental lengthening occurs for words in major grammatical categories in constituent-final position. The longer duration of nouns than of verbs, for example, was shown to be dependent not on grammatical category type per se, but rather on the difference in constituent position that these two category types typically occupy in English sentences. On the other hand, significant differences in duration were documented for major versus minor category types, suggesting the need for a binary distinction between these two classes of categories.

Informal observations of Romance languages also suggest that constituent position plays a role in determining the duration of a word belonging to a given grammatical category. For example, in

Table 3.5 *Mean durations (msec) and standard deviations of the italicized key words in experiment 5*

	$\bar{X}$	S_x
(19) (a) We heard Janice read *two* poems at the literary convention.	146.6	32.5
(b) We heard Janice read *to* poets at the literary convention.	71.2	18.2
(20) (a) I saw John run *two* kilometers last night.	139.2	25.8
(b) I saw John run *to* Canaveral last night.	71.5	15.8
(21) (a) Alice said she must write *two* pages this afternoon.	131.0	29.0
(b) Alice said she must write *to* Patty this afternoon.	72.7	17.3
(22) (a) Ted watched the couple walk *two* blocks down the street.[6]	126.4	25.9
(b) Ted watched the couple walk *to* Bob's down the street.	65.0	18.8

French it appears that adjectives are longer in postnominal versus prenominal position, though they are also typically accompanied by a change in meaning. In Spanish, Carmen Egido has pointed out to us that a phonemic contrast exists between semantically equivalent forms of the adjective "good" when these occur in prenominal versus postnominal position, as in:

Juan es un *buen* niño.   (John is a good boy.)
Juan es un niño *bueno.*   (John is a good boy.)

The longer version of the adjective occurs in constituent-final position, consistent with the results presented here. Further studies with other languages might be aimed at testing whether differences in duration among words in major grammatical categories are attributed to constituent position. Such studies would be particularly interesting with languages like Japanese, in which the verb typically appears in clause-final position.

By using the terms *lengthening* and *shortening* we have implied the existence of a fixed reference for durational rules. We postulate that the reference duration for a word can be defined as the duration of that word when it occurs as a major grammatical category in non-phrase-final position. For example, we considered the reference duration of /tu/ in experiment 4 to be the duration of "two" as it typically occurs in non-phrase-final position. Thus, the durational difference between this form and "too," when it occurs as a clause-final adverb, was described as lengthening. On the other hand, the durational effect for the preposition *"to,"* a minor grammatical category word, was described as shortening.

This classification of durational effects is in accord with our intuition about the underlying determinants of rules for speech timing. Major category words are lengthened in constituent-final position as a result of a marked slowdown of the speech processing machinery, a by-product of general relaxation upon completion of the constituent and/or the need to plan an upcoming constituent (see chapter 7). The shortening of minor categories, on the other hand, may be attributed to the very low information load carried by words belonging to this class, as evidenced by the fact that these words are typically omitted in instances in which there exist major constraints on speech processing—compare the "telegraphic" speech produced by young children (Brown and Bellugi, 1964) and Broca's aphasics (Goodglass and Hunt, 1958).

In summary, we can infer from the results obtained in this chapter that information about specific category membership does not play a major role at the stage of syntactic coding at which phrase structures influence segmental duration. However, this inference does not lead to the conclusion that the speaker fails to code information about specific category membership at *any* stage during the speech production process. On the contrary, evidence from word exchange errors in spontaneous speech (for example, "I've got to go home and give my *bath* a hot *back*"—Garrett, 1975, Example 15) suggests that speakers may represent words in terms of their category membership at a stage of processing that involves lexical insertion. Thus, while evidence from speech timing may be used to infer the existence of a certain form of mental representation involved at one particular stage of processing, the absence of timing effects cannot be taken as evidence to support the view that a particular form of representation is not coded at some other stage of speech processing. This principle applies to the results obtained throughout this study.

4 | Deletion Rules

I N THIS CHAPTER we begin to consider the possibility that more than a single level of syntactic coding is computed during speech production. As noted in chapter 1, the proposal of more than a single level of syntactic representation is one of the distinguishing properties of a transformational grammar. For a given sentence, such a grammar provides an underlying and a surface level of representation, mediated by transformational rules that move, add, or delete elements. A good deal of psychological research has been aimed at the question of whether these levels of linguistic description correspond to mental operations performed during sentence production and perception (for a review, see Fodor, Bever, and Garrett, 1974). The outcome of such research has provided some support for this analogy, but it remains unclear whether the underlying level of coding tapped by such research is syntactic or semantic (see also Garrett, 1975).

In chapters 2 and 3 we considered mainly sentences whose underlying and surface structures were isomorphic in all relevant respects. In chapter 2, for example, experiments with ambiguities provided information about the specific structural nodes computed by the speaker at a given level of coding, but they did not bear critically on the issue of whether speech timing may be influenced by more than a single level of syntactic coding. In fact, for reasons to be discussed in this chapter, it is extremely difficult to provide a critical test of this issue.

One type of sentence suited for this purpose involves a surface structure that, according to transformational grammar, has been derived via deletion transformations. We have conducted a series of experimental studies with such structures to determine whether effects on speech timing are produced at the site of deleted constituents, as suggested by informal observation in chapter 1. If effects can be properly attributed to such deletion sites, we can infer that at least some rules for speech timing are influenced by a nonsurface level of syntactic coding. For results involving any single rule of deletion, it is impossible to determine whether an effect on timing is due to the deletion site per se or to the particular form of derived surface structure; however, a consideration of different deletion types can provide a basis for choosing between these two alternatives.

In linguistics, research on deletion rules has been characterized by a high degree of controversy, even by the standards of this controversy-laden field. Early formulations of transformational grammar sported numerous syntactic deletions, but in recent years it has been argued, often convincingly, that many of these rules are actually semantic rather than syntactic (see, for example, Sampson, 1972; Wasow, 1972; Hankamer and Sag, 1976). In this chapter we begin by examining deletion rules that seem to have withstood these attacks and still appear to be valid syntactic transformations. We will also descend into the mire to examine some putative deletion rules that remain quite controversial on linguistic grounds.

Generally deletion rules can be subdivided into two major classes, known as *identity* and *free* deletions. Identity deletions can erase material from a linguistic string only when the same material appears at another specified location in the string, whereas free deletions can erase material that does not appear elsewhere. In general, identity deletions have a firmer syntactic basis than do free deletions, and we will focus on identity rules in the first two sections of this chapter.

Gapping Rules

In order to study the possible influence of identity deletion sites, we initially chose a structure that contains a deletion site but that is not altered drastically at the surface level of representation by virtue of the deletion. Later we shall discuss other deletion rules that produce very altered surface structures, making the interpretation of the data more difficult.

The type of deletion chosen for the following experiments is termed *Gapping* (Ross, 1970), mentioned in chapter 1 during the informal discussion of pausing. This deletion is distinguished from other identity deletions by the fact that it erases a constituent from the middle of a clause rather than from its beginning or end (Jackendoff, 1971). The deleted constituent typically consists of a verb, as in (1) below, or a noun, as in (2).

(1) I ate the chicken and Harry (ate) the peas.
(2) I drank prune juice for breakfast and orange (juice) for lunch.

The linguistic constraints on Gapping have been discussed by Ross (1970), Hankamer (1971), Jackendoff (1971), Kuno (1975), Stillings (1975), and Sag (1976), among others. Both Verb and Noun Gapping can be applied optionally when two conjoined clauses or phrases contain similar structures. Typically, as in (1) and (2), the conjoined structures differ by very few contrasting elements. Hankamer and Sag (1976) have shown that Gapping is properly regarded as a syntactic deletion, since the rule operates under syntactic but not pragmatic control.

The main purpose of the following experiments was to determine whether a difference in speech timing exists between structures that do or do not involve Gapping. Intuitively, it seemed that such a difference exists for the duration of the word immediately preceding the deletion site ("Harry" in (1), for example) and, as observed in chapter 1, for the duration of the pause following this word. We undertook experiments in which measurements could be made for both the word and the pause preceding the deletion site. The phonetic material surrounding the key region was matched as closely as possible in the members of each sentence pair to neutralize the influence of phonetic structure on speech timing.

EXPERIMENT 1: VERB GAPPING

The most common type of Gapping, in which a verb is deleted under identity, was examined in experiment 1. The main purpose was to determine whether the duration of a word segment and pause immediately preceding the deletion site differs from the duration of the same word segment and pause in a comparable sentence not containing a deletion site. Additional sentences were designed to test whether the magnitude of the effect at deletion sites might be a function of (i) the type of clause (main versus embedded) containing the deletion site, (ii) the number of words in the deleted constituent, and (iii) the number of syllables in this constituent. The first test was designed to assess whether any deletion site effect is influenced by the level of the involved clauses in the structural representation, whereas the latter two tests were included to determine whether any effect at deletion sites is independent of the particular phonetic and morphological structure of the deleted material.

Sentence Materials and Procedure

Twenty test sentences, designed so that pairwise sentence comparisons could be made for each of the issues (i)–(iii) mentioned above, were constructed.

The following two sentence pairs were designed to test the effect of deletion sites in main clauses:

(3) (a) My cousin Jane completed Allen's story and my Aunt *Kate* completed Ed's poem.

   (b) My cousin Jane completed Rita's story and my Aunt *Kate* Carmella's new poem.

(4) (a) Uncle Abraham confiscated Ed's motorcycle and my cousin *Pete* confiscated Bert's Chevy.

   (b) Uncle Abraham confiscated Ed's motorcycle and my cousin *Pete* Connie's baby blue Chevy.

In each case, the italicized name represents the key word whose duration is to be measured. Verb Gapping has applied in each of the (b) versions of (3)–(4), while no deletion accompanies the (a) versions. The sentences of each pair contain the same number of syllables and the same approximate stress contour. In addition, the phonetic environment in the region of the key material is matched closely enough to eliminate phonetic influences on the durations of the key segment and following pause.

Two additional pairs of sentences were constructed to test for the effect of deletion sites within embedded clauses:

(5) (a) I thought that Jane completed Allen's story and my friend *Kate* completed Ed's poem.

   (b) I thought that Jane completed Rita's story and my friend *Kate* Carmella's new poem.

(6) (a) I'm surprised that Sam confiscated Ed's motorcycle and my cousin *Pete* confiscated Bert's Chevy.

   (b) I'm surprised that Sam confiscated Ed's motorcycle and my cousin *Pete* Connie's baby blue Chevy.

The sentences were designed so that the embedded clauses of (5)–(6) could also be compared directly with the main clauses of (3)–(4), respectively. In the case of (6b), a disambiguating string was included at the end of the sentence to aid speakers in rendering the intended meaning: "I'm surprised at the actions of both Sam and my cousin Pete."

The instances of Verb Gapping in sentences (3)–(6) involved a single polysyllabic word. Additional sentences were constructed in which the deleted constituent included three words, including the verb and two other constituents of the Verb Phrase. The deletion sites were contained in main clauses in (7)–(8) and in embedded clauses in (9)–(10).

(7) (a) My cousin Jane could read me Allen's story and my Aunt *Kate* could read me Ed's poem.

(b) My cousin Jane could read me Rita's story and my Aunt *Kate* Carmella's new poem.

(8) (a) Uncle Abraham quickly sold me Ed's motorcycle and my cousin *Pete* quickly sold me Bert's Chevy.

(b) Uncle Abraham quickly sold me Ed's motorcycle and my cousin *Pete* Connie's baby blue Chevy.

(9) (a) I thought that Jane could read me Allen's story and my friend *Kate* could read me Ed's poem.

(b) I thought that Jane could read me Rita's story and my friend *Kate* Carmella's new poem.

(10) (a) I'm surprised that Sam quickly sold me Ed's motorcycle and my cousin *Pete* quickly sold me Bert's Chevy.

(b) I'm surprised that Sam quickly sold me Ed's motorcycle and my cousin *Pete* Connie's baby blue Chevy.

Disambiguating strings were provided for each (b) version: for example, (7b) "Jane and Kate could both read to me," and (8b) "Abraham and Pete each sold me a motor vehicle." Again, the sentences were constructed so that additional comparisons could be made with sentences (3)–(4) and (5)–(6).

Finally, sentences were constructed in which the deleted constituent involved a single monosyllabic verb. The verb was contained in a main clause in (11)–(12) and in an embedded clause in (13)–(14):

(11) My cousin Janet read Maria's story and my Aunt *Kate* Carmella's new poem.

(12) Uncle Abraham's nephew sold my friend's motorcycle and my cousin *Pete* Connie's baby blue Chevy.

(13) I thought that Janet read Maria's story and my friend *Kate* Carmella's new poem.

(14) I'm surprised that Sam's nephew sold my friend's motorcycle and my cousin *Pete* Connie's baby blue Chevy.

These sentences were also constructed so that they were comparable to (3)–(4). A disambiguating string was provided for (13): "I
thought that both Janet and Kate read the works."

The test sentences were presented, along with fillers, in pseudorandom order to ten speakers using the procedure described in
chapter 1. Acoustic measurements were obtained for the key segments /ke/ of "Kate" and /pi/ of "Pete" and for the silent interval following these segments. Any release burst at the end of the
key segment was included as part of the pause measurement.

Results

The mean durations and standard deviations of the word and
pause segments for each test sentence are presented in table 4.1. A
comparison of sentences containing deletion sites with corresponding sentences containing no deletion sites—that is, the (a)
versus (b) versions of sentences (3)–(10)—revealed systematic
lengthening of the word and pause segments immediately preceding the deletion sites. For the word segment, the duration was
significantly longer (at $p < 0.05$) in seven of eight cases. For the
eight sentence pairs, the t values ranged from 2.00 to 6.91, with
the lengthening for each pair averaging from 10 to 27 percent. The
duration of corresponding pauses preceding the deletion sites was
also longer in each of the eight (b) versions, and in three cases this
effect reached statistical significance (t values ranging from 1.39 to
4.55 for all eight pairs). The lengthening averaged from 27 to 66
percent for the pauses. A comparison of the data for word segments and pauses reveals the same dissociation shown in chapter
2—the percentage lengthening effect for the pauses is greater than
for the corresponding word segments, but the lengthening effect
for the word segments shows greater consistency across speakers,
as indicated by the statistical analysis.

The results of this experiment showed, as predicted, that
lengthening occurs at deletion sites. Additional statistical tests
were conducted to determine whether the amount of lengthening
was a function of the number of syllables or words in the deleted
constituent. The results, involving sentences (3)–(14), showed no
trends favoring either of these possibilities. In addition, a comparison of the effects for deletion sites in different clause types
(main and embedded) showed no consistent difference in magnitude.

In sum, the present data demonstrate the occurrence of segment
and pause lengthening immediately preceding deletion sites in the
case of Verb Gapping. The magnitude of this effect is dependent
neither on the phonetic structure of the deleted material (in terms

of its number of syllables), nor on the number of deleted words. Finally, the magnitude of the effect is approximately equal whether the deletion site occurs in main or in embedded clauses, indicating that such effects are not influenced by the type of clauses involved.

Although these data suggest that speech timing is influenced by deletion sites per se, other interpretations can be advanced to account for these data without the need to invoke a nonsurface level of syntactic coding. At present, we will mention two of the most superficial accounts, postponing a more detailed discussion until later in the chapter. According to one alternative, lengthening might be produced not by the presence of a deletion site, but by the presence of a surface sequence of NP + NP in the (b) versions of sentences (3)–(10), as opposed to a V + NP sequence in the (a) versions. This difference in the (a) and (b) versions is necessarily confounded with the nondeletion versus deletion contexts. In addition, lengthening may be produced by the presence of a proper noun immediately following the key material in each (b) version.

As noted at the outset of this chapter, a selection between a deletion interpretation of timing effects and a surface interpretation can only be made on the basis of experiments with more than one type of deletion. By turning our attention to Noun Gapping, it is possible to provide another test with deletion sites, a test not confounded with the two particular surface interpretations applicable to Verb Gapping.

EXPERIMENT 2: NOUN GAPPING

Sentence Materials and Procedure

Ten test sentences were constructed for experiment 2. Four pairs of test sentences, (15) through (18), included comparisons of structures involving no deletion in (a) and the deletion of a noun in (b). Of these, sentence pairs (15) and (16) involved a deletion operating across two main clauses, while (17) and (18) involved a deletion within a single clause in surface structure. This distinction was included as a test of the generality of any Noun Gapping effects. The test sentences appear below, with the key word italicized. Disambiguating strings were provided in parentheses for the (b) versions to aid the speaker in rendering the intended meaning.

(15) (a) Janet had prune juice today before lunch and I had *grape* juice last week.

Table 4.1 *Mean duration (msec) and standard deviations of key word segments and pauses for sentences in experiment 1 (standard deviations in parentheses)*

Test sentence	Nature of deleted material (in version (b), 3-10)	Clause type	Key word segment		Pause	
			Version (a)	Version (b)	Version (a)	Version (b)
(3)	single polysyllabic word	main	195.0 (30.8)	218.9 (32.7)	115.8 (34.2)	160.9 (88.1)
(4)		main	167.6 (22.0)	197.7 (29.0)	107.6 (12.3)	153.5 (36.3)
(5)		embedded	193.2 (28.9)	225.4 (26.8)	107.1 (21.7)	150.6 (64.9)
(6)		embedded	167.0 (31.4)	194.7 (30.8)	114.5 (24.7)	164.8 (115.1)
(7)	three words	main	202.0 (26.0)	229.8 (21.2)	107.2 (20.8)	164.8 (131.9)
(8)		main	156.6 (21.4)	198.5 (30.0)	109.4 (23.3)	154.9 (72.2)
(9)		embedded	208.1 (26.0)	228.6 (33.0)	99.6 (14.2)	138.2 (36.0)

		Key word segment		Pause	
(10)	embedded	163.1 (32.5)	198.4 (38.7)	123.9 (37.7)	157.8 (59.6)
(11)	single monosyllabic word	main	229.6 (33.2)		152.6 (54.1)
(12)		main	119.0 (40.1)		222.6 (157.8)
(13)		embedded	227.4 (41.4)		138.7 (53.4)
(14)		embedded	191.0 (38.6)		166.3 (128.5)

       (b)   Janet had prune juice today before lunch and I had
              grape just last week.
              (Janet drank prune juice and I drank grape juice.)

(16) (a)   Ann will send apricot jelly to Ron and Jeannette will
              send *peach* tapioca to Steve.

       (b)   Ann will send apricot jelly to Ron and Jeannette will
              send *peach* to Teresa and Steve.
              (Both apricot and peach jelly will be sent.)

(17) (a)   Janet made prune juice the day before yesterday and
              grape juice last week.

       (b)   Janet made prune juice the day before yesterday and
              grape just last week.
              (Janet made both prune and grape juice.)

(18) (a)   Ann will send apricot jelly to Angela's nephew and
              peach tapioca to Steve.

       (b)   Ann will send apricot jelly to Angela's nephew and
              peach to Teresa and Steve.
              (Ann will send both apricot and peach jelly.)

Ten speakers were tested using the procedure described in chapter 1. Acoustic measurements were obtained for the key segments /gre/ of "grape" and /pi/ of "peach," and for the following pauses, including any release burst in the pause measurement.

Results

The mean durations and standard deviations of the word segments and pauses for each sentence appear in table 4.2. The data show that the duration of the word segments and pauses was lengthened immediately before the deletion site in each of the (b) versions of (15)–(18). In each case, this effect was statistically significant for the word segment ($p < 0.001$, t values ranging from 4.47 to 6.86). The percentage of lengthening for the word durations averaged from 19 to 29 percent. For the pause durations, two of the four (b) sentences showed a statistically significant effect of lengthening ($p < 0.05$, t values of 2.56 and 3.40). Pause lengthening for the four sentences averaged from 1 to 60 percent. Comparison of the within-clause and across-clause instances of deletion revealed no consistent differences. The combined results for the word and pause durations indicate that lengthening is produced at the site of Noun Gapping. However, we still need to determine whether these effects should be attributed to the presence of a deletion site per se, or to the constituent-final position of the key material in surface structure arising from the operation of this particular deletion transformation. According to this latter alternative, lengthening in the deletion versions of (15)–(18) was produced not because of a deletion site per se, but because the key material occurred necessarily in phrase-final position in surface structure, unlike the key material in the corresponding nondeletion sentences.

To select between these alternative accounts of the timing effects obtained for (15)–(18), an additional experiment was conducted, comparing the duration of a noun-adjective homophone appearing (a) as an adjective at the site of Noun Gapping versus (b) as a head noun at the end of a noun phrase. Assuming a small, 10 msec durational difference for noun versus adjective on the basis of grammatical category membership, as obtained in chapter 3, we expect a slightly longer duration of the key word in the (b) version here if the earlier timing effects produced at the site of Noun Gapping are attributable solely to phrase-final lengthening. Alternatively, if the results obtained in experiment 2 are due to Gapping per se, we expect the duration of the key word to be longer in the (a) version, since, in addition to appearing in phrase-final position in surface structure, this word marks the site of Noun Gapping.

In an experiment involving two sentence pairs and eight speakers, the word durations in the (a) gapped sentences were significantly longer ($p < 0.01$, both pairs), by an average of 32 msec for one sentence pair and 42 msec for the other.[1] The results provide the clearest piece of evidence thus far that speakers lengthen a word's duration just prior to the site of a deletion.

In summary, the results for both experiments 1 and 2 indicate that segments and pauses are lengthened preceding deletion sites of Verb and Noun Gapping. While the results for Verb Gapping may alternatively be explained in terms of differences in surface

Table 4.2 *Mean duration (msec) and standard deviations of key word segments and pauses for sentences in experiment 2 (standard deviations in parentheses)*

Test sentence	Key word segment		Pause	
	Version (a)	Version (b)	Version (a)	Version (b)
(15)	177.6 (19.4)	221.0 (27.9)	80.3 (15.7)	128.2 (48.1)
(16)	226.6 (21.0)	286.2 (22.5)	35.9 (14.7)	36.3 (15.5)
(17)	180.3 (16.5)	232.0 (30.8)	82.2 (13.0)	122.3 (46.6)
(18)	244.4 (36.5)	291.5 (38.8)	35.4 (10.8)	53.0 (20.6)

structure, the effects obtained for Noun Gapping in the previous experiment seem more clearly attributable to the presence of the deletion site. We shall consider these Gapping rules further in chapter 6, where experiments are presented on the blocking of cross-word phonetic conditioning effects (see also Cooper and Sorensen, 1980, for F_0 effects).

SUBJECT DELETION

There exist other putative deletions whose validity is questionable on linguistic grounds, and experiments were undertaken to determine whether one such rule influences speech timing in a manner similar to Gapping. The experiments involved the putative rule of Subject Deletion, which optionally deletes the second occurrence of a main subject under identity in a conjoined sentence, as in (19b):

(19) (a) Craig bought a brand new truck and he painted it with pink enamel.
    (b) Craig bought a brand new truck and repainted it with pink enamel.

According to the interpretive hypothesis of Dougherty (1970), however, structures like (19b) are not derived from two conjoined clauses but consist simply of a single underlying clause containing conjoined verb phrases. If the hypothesis is correct, the duration of "truck" should be longer in (19a) than in (19b) under the assumption that lengthening is triggered by a major clause boundary. On the other hand, if the presence of a deletion site triggers lengthening here in the manner found for Gapping, the duration of "truck" in (19b) should actually be longer than in (19a), contrary to the interpretive prediction.

An experiment was conducted using ten speakers and five sentence pairs:

(20) (a) Craig bought a brand new *truck* and he painted it with pink enamel.
    (b) Craig bought a brand new *truck* and repainted it with pink enamel.
(21) (a) Professor Marcus showed a film to *Kate* and he cited one of Dante's works.
    (b) Professor Marcus showed a film to *Kate* and recited one of Dante's works.
(22) (a) Jake bought an old *couch* and he stored it in his studio.

    (b)   Jake bought an old *couch* and restored it in his studio.

(23) (a)   Dick wrote the *script* and he typed it on the IBM typewriter.

    (b)   Dick typed the *script* and retyped it on the IBM typewriter.

(24) (a)   John first taped the *talk* at 1 o'clock and he taped it five more times.

    (b)   John first taped the *talk* at 1 o'clock and retaped it five more times.

The speakers were instructed to place the same amount of stress on "he" and "re" in the (a) and (b) versions of each sentence, to ensure a close match for stress near the key word. To provide an additional test of possible stress differences, the speakers were instructed to read (24b) on separate readings with "re" receiving stress or not receiving stress.

The results for word durations failed to show any significant effects. The results of the control test for stress effects were also nonsignificant. The data do not support either the interpretive or the deletion hypothesis. An additional experiment was conducted to test the generality of these results for sentences in which the subject of the second clause in the (a) sentences was not coreferential with the subject of the first clause. The results for three sentence pairs with eight speakers again showed no significant effects. The data from both experiments thus provide no basis for selecting between the deletion and the interpretive hypotheses regarding the way in which a speaker represents these sentence structures.

Free Deletion and Tree Pruning

In addition to identity deletions, there exists a class of free deletions which drastically alter the surface structure of a sentence. The free deletions in one major subclass apply only within embedded clauses and reduce the status of the embedded material from a clause to a simple phrase (that is, the deletions "prune" the embedded S node). Linguistic evidence for the pruning convention was first put forth by Ross (1969); revisions of the convention have been proposed by Hankamer (1971) and Reis (1973), among others.

For our purposes, the pruning convention is of interest because it may provide a test of whether lengthening is determined at clause boundaries computed at underlying versus surface levels of coding. The test rests on a crucial assumption—that a small but detectable amount of lengthening occurs for a word segment immediately preceding an embedded clause. The discussion in chapter 1 suggests that segmental lengthening precedes main clauses, although no empirical evidence bears directly on the assumption made here for embedded clauses. If the assumption concerning preclausal lengthening for embedded clauses is correct, then a test of the underlying versus surface account of preclausal lengthening can be provided by studying the timing of words in sentences with or without a deletion rule that involves tree pruning. If preclausal lengthening is determined at an underlying level of coding, prior to the application of pruning, then there should be no difference in the duration of words in the two types of sentences. However, if such lengthening is determined at a surface level of coding, after the application of pruning, then the duration of the word in sentences without the deletion should be longer.

In two experiments we tested this hypothesis using a free deletion rule known as Whiz Deletion (Ross, 1967). This rule operates to optionally erase a WH subject and auxiliary in sentences like (25b).

(25) (a) The cat which is with my sister couldn't sleep.
      (b) The cat with my sister couldn't sleep.

In one experiment, two sentence pairs (26)–(27) were spoken by a group of twenty speakers.

(26) (a) The black *duck* which is swimming quacks loudly.
      (b) The black *duck* with my sister quacks loudly.
(27) (a) The little *chick* which was pecking couldn't find its mother.
      (b) The little *chick* with my cousin couldn't find its mother.

Acoustic measurements were obtained for the segments /dʊ/ of "duck" and /čɪ/ of "chick." The key segment was longer in the nondeletion (a) versions of both sentences. The amount of lengthening was negligible in (27), but in (26) it averaged 11 percent and was statistically significant ($p < 0.01$, $t = 2.98$, $df = 19$).

An additional experiment was conducted using sentence pairs (28)–(30) and ten speakers.

(28) (a) The little brown *chick* which is pecking couldn't find its mother.
      (b) The little brown *chick* with my nephew couldn't find its mother.

(29) (a) The baby *sheep* which is sleeping had wandered out of the pasture.

     (b) The baby *sheep* with my sister had wandered out of the pasture.

(30) (a) The little *duck* which is quacking likes to swim with the children.

     (b) The little *duck* with my cousin likes to swim with the children.

The word duration in the nondeletion (a) version was slightly longer in (28) and (29), averaging only 1 and 6 percent, respectively, whereas the duration was approximately equal for the (a) and (b) versions of (30). None of the differences reached statistical significance. Measurements of pauses following the key word also failed to show any significant effects. In summary, Whiz Deletion produces no highly systematic effects on the duration of immediately preceding word or pause segments.

The null results obtained here can of course be interpreted in more than one way. They may indicate that (i) preclausal lengthening is determined at an underlying as opposed to surface level of coding, (ii) Whiz Deletion is not a bona fide operation in speech production, or (iii) the assumption of preclausal lengthening for embedded clauses is unfounded. Of these three possibilities, (ii) and (iii) are the least interesting in terms of their implications, but happen to be the most plausible. In the case of (ii), independent linguistic evidence has cast doubt on the existence of Whiz Deletion as a grammatical rule (Wasow, 1972). If correct, the reason no effects were obtained may simply be that no deletion site (and hence no tree pruning) was present in either case.

Finally, it is conceivable that the present null results represent the cancellation of two opposing effects—one an effect of lengthening at the deletion site, the other an effect of shortening at the same site due to tree pruning. This possibility cannot be tested adequately, since there is no way to examine the effect of tree pruning independent of a coinciding deletion site. At present we can only say that the results of the experiment rule out any possibility that an effect of tree pruning (if it is present at all) overrides any competing effect produced by the deletion site per se.

Related experiments were conducted with another free deletion rule—Relative Clause Reduction—which deletes the relative pronoun at the beginning of an embedded relative clause, as in (31):

(31) (a) I saw the man that you hit in the nose.

     (b) I saw the man you hit in the nose.

According to one plausible version of the tree-pruning convention (Hankamer, 1971; Cooper, 1976a, chap. 2), this deletion serves to prune the embedded clause node from the surface structure, thus providing an additional test of the underlying versus surface accounts of preclausal lengthening.

Three experiments were conducted to test for differences in segment durations attributed to Relative Clause Reduction. In the first experiment (Cooper, 1976a, chap. 2), sixteen speakers read the two versions of (32) below, containing the key word "tape":

(32) (a) I have the *tape* that the officer erased.
     (b) I have the *tape* the officer erased.

The results showed a small but statistically significant lengthening of the segment /te/ of "tape" in the (a) nondeletion version of (32), as predicted by the surface structure hypothesis. The magnitude of the effect was small, averaging only 6 msec.

In a second experiment, fourteen speakers read versions of (33) and (34) below:

(33) (a) It was an agent like *Jack* who Dee-Dee owed her success to.
     (b) It was an agent like *Jack* Houdini owed his success to.
(34) (a) There is the *park* which Concord is famous for.
     (b) There is the *park* Wisconsin is famous for.

The results for these sentences showed a nonsignificant trend in the opposite direction, with the key word durations being somewhat longer in the deletion-containing (b) versions of (33) and (34). The results of this experiment thus conflict with those of the earlier one. It is conceivable that the present trend is due to a lengthening effect immediately preceding a proper noun in the (b) versions—a situation that did not exist in the earlier experiment.

A third experiment involving ten speakers was conducted to test this possibility with two additional sentence pairs. In (35) below, a proper noun immediately followed the deletion site in the (b) version, whereas in (36) no proper noun occurred in this location.

(35) (a) There is the *park* which Copley is famous for.
     (b) There is the *park* Wisconsin is famous for.
(36) (a) It was an agent like *Jack* who Frankie owed his success to.

(b)   It was an agent like *Jack* her father owed his success
to.

The results showed a small, nonsignificant lengthening of the
nondeletion (a) version of (35) and a small, nonsignificant lengthening of the deletion-containing (b) version of (36); this is in op-
position to the effects predicted on the basis of the hypothesis that
lengthening is triggered by the presence of a following proper
noun.

The combined results of the three experiments on Relative
Clause Reduction are in agreement with those obtained for Whiz
Deletion. In all cases, the absence of highly systematic differences
in the duration of segments in sentences with and without deletions seems to point to the conclusion that preclausal lengthening
does not exist and/or that Whiz Deletion and Relative Clause Reduction are not among the speaker's deletion rules.

Conclusion

It might well be said that in deciding to study deletion rules we
were looking for trouble. After reading the experimental studies
on this topic, one can certainly conclude that we have found it. A
general principle does emerge from a consideration of the various
results obtained above, however.

Of the putative deletion rules examined here, only two showed
systematic effects of lengthening at the deletion site, and both of
these deletion rules, involving Gapping, received independent
support as bona fide syntactic deletions. Of the remaining rules,
none except Relative Clause Reduction received strong independent support, and in this case the predicted deletion site effect was
confounded with the possibility of tree pruning. Consequently, it
is conceivable that a general principle does emerge from the various results obtained here, namely, that lengthening is produced at
bona fide deletion sites when such sites are not accompanied by
other confounding influences.

Before accepting this deletion-specific account, however, we
must consider at least four alternative accounts of the lengthening
effects, involving (i) the distinction between identity and free deletion, (ii) a no-ambiguity constraint, (iii) transitional phrase ac-
cessibilities, and (iv) the influence of semantic versus syntactic
factors. In the first case, it should be noted that both of the Gapping rules yielding lengthening effects were identity deletions,
whereas none of the free deletion rules studied produced systematic effects. We might ask, then, whether the effects for deletions
are restricted to the class of identity deletions.

It appears that at least one free deletion is accompanied by lengthening. In chapter 1, we noted that pausing typically accompanies certain conjoined adjectives like "tall, handsome." In examining previous studies of conjoined adjectives (Vendler, 1968; Martin, 1969), we discovered a striking relationship between the likelihood of pausing between the two adjectives and the acceptability of inserting a surface conjunction in lieu of a pause. In table 4.3 we present a sample of conjoined adjectives illustrating this tendency. For conjoined adjectives listed in the left-hand column, a brief pause is likely to accompany the adjectives in speech when a surface conjunction is not present; however, a conjunction may be inserted instead of a pause. For conjoined adjectives listed in the right-hand column, on the other hand, no pause typically accompanies the adjectives in speech, and a conjunction cannot be inserted between the adjectives (see Vendler, 1968). We have obtained informal support for this relationship by asking a group of twenty students for their intuitions about the acceptability of inserting a pause or a conjunction in each case.

Since the presence of pausing seems directly linked to the acceptability of inserting a conjunction between the adjectives, it is tempting to suggest that pausing in such cases serves as a replacement for a freely deleted conjunction. If so, then we have found an example of a free deletion that influences speech timing, rendering any distinction between identity and free deletions useless for characterizing the influence of deletion rules on segmental and pausal lengthening. At the same time, the addition of the pause rule for conjoined adjectives militates against the possibility that the lengthening effects obtained earlier for Gapping are simply due to surface structure. In the present case, the surface structures for conjoined adjectives in both the left- and right-hand columns of table 4.3 are identical, yet pausing is more likely to accompany the adjectives in the left-hand column. The only single hypothesis that can handle the data both for Gapping and for conjoined adjectives states that lengthening is produced at deletion sites per se.

The second alternative account of the deletion effects, involving

Table 4.3 *Two types of conjoined prenominal adjectives*

Type 1 (accompanied by pause or "and")	Type 2 (not accompanied by pause or "and")
thin sickly	rich Polish
deep narrow	red plastic
long lovely	large green
small tender	small round

the notion of a no-ambiguity constraint, states that lengthening is produced at a deletion site to avoid a modifying relation between the words bordering this site. To take an example, consider the case of Verb Gapping. According to the no-ambiguity account, lengthening was produced at the deletion site between "Kate" and "Carmella's" in sentence (7b) and between "Pete" and "Connie's" in sentence (8b) in order to avoid a reading in which "Kate Carmella's" or "Pete Connie's" referred to a single proper noun containing both first and last names. To be sure, "Carmella" and "Connie" are unlikely candidates for last names, but, for the sake of argument, let us assume that these words could be so construed by the listener. However, the no-ambiguity account fails to handle the lengthening effects produced at the site of Noun Gapping, as in the (b) versions of sentences (15)–(18). In these sentences a modifying relation between the words bordering the deletion site is impossible, and there exists no likely alternative reading up to the key site if we assume that the listener properly decodes the singular number assigned to the key word. Only if the listener incorrectly inserted a determiner just before the key word (for example, "a peach") or incorrectly assigned plural number to the key word (for example, "peaches") could any sort of ambiguity arise at the key site, and such misperceptions are highly unlikely to occur in such a situation. Consequently, the no-ambiguity account can plausibly handle only one of the two types of Gapping accompanied by lengthening here; for this reason the account will not be adopted.

Next, let us consider a possible account of the lengthening effects in terms of the notion of transitional accessibility. According to this account, lengthening is produced at the sites of Gapping because these locations are accompanied by low transitional accessibility between phrase types. That is, for reasons not yet understood, the speaker is assumed to select phrase types in a nonrandom fashion such that the selection of one phrase type produces differential accessibility to the next phrase type to be selected. In the case of Gapping, it is assumed that the phrase type following the deletion site is relatively inaccessible (accounting for the "awkwardness" commonly attributed to this region), such that the speaker produces lengthening at the deletion site to allow an extra fraction of time to access the upcoming phrase. In earlier work, Lounsbury (1954) and MacClay and Osgood (1959), among others, argued that pausing is commonly associated in spontaneous speech with relatively low transitional accessibility between adjacent lexical items. Here, however, the notion must be defined in terms of phrase types if it is to handle the results, but there exists no literature on the transitional accessibility of phrase types in speech production. Thus, the hypothesis as it stands offers little predictive value.

Finally, an attempt to account for the results obtained for Gapping provides a particularly clear example of the difficulty involved in distinguishing between syntactic and semantic factors. Heretofore we have discussed Gapping in terms of the deletion of a syntactic constituent and have accounted for its influence on speech timing accordingly. Alternatively, however, it may be that the effects produced at the site of Gapping are due to the information load carried by the deleted constituent. The information contained in the constituent deleted from the second clause of a gapped sentence is integral to the meaning of that clause, whereas the information contained in many other types of deleted constituent is not. It is thus conceivable that speakers produced lengthening effects at the site of Gapping but not at the sites of other deletions because lengthening is restricted to those deletion sites associated with high information load, possibly as an aid to the listener. However, this sort of account cannot readily handle the intuitions discussed above regarding the deletion of a conjunction between conjoined adjectives.

To summarize the discussion to this point, we have defended the deletion site account of lengthening against four possible alternatives, including accounts based on the distinction between identity and free deletion, a no-ambiguity constraint, transitional accessibility among phrase types, and information load. Although the deletion site account seems preferable to any of these alternatives, the evidence in its support is not compelling. For this reason, the results of the present study do not provide conclusive evidence in support of the existence of more than a single level of syntactic coding in speech production.

In psychological terms, exactly why lengthening accompanies deletion sites remains unclear. Perhaps the effect is produced at selected deletion sites to partially fill a time interval for the production of the missing constituent, originally allocated in underlying structure. Alternatively, the lengthening may serve instead, or additionally, as an intended cue for the listener to decode the missing constituent (see chapter 8 for further discussion). More experimentation with deletion rules must be conducted before we can select between these hypotheses.

Aside from this issue, the results of the experiments on deletions also bear on the hypothesis that English exhibits isochrony, the tendency for the durations between stressed syllables in an utterance to occur at constant intervals. There is no question that

English does not obey a strict isochrony rule (see, for example, Klatt, 1975; Lehiste, 1977); yet a tendency toward isochrony has often been argued for (see Lehiste, 1977).

The isochrony notion should be reconsidered in light of the data for Verb Gapping and Noun Gapping in experiments 1 and 2. For Verb Gapping, the deletion of the verb results in a closer syllabic proximity of two stressed nouns. Lehiste (personal communication) has suggested that pausing and lengthening may be produced at the site of Verb Gapping to maintain a more natural temporal spacing between the two stressed nouns. This hypothesis falters for Noun Gapping in experiment 2, however, where the same effects were observed despite the fact that their production actually increased the interstress intervals well beyond normal. It appears, then, that the timing effects at deletion sites are a reflection of deletion per se rather than rhythmic isochrony.

5 | Movement Rules

THE SCOPE of the discussion on underlying versus surface structure can be enlarged by studying another major class of transformations—movement rules. These transformations operate to move constituents forward or backward in a structure, as well as higher or lower (Langacker, 1974). Continuing our attempt to determine whether speakers code more than one level of syntactic structure, we shall examine how movement rules might influence speech timing.

Fronting Rules

With rules that move a constituent forward in a clause, there exist two locations where effects on speech timing might be observed. One location is the position originally occupied by the moved constituent in underlying structure, a position referred to as the movement site. The other location is the boundary between the location of the moved constituent in surface structure and other material in the sentence. In an earlier study (Cooper, 1976a), fronting rules were examined to determine whether the duration of a word segment immediately preceding the movement site might be affected by movement transformations. This possibility was of particular theoretical importance, because if such an effect were obtained it would provide rather direct support for the notion that a speaker's syntactic code involves an underlying as well as a surface level of computation. However, no systematic effect was observed at these sites. Lengthening did occur for the final segment of the preposed constituent, suggesting an influence of surface structure. The present study was conducted in an attempt to further document this lengthening effect and to extend the measurements to pauses immediately following the preposed material.

Sentence pairs (1)–(3) serve to introduce three different fronting rules.

(1) (a) Our cuckoo clock is very special.
     (b) Our cuckoo clock it's very special.
(2) (a) I like your mother's clock very much.
     (b) Your mother's clock I like very much.
(3) (a) I timed the racers with Charlie's clock.
     (b) With Charlie's clock I timed the racers.

In each pair, (b) contains approximately the same meaning as (a) but represents a departure from normal word order. In the (b) sentences, the preposed constituent ending with "clock" may be marked off from the rest of the sentence in speech by a pause, as suggested by a writer's inclination to insert a comma after "clock" (see also Emonds, 1976, p. 43).

The preposing rules involved in the (b) sentence of pairs (1)–(3) above are termed Left Dislocation, Topicalization, and Prepositional Phrase (PP) Preposing, respectively (Ross, 1967). Left Dislocation moves an NP to the front of a sentence and leaves a pronoun at the movement site, as in (1b); Topicalization moves a direct object NP to the front of a sentence, as in (2b); and PP Preposing moves a PP to the front, as in (3b). In each case, the transformation typically serves to place attention on the preposed constituent (Langacker, 1974; Ross and Cooper, 1979).

Each of the transformed structures noted above represents a surface word order that could not be generated by the underlying phrase structure rules of a transformational grammar (Emonds, 1976). The preposing rules studied here are termed *root* transformations, which operate to move a constituent and attach it to the root, or highest node, of a phrase structure tree. Structurally, a preposed root constituent is immediately followed by an S node that marks the beginning of the canonical main clause. Thus, it may be that lengthening effects observed at the end of a preposed root constituent are due to the presence of this upcoming clause.

In contrast to root transformations, some other preposing rules (for example, Passive) preserve a type of word order allowed in the base structure and are designated as *structure-preserving* transformations. Cooper (1976a) found no additional lengthening effects at the end of the preposed constituent with passive versus active sentences and suggested that the influence of preposing rules on speech timing may be limited to root transformations of the type studied here. We shall evaluate this hypothesis in more detail as experiments are presented.

PILOT EXPERIMENT

A pilot experiment was conducted with two groups of four sentences, each group containing one sentence with normal English word order and three sentences with preposed structures. The results for twenty speakers showed lengthening of the segment and pause at the end of the preposed constituents. However, the phonetic material and stress pattern in the key region were not tightly matched; such matching is particularly difficult to attain in the case of preposing. An additional experiment was conducted to independently assess the role of these other variables, and the results supported the notion that the original results were attributed to the influence of preposing. As we gained more experience in constructing matched sentence materials, however, it was possible to design sentences that provided a more direct test of preposing; the results of this effort are presented in the following experiment.

EXPERIMENT 1

Sentence Materials and Procedure

Two groups of three sentences were used in experiment 1. In each group, one sentence contained normal SVO order, while the other two contained Topicalized and PP Preposed structures. The sentences are listed below, along with descriptive labels.

(4) (a) Yvonne's friend Kate shares cots with the children. (SVO)
     (b) Yvonne's friend Kate Cher caught with the children. (Topicalization)
     (c) With Ron's friend Kate Cher coddled the children. (PP Preposing)
(5) (a) Our Sunday school class will ask for support. (SVO)
     (b) Our Sunday school class Will asked for support. (Topicalization)
     (c) In Sunday school class we'll ask for support. (PP Preposing)

In group (4) the key word segment was /ke/ of "Kate," and in group (5) the key word segment was /klæs/ ("class"). The immediate phonetic environment of the key words was identical for the sentences of each group. In addition, the sentences in each group contained the same approximate stress contour, except that greater stress was typically placed on "Cher" in (4b) and (4c) than on "shares" in (4a), and similarly "Will" and "we'll" in (5b) and (5c) often received greater stress than "will" in (5a). However, we shall see in experiment 2 that stress differences cannot account for the results of preposing.

Ten speakers were tested as in experiments in previous chapters. Measurements of duration were made for the key segments /ke/ and /klæs/, as well as for the silent intervals following each of these segments.

Results and Discussion

The mean durations of the key word segments and pauses are presented in table 5.1. A priori *t* tests for matched pairs showed that the key word segment was significantly longer in both Topicalization and PP Preposing than in SVO for both sentence groups (Topicalization versus SVO—group (4): $p < 0.05$, $t = 2.388$, $df = 9$; group (5): $p < 0.001$, $t = 6.526$, $df = 9$; PP Preposing versus SVO—group (4): $p < 0.05$, $t = 2.475$, $df = 9$; group (5): $p < 0.05$, $t = 2.338$, $df = 9$). In addition, the duration of the following pause was significantly longer for PP Preposing than for SVO in group (4) ($p < 0.05$, $t = 2.335$, $df = 9$). Nonsignificant trends in the same direction were obtained for the pauses of PP Preposing versus SVO in group (5) and for Topicalization versus SVO in both sentence groups (PP Preposing versus SVO—group (5): $0.10 > p > 0.05$, $t = 2.067$, $df = 9$; Topicalization versus SVO— group (4): $0.20 > p > 0.10$, $t = 1.453$, $df = 9$; group (5): $0.10 > p > 0.05$, $t = 2.161$, $df = 9$).

In sentence group (4) the magnitude of the lengthening effect for the word segment averaged 5 percent for Topicalization and 7 percent for PP Preposing. For group (5) the effect for the word segment averaged 11 percent for Topicalization and 7 percent for PP Preposing. The lengthening effect was considerably greater for the duration of the pauses. In group (4) the pause lengthening averaged 39 percent for Topicalization and 57 percent for PP Preposing, while in group (5) the effect averaged 231 percent for Topicalization and 195 percent for PP Preposing. The failure of the pause effects to achieve statistical significance in three of the four

Table 5.1 *Mean durations (msec) for word segments and pauses in experiment 1*

Sentence group	SVO	Topicalization	PP Preposing
Word segments			
(4)	268.9	283.1	287.5
(5)	387.2	432.5	414.4
Pauses			
(4)	71.2	99.6	112.0
(5)	26.7	88.5	79.0

test comparisons, despite the large percentage of average lengthening, may be attributed to systematic individual differences. For
the majority of speakers, considerable lengthening of pauses was
produced for both Topicalized and PP Preposed structures. For a
few speakers, however, pause lengthening was not observed for
either of the preposed structures. These results are in general
agreement with the comparisons of pausing and segmental
lengthening reported in chapters 2 and 4 (no pauses were measured in chapter 3). Speakers as a group lengthen pauses to a
greater extent than segments, but the lengthening of segments is
produced with greater consistency among the individual speakers.

Experiment 2

In experiment 2 we extended the study of phonetically matched
sentences to include Left Dislocation and to determine whether
the effects of preposing on speech timing are constrained by the
length and/or complexity of the preposed constituent. The latter
issue stems from the possibility that pauses at the end of a constituent are likely to be longer if the constituent itself contains a large
number of syllables. Following Lieberman (1967), it might be
supposed that longer pauses would accompany longer constituents because speakers are more likely to pause for a breath after
such constituents (cf. Grosjean and Collins, 1979, and chapter 7 of
this book).

Sentence Materials and Procedure

Two groups of four sentences were used in the experiment. In
each group, one sentence contained normal SVO order, while the
other three sentences contained Left Dislocated, Topicalized, and
PP Preposed constituents. The sentences of group (7) represented
versions of the sentences in group (6) in which the constituent
preceding the pause location was longer and more complex. The
sentences of each group, along with their descriptive labels, appear below.

(6) (a) The owner of the park shows gold to the children.
(SVO)
(b) The owner of the park she scolded the children. (Left
Dislocation)
(c) The statue in the park Cher showed to the children.
(Topicalization)
(d) At Brockton's city park Cher scolded the children.
(PP Preposing)

(7) (a) The ragged old woman planting flowers in the park shows photographs to the children. (SVO)

    (b) The ragged old woman planting flowers in the park she's photographing the children. (Left Dislocation)

    (c) The ragged old woman planting flowers in the park Cher photographed with the children. (Topicalization)

    (d) Inside the old building full of flowers in the park Cher's photographing the children. (PP Preposing)

In both groups, the key word segment was /par/ of "park."

Eight speakers were tested as in previous experiments. Measurements of duration were made for the key segment /par/ and for the following silent interval.

Results and Discussion

The mean durations of the key segments and following pauses for each sentence appear in table 5.2. From this table, it can be seen that the durations of both the key segment and the pause were longer in each of the three preposed structures than in the corresponding SVO sentence of each group. In addition, the segment and pause durations were generally longer for group (7), which contained the longer preposed constituents, than for group (6).

A two-way ANOVA showed significant main effects for sentence type and for sentence group (sentence type: $F_{(3,21)} = 4.389$, $p < 0.02$; sentence group: $F_{(1,17)} = 7.500$, $p < 0.05$). However, there was no significant interaction between sentence type and sentence group ($F_{(3,21)} = 1.054$, $p > 0.20$). Further analysis of the sentence type effect for each group showed the following: For group (6) the key word segment duration in the Left Dislocation sentence was significantly longer than in the SVO sentence (LD versus SVO: $p < 0.005$, $t = 4.527$, $df = 7$). Nonsignificant trends in the same direction were observed for both Topicalization and PP Preposing

Table 5.2 *Mean durations (msec) for word segments and pauses in experiment 2*

Sentence group	SVO	Left Dislocation	Topicalization	PP Preposing
Word segments				
(6)	203.1	227.0	223.2	217.6
(7)	212.2	223.1	232.4	226.7
Pauses				
(6)	59.0	114.0	71.7	88.0
(7)	72.1	123.3	134.5	121.6

(Topicalization versus SVO: $0.10 > p > 0.05$, $t = 2.311$, $df = 7$; PP Preposing versus SVO: $0.20 > p > 0.10$, $t = 1.609$, $df = 7$). For the pause duration in group (6), no significant effects were obtained, but nonsignificant lengthening was observed for all three of the preposed constituents compared with SVO.

In sentence group (7), which contained the longer preposed constituents, the word segments were significantly lengthened in both Topicalized and PP Preposed sentences compared with the SVO sentence (Topicalization versus SVO: $p < 0.02$, $t = 3.477$, $df = 7$; PP Preposing versus SVO: $p < 0.05$, $t = 2.638$, $df = 7$). A nonsignificant trend in the same direction was observed for Left Dislocation ($0.10 > p > 0.05$, $t = 2.055$, $df = 7$). For the pause durations of group (7), a significant lengthening effect was observed for Topicalization ($p < 0.05$, $t = 2.509$, $df = 7$), while nonsignificant lengthening trends were obtained for both PP Preposing and Left Dislocation (PP Preposing versus SVO: $0.20 > p > 0.10$, $t = 1.677$, $df = 7$; LD versus SVO: $0.10 > p > 0.05$, $t = 1.962$, $df = 7$). As in experiment 1, the mean lengthening effect for the pauses was considerable for all three preposed structures; yet some of the effects failed to reach significance because a few speakers did not exhibit pause lengthening for any of the sentences containing preposed constituents. For the majority of speakers a sizable pause lengthening effect was observed for each of the preposed structures, as indicated by the mean pauses in table 5.2.

Comparison of the word segment and pause durations in sentence groups (6) and (7) revealed only a nonsignificant trend for longer durations at the end of the longer preposed constituent in group (7). As shown in table 5.2, the word segments averaged only about 5 percent longer in three of the four sentences for group (7), while the average pause durations ranged from less than 10 percent to more than 40 percent longer in each of the four sentences of this group. The data for the pause durations provide some support for the notion that speakers insert longer pauses at the end of long versus short constituents, although the magnitude of the pauses for individual utterances was typically shorter than the 150 msec believed to be required to take a breath (Stevens, personal communication; Grosjean and Collins, 1979). The data thus suggest that pause duration may be influenced by the length of a constituent in the absence of breathing at this site.

Additional acoustic measurements were obtained for these utterances in order to assess the possible role of inherent differences in the stress of words in the key region. Cooper and Sorensen (1977) obtained measurements of the fundamental frequency (F_0)

for the key word "park" and for the words following it, "shows," "she('s)," and "Cher('s)." Measurements for "park" included the highest and lowest values of F_0, while measurements for the following words included the highest values of F_0. The results of this analysis suggested that inherent stress differences can account neither for the results obtained for duration in this study nor for the presence of consistent and large rises in F_0 following the preposed constituent (for an extended discussion, see Cooper and Sorensen, 1977, p. 690).

EXPERIMENT 3

In chapter 2 we discussed a variety of structurally ambiguous sentences that could be disambiguated by preposing. Recall that in each of the sentences studied in chapter 2 an ambiguity arose because a given constituent could modify either of two antecedent constituents. Preposing the modifying constituent in these ambiguities served to force the reading for which this constituent modified the higher of the two antecedent constituents in the hierarchical representation. In experiment 3 we tested the effects of preposing constituents similar to some of those discussed in chapter 2 on segment and pause durations at the site of preposing, as a means of determining the generality of the findings of experiment 2.

Sentence Materials and Procedure

Eight sentence pairs were constructed. Pairs (8)–(9) involve tests for preposing a vocative (see experiment 2 in chapter 2); pairs (10)–(12) involve tests of PP Preposing (see experiments 3 and 4 in chapter 2); pair (13) includes an adverbial phrase for which a preposing account is debatable on purely linguistic grounds; and pairs (14)–(15) involve preposing a subordinate clause under negative scope (see experiment 6 in chapter 2). In each case the italicized word occurs at the end of a constituent that is preposed in the (b) version.

(8) (a) *Clark* thought he had seen the Duke of Normandy.
    (b) *Clark* there is the famous Duke of Normandy.
(9) (a) Uncle *Jake* married a girl from my hometown.
    (b) Uncle *Jake* Mary's a girl from my hometown.
(10) (a) With a lead *pipe* in each hand the bandit confronted the bank teller.
    (b) With a lead *pipe* an old man attempted to scare the new bank teller.
(11) (a) With a *joke* pertaining to math I began the lecture.

(b) With a *joke* Professor McGrath will begin his lecture.

(12) (a) Warren didn't know the purpose of the *talk* Joe had with Mary.

(b) With a better understanding of the *talk* Joe left the meeting.

(13) (a) Walking through the *park* Jennifer likes Teresa made some friends. (the park that Jennifer likes)

(b) Walking through the *park* Jennifer looked for Lisa and her friends.

(14) (a) The Carsons' house was near the *park* John used to work at.

(b) Because the house was near the *park* John didn't buy it.

(15) (a) My cousin wanted to *bake* Pam a jelly roll and an apple pie.

(b) Because she knew how to *bake* Pam did not enroll in the cooking class.

The testing procedure for each of ten speakers was the same as for experiment 1. Acoustic measurements were obtained for the durations of the key word segments and following pauses in each sentence. The duration of the word segment was measured from the beginning of the consonant to the beginning of the silent interval for the word-final consonant.

Results and Discussion

The mean durations of the key segments and following pauses for each sentence appear in table 5.3. It can be seen that the segment durations were longer in the (b) versions of the eight sentence pairs. The lengthening that accompanied the end of the preposed constituent was statistically significant for both preposed vocatives ($p < 0.001$, t values of 5.26 and 7.46, $df = 9$); for all four sentences with preposed PPs ($p < 0.01$, t values ranging from 4.02 to 6.65, $df = 9$); and for one of the two preposed subordinate clauses ($p < 0.001$, $t = 10.3$, $df = 9$). For the eight sentence pairs, the amount of lengthening averaged from 7 to 39 percent.

The pause durations were also longer in the (b) versions of each of the eight sentence pairs. The pause lengthening reached statistical significance in both of the sentence pairs with preposed vocatives ($p < 0.01$, t values of 3.76 and 3.89, $df = 9$; in one of the sentence pairs with preposed PP ($p < 0.01$, $t = 3.89$, $df = 9$); and in one of the two preposed subordinate clauses ($p < 0.05$, $t = 2.49$, $df = 9$). The average pause lengthening for the eight sentences ranged from 43 to 179 percent. As in experiments 1 and 2, the

Table 5.3 *Mean durations (msec) for word segments and pauses in experiment 3*

Sentence pair	Key word segment		Pause	
	Version (a)	Version (b)	Version (a)	Version (b)
(8)	206.7	279.0	148.4	317.3
(9)	202.7	237.2	109.7	306.3
(10)	199.7	233.1	85.2	139.7
(11)	188.3	231.0	22.5	107.3
(12)	225.7	253.6	143.8	265.9
(13)	199.9	241.0	95.8	205.8
(14)	220.9	237.0	140.4	225.6
(15)	131.5	183.0	129.8	276.4

amount of lengthening was greater for the pause durations than for the segment durations, but the consistency of the lengthening among the different speakers was greater for the segment durations. For sentence pairs (8) and (9) the key word marked the end of a constituent that was identical for both the (a) and (b) versions of each pair. Thus, as with the previous two experiments, the lengthening accompanying the end of the preposed constituent (here, a vocative) may be attributed to differences in upcoming surface structure, specifically the presence of an upcoming clause in the (b) versions. The preposed constituent in each of pairs (10)–(15) also occurred just prior to a canonical main clause; however, due to the nature of the preposing rules being studied, the constituents ending with the key material were structurally different for the (a) and (b) versions of each sentence pair. Thus, the lengthening effects obtained for this latter group of sentences are also open to an alternative interpretation based on phrase-final lengthening, similar to that employed in chapters 2 and 3.

SUMMARY OF EXPERIMENTS ON FRONTING RULES

The results of these experiments indicate that syntactic rules of preposing exert a systematic influence on speech timing. The effect of preposing occurred most noticeably for the pause immediately following the preposed constituent. For nearly all of the fronted structures, the pause lengthening effect was substantial, averaging between 50 and 200 percent. Since a few speakers did not show the lengthening effect for the preposed structures, however, it must be concluded that the timing effect exerted by preposing is an optional rather than an obligatory feature of speech production. In addition to pause lengthening, the present results also showed small amounts of lengthening occurring for the word segment at the end of a preposed constituent.

Thus it appears that the major timing effect produced by preposing is an optional but substantial lengthening of the pause immediately following the preposed constituent. The effects obtained for both segmental lengthening and pausing seem to be programmed by the speaker at a level of coding that corresponds more nearly to surface than to underlying syntactic structure. For many of the sentences studied, these effects can be attributed to the influence of an S node that immediately follows this site, signaling the beginning of the canonical main clause (Emonds, 1976). It is possible that lengthening at the site of the moved constituent reflects the speaker's need to allow extra processing time for planning the upcoming clause. A related listener-oriented possibility is that the speaker endeavors to demarcate the preposed constituent from the remainder of the sentence by lengthening, thereby signaling to the listener that the preposed constituent is the focus of the sentence, while simultaneously indicating that the sentence represents a severe departure from normal word order. These alternative explanations will be discussed further in chapters 7 and 8 as they relate to speech timing effects in general.

Backing Rules

Whereas preposing rules move a constituent to the front of a sentence, another class of movement rules serves to reorder a constituent to the end. These so-called postposing or backing rules include Right Dislocation, Extraposition, and Relative Clause Extraposition (Ross, 1967; Langacker, 1974). The following experiments were conducted to determine whether structures derived from these transformational rules exhibit temporal effects in speech. We shall again focus on timing at one or two key locations: (i) the boundary separating the moved constituent from the rest of the sentence, and (ii) the location that the moved constituent presumably occupied in the underlying structure of the sentence.

Experiment 1: Right Dislocation

The rule of Right Dislocation is a root transformation that operates by replacing an NP with a pronoun and moving the NP to the end of the sentence, in a manner that mirrors the preposing rule of Left Dislocation (Ross, 1967; Emonds, 1976). For example, (16b) is derived from (16a) by Right Dislocation.

(16)　(a)　This cake has been eaten.
　　　(b)　It's been eaten, this cake.

In written English the moved constituent is separated from the rest of the sentence by a comma, suggesting the presence of a pause in speech at this location. Experiment 1 was designed to investigate speech timing effects for Right Dislocation, with moved subject NPs originating from within both main and embedded clauses.

Sentence Materials and Procedure

Two triplets of sentences were constructed for the experiment. Each triplet included: (a) a control sentence not involving postposing, (b) a sentence involving Right Dislocation of a main clause subject, and (c) a sentence involving Right Dislocation of a subordinate clause subject. These latter two sentence types were included as a test of generality of any obtained effects of postposing. The sentences appear below, along with their surface structure labels.

(17) (a) I think that Ellen *touched* this cake.
(SVO)
(b) It seems to have been *touched* this cake.
(Right Dislocation, main clause subject)
(c) I think that it's been *touched* this cake.
(Right Dislocation, subordinate clause subject)
(18) (a) My mother thinks that Marion *tricked* that detective.
(SVO)
(b) He seems to think the judge has been *tricked* that detective.
(Right Dislocation, main clause subject)
(c) My mother thinks he might have been *tricked* that detective.
(Right Dislocation, subordinate clause subject)

The testing procedure for each of ten speakers was the same as in previous experiments. No commas were inserted in the sentence materials, as with the experiments on preposing. Acoustic measurements were obtained for the segments /tʊ/ of "touched" and /trɪ/ of "tricked," as well as for the following interval of silence and release burst until the beginning of the next word.

Results and Discussion

The mean segment and pause durations for each sentence are shown in table 5.4. The four instances of sentences involving Right Dislocation showed considerable lengthening of the word

Table 5.4 *Mean durations (msec) for word segments and pauses in experiment 1*

Sentence group	SVO	Right Dislocation, main clause subject	Right Dislocation, subordinate clause subject
Word segments			
(17)	263.0	336.2	344.9
(18)	158.6	207.4	211.9
Pauses			
(17)	75.7	215.5	203.9
(18)	152.6	289.2	315.8

segment and pause compared to the associated control sentences. This effect was independent of whether the postposed constituent served as a main or a subordinate clause subject NP. For the word segment and pause, each of these lengthening effects was statistically significant (word segment: $p < 0.005$, t values ranging from 4.63 to 5.86, $df = 9$; pause: $p < 0.02$, t values ranging from 3.15 to 4.19, $df = 9$). The average lengthening of the word segment in the different sentences ranged from 28 to 34 percent, while the average lengthening of the pause ranged from 90 to 185 percent. The results of this experiment provide a clear demonstration that the boundary between a right dislocated constituent and the rest of the sentence is marked by a large amount of lengthening for both word segment and pause. This effect can be attributed to the clause-final position of the key word in the sentences containing Right Dislocation.

EXPERIMENT 2: EXTRAPOSITION

The rule of Extraposition moves a subject clause to the end of a sentence (Rosenbaum, 1967; Ross, 1967), as in (19b).

(19)   (a)   That John left Mary is obvious.
       (b)   It is obvious that John left Mary.

Extraposition differs from Right Dislocation in that it is not considered a root transformation (Emonds, 1976). Instead, it is termed *structure-preserving* because it reorders constituents in such a way as to preserve the basic structural nodes found in underlying structure. In addition, extraposed constituents are not set off by a comma in writing, and there is no intuitive basis for expecting that lengthening is exhibited at this boundary. Experiment 2 was conducted to determine whether, as seems to be the case with fronting rules, the lengthening effects for backing rules are restricted to root transformations.

Sentence Materials and Procedure

Two pairs of sentences were constructed for this experiment. Each pair included a control sentence not involving postposing (a) and a sentence involving Extraposition (b). The italicized key word in each sentence appears as the last word before the postposed material.

(20) (a) I reminded *Jake* that his mother was taking him to the park.
     (b) It excited *Jake* that his mother was taking him to the park.
(21) (a) Mary told *Clark* that the publisher rejected his book.
     (b) It appalled *Clark* that the publisher rejected his book.

The usual testing procedure was adopted for each of the eleven speakers tested. Acoustic measurements were obtained for the word segments /je/ of "Jake" and /klar/ of "Clark" as well as for the following silent interval.

Results

The mean durations for each sentence are shown in table 5.5. The word segments for the (a) and (b) versions of each sentence pair were approximately equal, and the difference between them did not approach statistical significance. The pause durations were slightly longer in the (b) versions of both sentence pairs, averaging 4 and 12 percent lengthening for (20b) and (21b), respectively. For (20b) pause lengthening reached statistical significance ($p < 0.05$, $t = 2.52$, $df = 10$). Overall, however, the results of this experiment indicate that Extraposition produces no major consistent effect on speech timing at the boundary between the moved constituent and the rest of the sentence, in contrast to the marked effect of Right Dislocation in experiment 1. Thus, we can tentatively conclude that the lengthening effects for both fronting and backing rules are largely restricted to root transformations.

Table 5.5 *Mean durations (msec) for word segments and pauses in experiment 2*

Sentence pair	Key word segment		Pause	
	Version (a)	Version (b)	Version (a)	Version (b)
(20)	209.9	209.2	115.2	128.8
(21)	254.2	253.5	41.4	129.0

EXPERIMENT 3: EXTRAPOSITION FROM NOUN PHRASE

The rule of Extraposition from Noun Phrase moves a relative clause to clause-final position, away from its head. This rule is structure-preserving (Emonds, 1976) and is most likely to apply when the relative clause is long and complex, as in (22b).

(22) (a) Tom presented a bear which had five cubs to Marcia.
　　　(b) Tom presented a bear to Marcia which had five cubs.

Experiment 3 was designed to permit measurements of duration at two locations, the site occupied by the postposed constituent in underlying structure and the boundary between the postposed constituent and the rest of the sentence.

Sentence Materials and Procedure

Two pairs of test sentences, each pair containing a control sentence not involving postposing (a) and a sentence involving Extraposition from Noun Phrase (b), were constructed for the experiment.

(23) (a) Mary gave a *plaque* to *Clark* when she went to the festival downtown.
　　　(b) Mary gave a *plaque* to *Clark* which she bought at the festival downtown.
(24) (a) I gave an antique *clock* to *Jake* when he came to repair the roof on the back porch.
　　　(b) I gave an antique *clock* to *Jake* which I found under some old rags on the back porch.

The testing procedure for each of ten speakers and the acoustic measurements were similar to previous experiments.

Results

The mean durations of the word segments and pauses for each sentence appear in table 5.6. The results for all word segments and pauses failed to show any systematic or significant effects ($p > 0.20$).

SUMMARY OF EXPERIMENTS ON FRONTING AND BACKING RULES

The experiments on fronting and backing rules have revealed a variety of systematic effects on speech timing, as well as many

Table 5.6 *Mean durations (msec) for word segments and pauses in experiment 3*

Sentence pair	Key word segments		Pauses	
	Version (a)	Version (b)	Version (a)	Version (b)
(23)				
"plaque"	215.8	210.2	112.8	112.0
"Clark"	275.9	273.0	177.9	190.5
(24)				
"clock"	235.5	238.9	112.1	110.7
"Jake"	231.1	217.5	190.9	217.0

null results. Any comprehensive theory of speech production must ultimately be able to account for both kinds of data.

At the outset we noted two particular locations in a sentence where interesting effects on speech timing might be revealed for strings derived via movement rules. One location was the site where the moved constituent appeared originally in underlying structure; the other was the boundary between the moved constituent in its surface position and other material in the sentence. At the first location there was no intuitive basis for expecting significant effects on speech timing; yet we sought to find such effects because their existence would be important evidence of a kind of syntactic code in speech production that would include both underlying and surface levels of representation. In general, our results failed to show systematic effects on speech timing at the movement site. The typical occurrence of null results at this site does not of course preclude the existence of a two-level type of syntactic coding. What it does indicate is that if an underlying level of representation is coded by the speaker, this representation exerts little direct influence on speech timing (see also chapter 6).

While the results at movement sites generally produced no systematic effects, the results at the surface boundary between the moved constituent and the rest of the sentence did show lengthening of both segments and pauses. These effects are quite robust for some sentence structures. The effects appear to represent the speaker's intent to demarcate the moved constituent from the rest of the sentence, either for reasons internal to the speech production process or as a cue to the listener that the sentence does not conform to the canonical order of English constituents.

Raising

Movement rules that raise a constituent into a higher clause provide yet another approach to the issue of whether lengthening might be sensitive to the distinction between surface and underlying structure. Linguistic hypotheses distinguishing underlying and surface representations have been particularly explicit in the case of complement clauses (Rosenbaum, 1967; Chomsky, 1973; Postal, 1974); moreover, the analysis of complement structure is considered by some linguists to be pivotal in the current controversy over the general form that grammatical rules and constraints on such rules should take (for reviews, see Bresnan, 1976; Bach, 1977). Thus, in addition to providing a further means of testing whether syllable timing is primarily controlled at an underlying or surface level of syntactic representation, the study of complementation affords an opportunity to test the relevance of competing linguistic analyses for developing a performance model of the kinds of computations carried out at these processing levels.

Although the clausal analysis of complements does provide a strong linguistic backdrop to the present study, there is no assurance a priori that complement clauses are accompanied by syllable lengthening in speech production. Coordinate clauses, nonrestrictive relatives, and conditionals are marked by a comma in written English and are bounded by perceptible syllable lengthening and pauses in spontaneous speech; by contrast, complement clauses are accompanied neither by a comma in writing nor by a perceptible terminal lengthening in speech.

"EXPECT" VERSUS "PERSUADE": UNDERLYING STRUCTURE

A major distinction between the underlying structures of two types of complement was pointed out by Chomsky (1965) and is illustrated by sentences (25) and (26), containing the verbs "expect" and "persuade."

(25) The host expected Kate to be at breakfast.
(26) The host persuaded Kate to be at breakfast.

Although these two sentences are quite similar superficially in their word order, they have quite different logical structures. The difference becomes clear when one considers the meanings of passive sentences containing "expect" or "persuade," as in (27) and (28).

(27) The host expected Kate to be brought by an escort.
(28) The host persuaded Kate to be brought by an escort.

Sentence (27) is synonymous with the active sentence "The host expected an escort to bring Kate," whereas sentence (28) is not synonymous with the corresponding "The host persuaded an escort to bring Kate." The logical distinction underlying this difference is that "expect Kate X" does not entail "expect Kate," whereas "persuade Kate X" does entail "persuade Kate."

The question of how this underlying distinction between the complements of "expect" and "persuade" is to be represented (in the underlying structure of the syntactic component of grammar or in a separate component marking logical relations) remains to some extent problematic. If the distinction is represented in the syntactic component, according to the proposal of Rosenbaum (1967), then the complements of the two verbs are assigned different clause status. Thus, to the extent that the underlying clause representation of complements determines syllable lengthening, the complements of "expect" and "persuade" should produce an observable difference in speech timing.

In particular, Rosenbaum proposed that sentences like (25) and (26) have underlying structures like those shown in figure 5.1. Under this proposal, the critical distinction between the complements is that the EXPECT complement is immediately dominated by an NP node in underlying structure, whereas the PERSUADE complement is immediately dominated by a VP node. Consequently, "Kate" is a member of the superordinate clause in the structure of the PERSUADE sentence but is a member of the subordinate clause in the structure of the EXPECT sentence. Put another way, the major clause boundary for the PERSUADE sentence occurs immediately after "Kate," whereas the major boundary for the EXPECT sentence occurs immediately before "Kate," just after the verb "expect." If the underlying clause structure of complements influences syllable timing, then lengthening should be observed for "Kate" in sentence (26) and for "expect" in sentence (25), relative to some reference duration.

"EXPECT" VERSUS "PERSUADE": SURFACE STRUCTURE

The underlying structures shown in figure 5.1 can be converted into surface structures by application of transformational rules that move or delete elements (Chomsky, 1965). For a verb such as "expect," the underlying structure can be converted into two types of surface complement—an infinitival complement (introduced by "to"), as in sentence (25), or a THAT complement (introduced optionally by "that"), as in sentence (29) below:

(29)   The host expected (that) Kate would be at breakfast.

Generative grammarians agree that the surface structure of THAT complements, as in (29), preserves the constituent structure of the

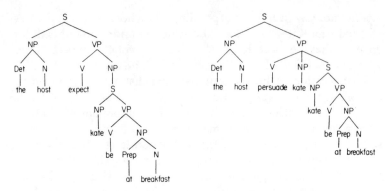

Figure 5.1 *Hierarchical tree diagram representing the underlying structure of sentences (28) and (29), according to the analysis of complements provided by Rosenbaum (1967).*

underlying representation shown in figure 5.1. In bracketed form, the constituent structure of (29) can thus be represented by (29′):

(29′) $[_S[_{NP}$the host] $[_{VP}$expect] $[_S[_{NP}$Kate] $[_{VP}$be at breakfast]]]

According to this analysis, there is a major clause boundary immediately after the verb "expected" in sentence (29) both in surface and underlying structure.

For infinitival complements with "expected," however, there exist two major alternative ways of describing the surface representation. According to one alternative, advocated principally by Rosenbaum (1967) and Postal (1974), the surface structure of infinitival complements differs from its underlying structure, and hence differs from the surface structure of THAT complements as well. Rosenbaum and Postal propose that the noun "Kate" in infinitival complements like (25) has been moved (raised) from its position as the subject of the subordinate clause in underlying structure (see figure 5.1) into the object position of the higher clause in surface structure. The transformational rule proposed to account for this movement is termed *Raising* (from subject to object).[1]

Note that according to the Raising analysis of infinitival complements, the surface structure of (25) contains a subordinate clause boundary immediately after the noun "Kate"; in contrast, the surface structure of THAT complements contains a subordinate clause boundary after the main verb, just prior to "Kate." The bracketed surface form of (25) is represented by (25′) below, assuming the Raising analysis.[2]

(25') [$_S$[$_{NP}$the host] [$_{VP}$expect Kate] [$_S$[$_{NP}$Ø] [$_{VP}$be at breakfast]]]

The Raising analysis of infinitivals was motivated by the need to account for a number of differences in grammaticality between infinitival and THAT complements under the application of certain transformations (for example, Passive) and constraints on transformations (for example, Inclusion Constraint—see Postal, 1974, and Cooper, 1976b, for discussion). However, another plausible account of infinitival complements has been proposed by Chomsky (1973) to account for the same range of facts. According to Chomsky's analysis, the surface structure of (25) is the same as (29) insofar as major constituency relations are concerned. To account for the variety of differences in grammaticality between infinitival and THAT complements, Chomsky proposed that a distinction be made between finite and infinitival clauses, and that a universal condition on transformations, the Tensed-S Condition, be used to account for the differences between the complement types.

At present, the linguistic controversy surrounding the two alternative accounts of infinitival complements is not settled. However, it is of independent interest to ask which of these two proposals provides a better model of performance in sentence production. This question can be tested in this study of syllable lengthening, under the assumption (requiring independent verification) that a surface as opposed to an underlying level of representation controls such lengthening, at least in part. According to the Raising analysis, lengthening should appear on the noun "Kate" of an infinitival complement with "expect" but on the main verb of the corresponding THAT complement; in contrast, according to Chomsky's Tensed-S account, lengthening should appear on the main verb for both types of complement.

We turn now to consider the surface structure of PERSUADE complements. Unlike "expect," the verb "persuade" takes only infinitival complements, with an underlying structure like that shown in figure 5.1. The infinitival sentence in (26), repeated below for convenience, is the relevant form.

(26) The host persuaded Kate to be at breakfast.

Given the underlying representation of figure 5.1, a transformational rule must be postulated to delete one of the two occurrences of the noun "Kate" to convert the underlying structure into a surface form. Generative grammarians agree for the most part that the correct formulation involves deleting the subordinate occurrence of "Kate," under identity with the superordinate one, by a rule known as Equi-NP Deletion. After this rule has been applied, the surface structure of (26) takes the bracketed form shown in (26').[3]

(26')　[s[NPthe host] [VPpersuaded Kate] [s[NP∅] [VPbe at breakfast]]]

The subordinate clause break of this structure appears immediately after the noun "Kate." Thus, syllable lengthening should be observed for this noun to the extent that such lengthening is determined by either underlying or surface structure.

Note that according to the Raising analysis the clause boundary for the PERSUADE infinitival occurs at the same location as for the EXPECT infinitival in surface structure, namely after "Kate." But, according to Chomsky's analysis, a difference in the boundary locations for EXPECT versus PERSUADE infinitivals exists, with the boundary occurring after the main verb for EXPECT but after "Kate" for the PERSUADE complement. By including PERSUADE infinitivals in this study, it was thus possible to provide another test of the merits of the two proposals in accounting for syllable lengthening in speech.

A summary of the clausal analysis of EXPECT and PERSUADE complements is provided in table 5.7, indicating the subordinate clause boundaries predicted by the Raising and Tensed-S proposals.

"TO BE" DELETION

Since the Raising and Tensed-S analyses make conflicting predictions about the locations of clause boundaries for the surface

Table 5.7 *Syntactic clause boundaries predicted on the basis of two linguistic analyses*

Linguistic analysis	Complement type		
	expect to	expect that	persuade to
Rosenbaum-Postal			
(a) underlying structure	expect◠	expect◠	Kate◠
(b) surface structure	Kate◠	expect◠	Kate◠
Chomsky			
(a) underlying structure	expect◠	expect◠	Kate◠
(b) surface structure	expect◠	expect◠	Kate◠

Based on the sentences "The host expected Kate to be at breakfast," "The host expected that Kate would be at breakfast," and "The host persuaded Kate to be at breakfast." Clause boundaries are denoted by " ◠ ."

but *not* the underlying representations of complements, it is necessary to try to provide an independent test of whether syllable
lengthening is primarily determined by one or the other of these
two levels of representation. Fortunately, evidence from a variety
of other experiments using the same testing procedure as the
present study indicates the presence of syntactic effects that can
be attributed to surface but not underlying structural relations.
However, none of these other experiments involved complement
structures, so a further test of surface structure effects was desired
here.

Consider sentence (30), which contains no complement clause
in surface structure.

(30)   The host expected Kate at breakfast.

This sentence is nearly synonymous with sentence (25), "The host
expected Kate to be at breakfast." Until recently, it was assumed
that (30) and (25) contained identical underlying structures, with
(30) being derived by application of a rule that deletes "to be."
Under such an analysis, a comparison of sentences like (25) and
(30) would provide the desired independent test of the role of
surface versus underlying structure as a determinant of syllable
lengthening. Borkin (1973) has shown that a slight difference in
meaning is usually associated with sentences (25) and (30), however: the version in which "to be" has been deleted has a greater
tendency to denote personal experience on the part of the subject.
Sentences (31) and (32) bring out Borkin's point clearly.

(31)   I find this chair to be uncomfortable. (= Borkin's 10b)
(32)   I find this chair uncomfortable.   (= Borkin's 10c)

Borkin notes that either (31) or (32) would be appropriate for a
speaker who is reporting on his personal experience with the
chair, whereas only (31) would be appropriate for a speaker who
is reporting the results of a consumer reaction test in which he
himself did not have experience with the chair. Since both (31)
and (32) can be used in the former circumstance, however, it can
still be maintained that the sentence pair (25) and (30) and the pair
(31) and (32) are derived from the same underlying structure on
their most common reading. Assuming this analysis,[4] if syllable
lengthening is controlled primarily by surface as opposed to underlying structure in the case of complements, lengthening should
be observed for the verb "expected" in (25) versus (30), since only
in the former sentence does the underlying complement clause

exist in surface structure. For (30) the subordinate sentence node in underlying structure is presumably deleted by the condition of S node pruning (Ross, 1969; Hankamer, 1971; Reis, 1973), a convention which, according to its original formulation, deletes all subordinate S nodes from surface structure which do not branch into a verb phrase and some other constituent.

Unlike the situation for "expect," the optional deletion of "to be" is not permitted for the complement of a verb such as "persuade," as evidenced by the major difference in meaning between sentences (33) below and (26).

(33)   The host persuaded Kate at breakfast.

Unlike (26), "The host persuaded Kate to be at breakfast," (33) is assumed to contain a single clause in underlying as well as surface structure. In addition to the surface structure contrast between EX-PECT sentences such as (25) and (30), it was decided to include the contrast between PERSUADE sentences such as (26) and (33) in the present study. Because (26) and (33) differ greatly in their meaning as well as in their constituent structure at both underlying and surface levels, however, it was not possible to make any firm predictions about the effects of this comparison on syllable timing. The absence of prediction in this case resulted from a lack of prior knowledge about any effects that semantic representation might have on timing.

EXPERIMENT 1

In experiment 1 the durations of syllables in five sentences were measured to determine whether differences in the syntactic structure of complements following the verbs "expected" and "persuaded" would produce differences in syllable timing. The verb and the following noun of each sentence were chosen as the key words for measurement, since the locations of the major syntactic boundaries postulated according to both major linguistic analyses of complementation occurred immediately after one of these two words. For the noun, the following word, of necessity, covaried with the syntactic structure of the sentence. For this reason an independent test (experiment 2) was required to determine whether any effects of syllable duration observed for the noun in this experiment were due to phonetic as opposed to syntactic influences.

Sentence Materials and Procedure

The sentences used in the experiment are listed below, along with their descriptive labels.

(a) The host expected Kate to be at breakfast.
    (EXPECT-INF = "expect" infinitival complement)
(b) The host expected Kate would be at breakfast.
    (EXPECT-THAT = "expect that" complement)
(c) The host expected Kate at the big breakfast.
    (EXPECT-SIMPLE = "expect" single surface clause)
(d) The host persuaded Kate to be at breakfast.
    (PERSUADE-INF = "persuade" infinitival complement)
(e) The host persuaded Kate at the big breakfast.
    (PERSUADE-SIMPLE = "persuade" single surface clause)

Each of these five sentences contains eight words and eleven syllables. All sentences have the same approximate sentence stress
contour, with primary stress on "Kate."[5] Sentences (a) and (d) are
equivalent to sentences (25) and (26) discussed previously. Sentences (c) and (e) have the same structure as (30) and (33); sentence (b) represents a version of (29) in which the THAT complementizer has been deleted so that the immediate phonetic
environment of the verb is identical for all five sentences.

Each of fifteen speakers read each sentence six times, following
the standard procedure. The first five occurrences of each sentence, excluding false starts, mispronunciations, and sentences
containing contrastive or emphatic stress, were analyzed as in previous experiments. Measurements were made for the bisyllabic
segments /spɛktəd/ and /swedəd/ of the verbs "expected" and
"persuaded" as well as of the monosyllabic /ket/ of "Kate."

The onset of visible frication following the closure gap of the
first /k/ in "expected" was taken as the onset of the final two syllables of this word.[6] For some speakers, a /k/ release burst was
discernible in the waveform and in such cases this burst was not
included as part of the measured bisyllabic segment, since including the burst durations would have introduced greater variability into the data.

The onset of visible frication following the /r/ in "persuaded"
was similarly taken as the onset of the bisyllabic segment for this
verb. The offset of the bisyllabic segments for both verbs was
measured to be the termination of visible glottal pulsing in the
unstressed syllable /əd/, not including the following closure interval of any /d/ release burst. As above, the decision not to include portions of the waveform as part of the bisyllabic segment
was based upon the undesirability of increasing the measurement
variability.

The onset of the monosyllable "Kate" was measured at the release burst of /k/, and the offset of the syllable was measured at

the termination of visible glottal pulsing. The onset release burst
was included in the measurements of "Kate" because this burst
was clearly discernible in the waveforms of all speakers and did
not increase the variability of the data appreciably. The closure
interval of the /t/ or any /t/ offset burst was not included as part
of the duration of "Kate."

Results and Discussion of Verb Duration

The mean durations of the verb segments for "expected" and
"persuaded" are presented for the individual speakers in table
5.8. Two-tailed *t* tests for correlated observations were applied to
the mean durations for the set of speakers to determine whether
any differences in these durations were statistically significant.
The analysis for the bisyllabic segment of the verb "expected"
showed that the segment in both sentence (a) EXPECT-INF and sentence (b) EXPECT-THAT were significantly longer than the segment
in sentence (c) EXPECT-SIMPLE (EXPECT-INF versus EXPECT-SIMPLE:
$p < 0.01$, $t = 2.675$, $df = 14$; EXPECT-THAT versus EXPECT-SIMPLE:
$p < 0.02$, $t = 2.487$, $df = 14$). The average duration of the bisyllabic
segment for EXPECT-INF was 13.3 msec longer than for EXPECT-SIM-
PLE, while the average duration of the segment for EXPECT-THAT
was 9.8 msec longer than for EXPECT-SIMPLE.

Table 5.8 *Mean durations (msec) of the last two syllables of the main verbs in experiment 1, sentences (a)–(e)*

Subject	(a)	(b)	(c)	(d)	(e)
I.B.	407.6	402.4	396.2	391.8	392.4
R.B.	326.5	317.6	310.2	305.3	309.0
L.C.	376.2	363.2	351.7	371.6	328.3
B.F.	415.6	381.2	367.8	380.1	432.7
P.F.	358.3	335.9	330.9	342.2	325.8
R.F.	378.7	399.0	368.5	349.0	325.5
J.G.	381.3	384.5	363.5	354.8	328.1
R.G.	422.3	435.0	411.7	349.7	358.5
L.H.	366.3	365.6	366.9	368.8	343.1
M.J.	357.9	378.0	341.3	349.2	323.1
S.K.	353.5	353.5	355.5	314.3	364.2
B.P.	350.4	349.8	352.8	345.0	350.5
J.P.	369.7	362.4	370.9	357.8	350.1
R.T.	339.6	317.3	335.1	316.7	334.8
P.V.	342.9	348.9	323.8	326.5	306.9
Grand mean	369.8	366.3	356.5	348.2	344.9

(a) = EXPECT-INF. (b) = EXPECT-THAT. (c) = EXPECT-SIMPLE. (d) = PER-
SUADE-INF. (e) = PERSUADE-SIMPLE.

The significant lengthening of the verb segment for the sentences (a) and (b), which contain surface complement clauses, versus sentence (c), which has the same meaning as the other two sentences and presumably the same underlying syntactic structure as well, suggests that complement clause boundaries in surface structure are among the types of syntactic boundaries that help to determine segmental lengthening. As expected, however, the lengthening observed for surface complements was small compared with the effects observed at the boundaries of other clause types such as coordinates and conditionals (Cooper, 1976a).

No significant difference was found with the duration of the verb segment for "expected" between the two complement types, EXPECT-INF and EXPECT-THAT ($p > 0.20$, $t = 0.856$, $df = 14$). The average duration of the segment in EXPECT-INF was longer than the duration in EXPECT-THAT by 3.3 msec. According to the Raising analysis of complementation, whereby a major clause boundary exists immediately after "expected" for EXPECT-THAT but not for EXPECT-INF, the duration of the verb segment for EXPECT-THAT should have been longer. Since the data in fact show a slight trend in the opposite direction, the results provide no support for a syntactic level of computation in speech production that corresponds to the surface representations proposed by the Raising analysis. This finding is paralleled in speech perception by a recent study of click location in which a test for Raising also failed to show support for such an analysis (Fodor, Fodor, Garrett, and Lackner, 1974).

The lack of a significant difference between EXPECT-INF and EXPECT-THAT is, on the other hand, consistent with the analysis of complement clause structure proposed by Chomsky (1973), whereby infinitival and "that" complements have the same surface as well as underlying constituent structure. However, the present data cannot be taken as very strong support for a performance analog of Chomsky's analysis, given the possibility of a Type II statistical error.

We will now consider the bisyllabic segment durations for the verb "persuaded." These durations were generally about 10–12 msec shorter than the durations of the corresponding segment of the verb "expected."[7]

The average duration of the verb segment in PERSUADE-INF was 3.3 msec longer than the average duration of the segment in PERSUADE-SIMPLE. The difference in duration for the set of subjects was not statistically significant ($p > 0.20$, $t = 1.149$, $df = 14$). Acceptance of the null hypothesis here is consistent with the predictions of both major analyses of complementation, since no major clause boundary occurred immediately after "persuaded" in either the underlying or surface structure of these two sentences.

According to either linguistic analysis of complementation, it was anticipated that some difference in the duration of the EXPECT sentences would occur, whereas no such differences would occur for the PERSUADE sentences. In fact, the only statistically significant effect obtained in the experiment was for the EXPECT sentences, providing support for the notion that syllable timing is conditioned in part by complement clause structure in a manner corresponding at a general level to a syntactic clause analysis.

The difference obtained for EXPECT-INF and EXPECT-THAT versus EXPECT-SIMPLE provides some evidence that the site of syntactic computation which controls syllable timing computes a clausal representation corresponding approximately to surface as opposed to underlying structure. Since a valid test of the Raising account of the possible difference between EXPECT-INF and EXPECT-THAT rested on the assumption that syllable lengthening is controlled in part at a surface as opposed to an underlying level of representation, the absence of a difference between infinitival and THAT complements must be considered problematic for the view that speakers generally compute a syntactic representation of complements corresponding to the Raising analysis.

Results and Discussion of Noun Duration

The results of the duration measurements for the noun "Kate" are presented in table 5.9. Unlike the durations for the verb segments, the data for the noun can be compared for a phonetically fixed environment in the case of sentences (a) versus (d) only, the infinitival complements for "expected" and "persuaded." In both sentences "Kate" was preceded by the unstressed syllable /əd/ and was followed by the infinitive "to." The results showed that the average duration of "Kate" for PERSUADE-INF was 2.5 msec longer than the average duration of "Kate" for EXPECT-INF. The difference in duration between these two test conditions was not statistically significant ($p > 0.20$, $t = 1.134$, $df = 14$). The slight trend for the noun following "persuaded" to be longer than the noun following "expected" is consistent with the notion that speakers compute the structural representations of the two complements according to Chomsky's (1973) account of infinitivals, whereby a major clause boundary exists immediately after the noun for "persuaded" but after the verb for "expected." On the other hand, the absence of a statistically significant difference between the two complement types is consistent with a Raising anal-

Table 5.9   *Mean durations (msec) for the noun "Kate" in experiment 1, sentences (a)–(e)*

Subject	(a)	(b)	(c)	(d)	(e)
I.B.	194.5	210.9	208.4	192.7	190.4
R.B.	169.7	163.1	181.5	161.8	167.3
L.C.	171.9	184.8	178.6	159.2	187.3
B.F.	196.0	214.0	227.6	211.0	261.4
P.F.	212.4	211.9	228.1	223.2	244.5
R.F.	156.8	149.2	214.3	160.5	179.8
J.G.	168.6	164.3	200.5	175.3	184.7
R.G.	177.2	194.9	194.0	187.5	223.1
L.H.	168.7	167.5	172.4	162.1	158.2
M.J.	191.9	187.9	176.2	180.8	179.1
S.K.	172.4	174.9	194.7	182.6	209.3
B.P.	161.0	164.1	197.0	172.8	210.9
J.P.	157.7	163.9	153.1	161.6	147.9
R.T.	143.3	149.7	172.5	143.1	167.7
P.V.	167.2	172.8	170.9	172.9	177.5
Grand mean	174.0	178.3	191.3	176.5	192.6

(a) = EXPECT-INF.   (b) = EXPECT-THAT.   (c) = EXPECT-SIMPLE.   (d) = PERSUADE-INF.   (e) = PERSUADE-SIMPLE.

ysis, whereby a major clause boundary exists immediately after the verb for both "persuaded" and "expected." In summary, then, the data for the noun durations of EXPECT-INF versus PERSUADE-INF provide no independent basis for distinguishing the merits of the Chomsky and the Rosenbaum and Postal proposals as models of speech performance.

In addition to the single comparison between phonetically stable nouns in EXPECT-INF versus PERSUADE-INF, other comparisons were made for the noun duration data. These comparisons revealed some significant differences, potentially attributable to the effects of the immediate phonetic environment. In particular, the durations of "Kate" before "at" in EXPECT-SIMPLE and PERSUADE-SIMPLE were significantly longer than the durations of "Kate" before "to" in EXPECT-INF and PERSUADE-INF and longer than the duration of "Kate" before "would" in EXPECT-THAT ($p < 0.05$ in each case). The average duration of "Kate" before "at" in the SIMPLE sentences was about 15 msec longer than before "to" and "would" in the complements.

EXPERIMENT 2

It is known that the duration of a vowel is longer when it is followed immediately by a voiced than by a voiceless phonetic segment occurring within the same word (Peterson and Lehiste, 1960; House, 1961; Delattre, 1966). In addition, Barnwell (1971) has shown that this effect of phonetic environment is stronger within a word than across a word boundary; however, his data base was not sufficiently large and his sentence materials were not sufficiently well matched to test the possibility that the phonetic effect does operate across a word boundary to some extent. The data for the noun "Kate" in experiment 1, regarding the difference between simple and complement sentences, could be accounted for by a similar effect, as opposed to some unexpected difference in syntactic structure. Of necessity, the structural differences of interest in experiment 1 made it impossible to control for the phonetic environment of the noun "Kate," unlike the verb. In experiment 2 an independent test was carried out to examine the possibility of a phonetic effect across word boundaries of the type that would directly account for the results for "Kate" in the previous experiment.

Sentence Materials and Procedure

The following three sentences were used in the experiment:

(a) We skate to the farm.
(b) We skate with the crowd.
(c) We skate at the pond.

The underlying and surface structure representations of each of these sentences were identical with regard to major constituent relations, consisting of a subject noun phrase and a verb phrase dominating a verb and a prepositional noun phrase.

Each sentence contained the key word "skate," immediately followed by a word beginning with /t/, /w/, or /æ/. These three segments corresponded to the three segments immediately following the word "Kate" in experiment 1. It was decided to use the above sentences for the test rather than simple phrases like "Kate to," "Kate would," and "Kate at" (taken directly from the sentences of experiment 1) so as to preserve a sentence context.

The procedure for testing described previously was used for this experiment. Ten speakers read each sentence in the list (a) through (c) six times, beginning with sentence (a) or (c) according to a randomized assignment. The durations of the monosyllabic words "we" and "skate" were measured using the same general procedure as in experiment 1.

Results and Discussion

The mean durations for the words "we" and "skate" are presented in table 5.10. The average durations of "we" in the three sentences were all within 3.5 msec of one another, and the differences among these durations for the set of subjects were not statistically significant ($p > 0.20$ in each case). These results are consistent with the notion that the duration of a word is not significantly influenced by the phonetic structure of another word that is two words removed from it.

The average duration of "skate" in the three sentences showed systematic differences. The word "skate" was longest preceding "at," somewhat shorter preceding "with," and shortest preceding "to," covering an average range of more than 24 msec. Statistical tests showed that the duration of "skate" before "at" was significantly longer than the duration of "skate" before "to" ($p < 0.01$, $t = 3.683$, $df = 9$) and that the duration of "skate" before "with" was also significantly longer than the duration of "skate" before "to" ($p < 0.001$, $t = 7.043$, $df = 9$). On the other hand, the duration of "skate" before "at" was not significantly longer than the duration of "skate" before "with" ($p > 0.20$, $t = 1.246$, $df = 9$).

The results of this experiment indicate that the duration of "skate" is significantly longer when the following word begins with either of the voiced segments /æ/ or /w/, in comparison

Table 5.10 *Mean durations (msec) of the pronoun "we" and the verb "skate" in experiment 2, sentences (a)–(c)*

Subject	"we"			"skate"		
	(a)	(b)	(c)	(a)	(b)	(c)
A.B.	165.1	175.2	162.6	391.0	419.1	401.9
D.B.	99.6	57.2	63.9	283.9	301.1	324.4
I.B.	127.6	135.8	129.1	366.1	384.5	403.9
J.B.	127.5	96.3	91.1	290.3	308.2	281.3
M.I.	61.9	66.5	70.7	254.9	267.1	274.1
C.K.	99.1	108.0	126.8	361.7	365.6	363.3
J.L.	59.7	96.7	83.0	282.2	293.5	325.7
S.L.	98.6	91.3	61.3	295.5	316.1	313.9
C.P.	128.3	115.5	144.3	390.4	399.2	411.3
J.P.	77.5	77.2	77.5	395.1	419.3	454.6
Grand mean	104.5	102.0	101.0	331.1	347.4	355.4

(a) = "We skate to the farm." (b) = "We skate with the crowd." (c) = "We skate at the pond."

with the voiceless segment /t/. This pattern of results demonstrates that the conditioning effect of following voiced versus
voiceless segments extends across a word boundary. This effect is
of the same order of magnitude as the effects observed in experiment 1. We can thus conclude that most, if not all, of the segmental lengthening observed for that noun was attributable to the
phonetic structure of the following segment rather than to the
distinction between simple and complement sentences.[8]

Post Hoc Analysis of Individual Speakers' Data for Experiment 1

Based on the results of experiment 2, a post hoc analysis was
carried out on the data of experiment 1 to determine whether any
individual speakers showed a pattern of results that was strikingly
consistent with either a Raising or Tensed-S analysis of complementation. If a speaker computed syntactic representations for
infinitival versus THAT complements according to a Raising analysis, then the duration of the verb segment of "expected" should
have been longer for EXPECT-THAT than for EXPECT-INF. In addition,
based on a consideration of the results of experiment 2, the duration of the noun following "expected" in EXPECT-INF should have
been longer than the duration of the noun in EXPECT-THAT,
whereas the duration of the noun in EXPECT-INF should have been
equal to the duration of the noun in PERSUADE-INF. Two of the fifteen speakers of experiment 1, R.F. and M.J. (see table 5.8),
showed this pattern of results. Thus, while a Raising analysis appears incapable of accounting for the results of the speakers as a
group, it is possible that this analysis is represented as a level of
speech computation for two of the fifteen speakers. Further research is required to test the possibility that the particular pattern
of results obtained for these two speakers was not coincidental.

A similar analysis of individual speakers' data was conducted
in search of speakers who showed a pattern of results corresponding to Chomsky's Tensed-S proposal. As noted earlier,
speakers who computed a syntactic representation of infinitival
and THAT complements according to the Tensed-S account should
have produced approximately equal durations for the verb segment of "expected" in EXPECT-INF and EXPECT-THAT. Furthermore,
taking into account the results of experiment 2, the speakers
should have produced a noun duration for EXPECT-THAT longer
than that for PERSUADE-INF, while the noun durations for EXPECT-
THAT and PERSUADE-INF should have been about equal. None of
the speakers of experiment 1 showed this particular pattern of results. The post hoc analysis of individual speakers' data thus provides no support for the notion that speakers represent the struc-

ture of complements in a manner like that proposed under a Tensed-S analysis and only very marginal support for the notion that some speakers represent the complements in a manner corresponding to a Raising analysis.

EXPERIMENT 3

The single result thus far providing any strong support for the notion that a surface structure representation of complements affects syllable timing was the significant lengthening of the verb segment in experiment 1 for the complements EXPECT-INF and EXPECT-THAT, in comparison with the duration of EXPECT-SIMPLE. To test whether this difference reflected an improbable chance result of some idiosyncratic property of the verb "expected," it was decided to conduct an experiment similar to experiment 1 but using different verbs.

There exist some verbs which trigger the same complement structures as "expect" but which, unlike "expect," can also occur as main verbs in sentences containing a single underlying clause. "Believe" is such a verb; it was used in this experiment in both single-clause and complement sentences.

Sentence Materials and Procedure

The sentences used in experiment 3 were divided into three categories: EXPECT-type 1, EXPECT-type 2, and PERSUADE-type 1. The EXPECT-type 1 sentences contained comparisons between infinitival complements and single-clause structures from which "to be" had presumably been deleted (see Borkin, 1973). Four different verbs were used, each triggering complements in the same manner as "expect" with regard to the major constituency relations of relevance (Bresnan, 1972). The resulting eight sentences appear below.

EXPECT-type 1
(a) We believed Kate to be crazy.
(b) We believed Kate crazy at times.
(c) We considered Kate to be crazy.
(d) We considered Kate crazy at times.
(e) The boss wants Ted to be at the station by 3 o'clock.
(f) The boss wants Ted at the old train station by 3 o'clock.
(g) The boss needs Ted to be at the station by 3 o'clock.
(h) The boss needs Ted at the old train station by 3 o'clock.

The list of EXPECT-type 2 sentences included three-way comparisons among infinitival complements, THAT complements, and single-clause sentences considered to contain a single clause in underlying as well as in surface structure. Three different verbs triggering complements in the same manner as "expect" were used, making a total of nine sentences.

EXPECT-type 2
(i)   Kate believed John to be at the trial.
(j)   Kate believed John was at the trial.
(k)   Kate believed John at the trial last week.
(l)   Kate understood John to be at the trial.
(m)   Kate understood John was at the last trial.
(n)   Kate understood John at the trial last week.
(o)   John proved Bayes' Theorem to be applicable to my sampling problem.
(p)   John proved Bayes' Theorem was applicable to my sampling procedure.
(q)   John proved Bayes' Theorem at the conference on statistical procedures.

Finally, the list of PERSUADE-type 1 sentences included two-way comparisons between infinitival complements and single-clause sentences considered to contain a single clause in both underlying and surface structure. These sentences used two verbs that trigger complements in the same manner as "persuade" (Bresnan, 1972).

PERSUADE-type 1
(r)   We convinced Kate to be at breakfast.
(s)   We convinced Kate at the big breakfast.
(t)   Ted challenged Kate to be at breakfast.
(u)   Ted challenged Kate at the big breakfast.

In summary, the EXPECT-type 1 and PERSUADE-type 1 sentences were comparable to sentences used for "expect" and "persuade" in experiment 1. The EXPECT-type 2 sentences, however, contained verbs like "expect" in single-clause sentences of the same kind as the sentences with verbs like "persuade."

The same testing procedure as in previous experiments was used to test seven speakers. The sentences appeared on three separate sentence lists. The durations of the verbs were measured using the general technique described earlier. Unlike in experiment 1, here the duration of the entire verb segment, excluding terminal gaps and offset bursts, was measured.

Results and Discussion

For the four EXPECT-type 1 verbs, three verbs showed an average lengthening effect in the infinitival complement versus single-clause sentences for the set of seven speakers. The average lengthening effect for "believe" was 20.1 msec, for "want" 5.1 msec, and for "need" only 0.2 msec. For the verb "consider" an average shortening of 7.9 msec was obtained, although, unlike the data for the other verbs, the average effect for "consider" was heavily influenced by the effect for a single speaker. We conclude from these results that the effect observed in experiment 1 generalizes to some extent to other verbs in the context of synonymous complement versus single-clause sentences, although a much larger data base would be required to test generality in a definitive manner.[9]

In contrast to the trend observed for the data of EXPECT-type 1 sentences, the duration of the main verb for EXPECT-type 2 sentences was either shorter for the complement than single-clause structures or was about equal. For the verb "believe," which showed a sizable lengthening effect for the complement in EXPECT-type 1 sentences, an equally sizable lengthening effect was observed for the single-clause sentence when this verb occurred in an EXPECT-type 2 context. The average duration of the verb in the single-clause sentence for "believe" in the latter context was 27.0 msec longer than the duration of the verb with an infinitival complement and 27.4 msec longer than the duration of the verb with a THAT complement. An average lengthening effect for the single-clause sentence was also observed for "understood," amounting to slightly more than 12 msec in comparison to each complement. For the verb "proved," however, the verb of the single clause was shorter than the verb in the infinitival complement by 11.3 msec and was longer than the verb in the THAT complement by 3.4 msec. In summary, it appears that the verb duration data for EXPECT-type 2 sentences differs from that of EXPECT-type 1 sentences in the predicted direction. The lengthening for the single-clause sentences of EXPECT-type 2 is unaccountable in terms of clausal analysis but may well reflect semantic differences of focus that will need to be studied further. Since the present data base is small and subject to idiosyncrasies, we will not pursue a discussion of the possible significance of the single-clause lengthening of EXPECT-type 2 sentences here.[10]

The data for the two PERSUADE-type 1 verbs, "convinced" and "challenged," showed approximately equal average durations for the single-clause and complement sentences. The average differ-ence in duration was within 2 msec for both verbs. These results indicate that the results for "persuaded" in experiment 1 general-ize to these other verbs of the same structural classification.

GENERAL DISCUSSION

These experiments have provided evidence for the existence of both syntactic and phonetic effects on syllable timing. At a syn-tactic level, speakers lengthened the duration of the last two sylla-bles of the verb "expected" when this verb was followed by a complement clause in the surface structure of the sentence, as compared with when it was followed in surface structure by a simple phrase which, according to one linguistic analysis, was derived from a full complement in underlying structure. This finding suggests that a speaker's surface structure representation of an utterance is the *primary* level of syntactic representation that exercises control over syllable timing.

The effect observed for full versus reduced complements is noteworthy also because the verb in both sentences occurred two words prior to the point in the sentences at which the distinction between the surface structures became apparent. This fact sug-gests that, as was the case in the study of preposing, the speakers in this study were computing the duration of syllables in part on the basis of the structure of material yet to be spoken. This indi-cation of planning is not too surprising in light of the speakers' practice, but the result does show that speakers can utilize hierar-chical structure in programming segment durations (see also chapter 7).

Conclusion

The studies of movement rules have revealed a variety of sys-tematic effects on speech timing. In nearly all cases, these effects seem to reflect the influence of a stage of the speaker's syntactic coding corresponding to a surface as opposed to an underlying level of linguistic representation. The results with movement rules, as with deletions, provide little evidence for a system of speech processing involving operations analogous to transforma-tional rules in a generative grammar. In view of this outcome it is interesting to consider another important source of evidence per-taining to the occurrence of syntactic transformations, involving spontaneous speech errors. In a careful analysis of errors, Fay (1977, 1980) observes cases in which a WH word is displaced to the location that it would have occupied at an underlying level of coding. To illustrate, consider the speech errors below.

(34) Target: Look at how fast those clouds are moving.
     Error: Look at those clouds are moving how fast.
     (= Fay, 1977, Example 9c)
(35) Target: Linda, which ear do you talk on the telephone with?
     Error: Linda, do you talk on the telephone with which ear?
     (= Fay, 1977, Example 9d)

In these cases, the WH word appears at the location where it is postulated to occur at an underlying level of structure (Chomsky, 1977). It seems very unlikely that the WH word would be displaced to this particular location by chance, although this possibility needs to be confirmed by an examination of a much larger body of errors of this general type than was available to Fay. The most likely interpretation of this type of error is that a speaker does compute an underlying representation of the string and that the WH movement transformation which normally applies to this representation fails to do so in the case of this error pattern.

A related type of error involves the improper duplication of the NP contained in the WH phrase. One occurrence of this NP appears in its properly fronted position, presumably derived via WH-Fronting. The second occurrence appears in the position presumably occupied by the NP in underlying structure. An example of this type of error appears below, involving duplication of the NP "a boy":

(36) Target: A boy who I know has hair down to here.
     Error: A boy who I know a boy has hair down to here.
     (= Fay, 1977, Example 12a)

As Fay points out, the second occurrence of the NP appears in the precise location occupied in underlying structure, suggesting that the speaker correctly copied this NP and preposed it via WH-Fronting but failed to erase the original representation of the NP. The existence of this type of error seems to add support for the transformationalist position.

A third related type of speech error appears to involve leaving a portion of the WH phrase in its underlying position while correctly moving another portion of the same phrase. Such movement of only part of the WH phrase violates a constraint on the WH-movement transformation (Ross, 1967). Examples of this kind of error appear below, in which the word "else" is apparently left behind in its underlying position when the WH word is moved.

(37) Target: Go ahead and do what else you're going to do
and I'll be there in a minute.
Error: Go ahead and do what you're going to do else
and I'll be there in a minute.
(= Fay, 1980, Example 15)

(38) Target: Who else did I think had left?
Error: Who did I think else had left?
(= Fay, 1980, Example 16)

The three types of WH errors observed by Fay may indeed be accounted for by a transformational malfunction; yet even in these cases the evidence pointing to a transformational framework is not compelling. First, these critical error types occur very infrequently in the large sample of errors collected to date. In addition, there remains some possibility that the errors noted above may reflect an entirely different sort of processing than one involving transformations. In particular, the errors may represent the blending of two competing surface structures that were simultaneously available to the speaker; blending of a similar sort is widely known to occur in errors involving lexical selection (for example, Garrett, 1975; Shattuck-Hufnagel, 1979). The blending hypothesis would require strong constraints in order to make adequate predictions about the specific locations of misplaced words, but this drawback may be overcome when this hypothesis is given proper consideration.

At the end of chapter 6 we shall consider some prosodic effects for traces in WH questions, involving the blocking of phonological rules and differences in segmental timing. The presence of such effects suggests that speakers might code more than a single level of syntactic representation in the case of particular WH structures, although an account has yet to be provided for why these structures yield prosodic effects at trace sites whereas structures involving most other movement rules do not. The results of this chapter have, for the most part, provided further evidence that surface structure influences speech timing. Particularly large and systematic effects of lengthening were noted at the boundaries between the moved constituent and the rest of the sentence for structures derived via root transformations. Some of the effects reported in this chapter, particularly those accompanying surface structures derived via backing rules (for example, Right Dislocation), can be attributed to the constituent structure preceding the relevant boundary. Such effects are explained in terms of constituent-final lengthening, a phenomenon invoked in previous chapters to account for timing effects for structurally ambiguous sentences and words belonging to different grammatical categories. Other timing effects at the site of a moved constituent, such as those observed in many preposed constructions, seem attributable to the influence of upcoming constituent structure. It seems likely that this latter type of effect may be programmed by the speaker in order to allow more time to plan the structure of material yet to be spoken, a possibility to be discussed more fully in chapter 7. In addition, the timing effects produced at the site of a moved constituent may serve as a cue to the listener that will aid in recovering the sentence structure during perception, as discussed in chapter 8. Whether or not the speaker produces such effects with this latter intention, such cues may be particularly helpful to the listener in the case of root transformational sentences, in which the derived surface form differs radically from canonical syntactic structure.

6 | Blocking of Phonological Rules

I N AN EARLY scene from the 1977 Oscar-winning movie *Annie Hall*, Woody Allen complains to his friend Tony Roberts that someone has expressed anti-Semitism toward Woody by rhetorically asking, "Jew eat?" Phonetically, /ju#it/ is a typical form of reduction for the question "Did you eat?" Woody has, characteristically, displayed his own paranoia by mistakenly comprehending the phonological reduction /ju#it/ as "Jew eat?"

How, we may ask, does the phrase "did you" become reduced to the monosyllable /ju/? The speaker has apparently deleted the word "did" altogether; but then why does the speech output contain a /ǰ/? This segment is derived via a common phonological rule known as *Palatalization*, which operates to change a /d/ to a /ǰ/ when it is immediately followed by a palatal like /y/. In this case, the word-final /d/ of "did" has been palatalized.

For our purposes, the interesting feature of phonological rules such as Palatalization is that they may operate across word boundaries as well as within words. That is, the specific conditioning environment which permits Palatalization to apply, namely the presence of a /d/ or /t/ immediately followed by a /y/, may bridge the boundary between two words, as in "did you."

Intuitively, it seems likely that a rule like Palatalization might be blocked from applying when a major syntactic boundary intervenes between the two key words. Since the normal application of such a rule requires that the phonetic segments lying on both sides of the boundary be of a specific type (for example, Palatalization cannot apply for /d#w/ or for /g#y/), the rule's application should be blocked if the speaker does not have simultaneous access to both key segments within the same processing domain. This intuition has already been examined to some extent from a linguistic standpoint (for example, Stanley, 1973; Selkirk, 1974).

According to this view, conditioning rules are applied over a given syntactic domain such that phonetic material lying outside the domain cannot be taken into consideration during the application of such rules. For example, if the coding system is currently dealing with a constituent domain D containing words $w_1, w_2, w_3, \ldots, w_n$, then cross-word phonetic rules operating on word w_n may involve another word or words only if such words also lie within domain D. Thus, a cross-word conditioning rule *cannot* involve word w_n and word w_{n+1} (where w_{n+1} follows w_n in the linear string of the sentence), if the two words belong to different domains D. The study of which syntactic boundaries block the operation of cross-word phonetic conditioning should thus provide information about the kinds of syntactic domains computed by the speaker. We set out in this chapter to examine possible syntactic constraints on the operation of three conditioning rules.

Study 1: Trochaic Shortening

In study 1 we investigate a cross-word conditioning effect that influences the duration of a word preceding the boundary but does not alter (as Palatalization does) its phonemic identity. An example of such a durational effect has already been discussed in experiment 2 of the study on Raising in the previous chapter, where the duration of "skate" was shown to be longer in the environment of a following "at" or "with" as opposed to a following "to" within the verb phrase. In that experiment the durational influence on "skate" appeared to be produced by the voiced-voiceless contrast at the beginning of the next word. Here we focus on another type of durational effect, involving conditioning produced by a difference in stress pattern.

When a stressed syllable is followed by an unstressed syllable, the stress pattern is termed a *trochee,* as will be recalled from an introduction to poetry. The duration of a stressed syllable in such a pattern is normally shortened relative to its duration as a monosyllable (Lindblom, 1964; Barnwell, 1971).[1] Huggins (1974, 1975) showed that this shortening operates across word boundaries, but not when the words are separated by a major syntactic boundary, such as the break between the subject noun phrase and the verb phrase of a single-clause sentence. The syntactic blocking effect was not observed with much consistency across different sentences, however; this failure may be traced to a lack of control for phonetic environment in the immediate vicinity of the measured segment. In this study, we attempted to establish whether the effect of syntactic blocking would occur with better-controlled sentence materials and, if so, which of a variety of syntactic boundaries would serve as processing junctures.

PILOT EXPERIMENTS

Three pilot experiments were conducted to determine whether a number of different syntactic boundaries blocked the durational rule referred to above (hereafter termed the *Trochaic Shortening rule*, TSR). A group of ten speakers participated in these pilot experiments, and the sentence materials and procedures were similar to those described previously. In a few sentence pairs, however, the boundaries of key segments could not be measured with much accuracy due to coarticulation; these key segments were replaced by others in the experiments reported below. The results of the pilot work for segments that could be measured with a high degree of reliability are summarized below in the context of results with new speakers for identical sentences.

EXPERIMENT 1

Sentence Materials and Procedure

Three sentence pairs were used in experiment 1. Each sentence contained a subject noun phrase (NP), a verb, a direct object NP or an indirect object prepositional phrase (PP), and, finally, a temporal PP, optionally containing an internal clause. The key segment in each sentence was /klɪn/, taken from the word "Clint" or "Clinton," which immediately preceded the temporal PP. In each sentence pair, the (a) sentence represented a test for a cross-word boundary durational effect of TSR, while the (b) version represented a test for a within-word TSR. Each of the pairs represented below is preceded by a descriptive label, signifying the type of syntactic constituents that bordered the syntactic boundary occurring just after "Clint(on)."

(1) NP-PP   (a)   The police kept Clint until nine o'clock that night.

(b)   The police kept Clinton till nine o'clock that night.

(2) PP-PP   (a)   The commissioner talked to Clint until the sunset.

(b)   The commissioner talked to Clinton till the sunset.

(3) PP-S   (a)   The commissioner talked to Clint until the sun set.

(b)   The commissioner talked to Clinton till the sun set.

We have labeled sentence pair (3) as PP-S (S = clause) to contrast the boundary for this pair with (2), despite the fact that the adverbial clause to the right of the boundary in (3), "until the sun set" or "till the sun set," is also considered a PP at its most inclusive (maximal) phrase level, containing the preposition "until" or "till" and an internal complement clause "the sun set" (Emonds, 1970; Jackendoff, 1973).

The (a) sentences in all three pairs contained the monosyllable "Clint" in phrase-final position and the iambic bisyllable "until" at the beginning of the next phrase; the (b) sentences contained the trochaic bisyllable "Clinton" and the monosyllable "till." By constructing the sentence pairs in this way, the immediate phonetic environment of the key segment /klɪn/ was kept as similar as possible for the two members of each pair.[2] In addition, the members of each pair contained the same approximate stress contour when spoken without contrastive or emphatic stress.

Eleven speakers were tested according to the procedure described in chapter 1. Measurements of the duration of the key segment /klɪn/ were taken for the first utterance of each sentence type. The accuracy of most measurements was within ±3 msec. For a few cases in which the measurement error was considered to exceed ±5 msec, the second utterance of the sentence type was measured instead.

For each of the three sentence pairs, the duration of the key segment was significantly shorter in the (b) sentence, testing within-word TSR (pair (1), NP-PP: $p < 0.05$, $t = 2.546$, $df = 10$; pair (2), PP-PP: $p < 0.01$, $t = 5.026$, $df = 10$; pair (3), PP-S: $p < 0.01$, $t = 3.715$, $df = 10$; two-tailed t tests for matched pairs). The average magnitude of the shortening in (b) relative to (a) sentences was as follows: 48.3 msec or 19 percent for pair (1), 35.9 msec or 14 percent for pair (2), and 44.5 msec or 18 percent for pair (3).

The results suggest that all three syntactic boundary types, NP-PP, PP-PP, and PP-S, serve to block TSR from applying across a word boundary. It is not possible to determine whether this blocking effect is complete or partial.[3] The magnitude of TSR for a vowel in a bisyllabic trochee compared with a similar monosyllable averages about 30 percent (Barnwell, 1971; Huggins, 1974; Lehiste, 1972). This average is somewhat greater than the blocking effect observed for the segment /klɪn/.

The similar magnitude of effect for sentence pairs (2) and (3) suggests that the degree of blocking is determined more by the most inclusive phrase types bordering the syntactic boundary than by the internal structure of such phrases. A slightly larger percent effect was observed in (3), however, suggesting that internal structure may play a minor role.

EXPERIMENT 2

The same procedure was applied to five new sentence pairs containing a key segment in the environment of various syntactic boundaries. The pairs (4)–(6) include syntactic boundaries similar to those in experiment 1, but here the constituent to the left of the boundary has been moved, in transformational grammar terms, by application of a syntactic transformation (Chomsky, 1965; Ross, 1967). Pairs (7) and (8) contain syntactic boundaries within the main clause VP not tested in experiment 1.

Sentence Materials and Procedure

The key segment, italicized in the sentences below, differed across the five sentence pairs used in experiment 2.

(4) PPP–S (a) With *Chuck* emotion is a way of life.
           (b) With *Chucky* motion is a way of life.
(5) PPP–S (a) As for *Trix* equality is a prime consideration.
           (b) As for *Trixie* quality is a prime consideration.
(6) PPP–NP (a) Dr. Zero made with *co*ke a medicine to cure all ills.
           (b) Dr. Zero made with *co*ca medicines to cure all ills.
(7) NP–NP (a) Horace bought *Clint* an enormous turtle.
           (b) Horace bought *Clint*on enormous turtles.
(8) V–NP (a) The longshoreman must *light* an inflammable carton.
           (b) The longshoremen must *light*en inflammable cartons.

The descriptive label PPP in pairs (4)–(6) refers to a preposed prepositional phrase. In these sentences PPs have been moved from the rightmost position in the constituent structure of the underlying syntactic representation to the left by a transformational rule of PP preposing in pairs (4) and (5) and by a rule of heavy NP shift in pair (6) (Ross, 1967; Emonds, 1970). In pair (6) the rule actually moves the direct object NP to the right of the PP rather than moving the PP to the left.

The same eleven subjects who particpated in experiment 1 were tested using the procedure described previously. Measurements of duration were obtained for the key segment /čʌ/ in pair (4),

/trɪ/ in pair (5), /koʷ/ in pair (6), /klɪn/ in pair (7), and /laⁱ/ in
pair (8), using the analysis procedure described in experiment 1.
In this experiment the measurement error for a few sentences exceeded ±5 msec for both sentence tokens; in such cases the
datum for the speaker was not included in the statistical analysis,
as indicated by the degrees of freedom (*df*) below.

Results and Discussion

The duration of the key segment was significantly shorter in the
(b) sentence for the three pairs containing preposed PPs (pair (4),
PPP-S: $p < 0.01$, $t = 4.122$, $df = 9$; pair (5), PPP-S: $p < 0.01$, $t = 5.556$,
$df = 8$; pair (6), PPP-NP: $p < 0.02$, $t = 3.183$, $df = 9$). No significant
effects were obtained for the other two sentence pairs (pair (7),
NP-NP: $p > 0.20$, $t = 0.758$, $df = 8$; pair (8), V-NP: $p > 0.20$, $t = 0.249$,
$df = 7$).

The average shortening effects for the three preposed PPs were
49.0 msec or 19 percent for pair (4), 55.2 msec or 22 percent for
pair (5), and 44.6 msec or 19 percent for pair (6). In the corresponding pilot experiment, shortening effects for these same pairs
averaged 16, 20, and 13 percent, respectively.

The similar effects observed for preposed PPs in this experiment and for PPs in normal position in experiment 1 suggest that
the degree of TSR blocking is determined more by the surface
structure constituent types that border the syntactic boundary
than by the transformational history of such constituents, if indeed mental operations analogous to syntactic transformations
are carried out at some stage of sentence processing.

The similarity between the effects in experiments 1 and 2 is of
interest from another standpoint. For the preposed PPs in this experiment, but not for the PPs in experiment 1, the end of the PP
may be accompanied by a pause in speech, and pauses were in
fact observed for some speakers in this experiment. Yet the degree to which TSR was blocked was no greater in this experiment
than in experiment 1. This finding suggests that the blocking of
TSR is influenced by the status of the syntactic boundary per se as
a juncture in the processing of timing relations, not via the mediating influence of a pause that may be induced by the syntactic
boundary.

Finally, the contrast between the significant effects for pairs
(4)–(6) and the lack of effects for pairs (7) and (8) suggests that
only certain syntactic boundaries act to block TSR. We will provide a structural account of this difference in the general discussion.

EXPERIMENT 3

In experiment 3 the same test procedure was applied to sentence structures of greater complexity. Each sentence contained two clauses, one main clause and one subordinate clause. The subordinate clause was either an adverbial, a complement, or a restrictive relative.

Sentence Materials and Procedure

The following five pairs of sentences were used in this experiment. The key segment in each sentence is in italics.

(9)	PS-S	(a)	After the governor appointed *Chuck* equality was ignored.
		(b)	After the governor appointed *Chucky* quality was ignored.
(10)	PS-S	(a)	Before the NRC interviewed *Trix* eradiation from the plant was three times as great.
		(b)	Before the NRC interviewed *Trixie* radiation from the plant was three times as great.
(11)	NP-S (REL)	(a)	The *coke* Adele sold was worth thousands.
		(b)	The *coca* Dell sold was worth thousands.
(12)	NP-S (COMPL)	(a)	George was trying to tell *Trix* erasers can't stand that much pressure.
		(b)	George was trying to tell *Trixie* racers can't stand that much pressure.
(13)	NP-VP	(a)	The woman who kissed *Chuck* erased the boards.
		(b)	The woman who kissed *Chucky* raced the boys.

The descriptive label PS symbolizes a preposed clause, moved from a position to the right of the main clause in underlying structure. The labels S (REL) and S (COMPL) refer to relative and complement subordinate clauses.

The same eleven subjects who participated previously were tested following the procedure described earlier. Measurements of duration were made for the key segments /čʌ/, /trɪ/, and /koʷ/.

Results and Discussion

The duration of the key segment in (b) was significantly shorter for each of the five sentence pairs (pair (9), PS-S: $p < 0.05$, $t = 2.370$, $df = 9$; pair (10), PS-S: $p < 0.01$, $t = 6.129$, $df = 9$; pair (11), NP-S (REL): $p < 0.01$, $t = 3.815$, $df = 9$; pair (12), NP-S (COMPL): $p < 0.01$, $t = 4.236$, $df = 9$; pair (13), NP-VP: $p < 0.01$, $t = 3.830$, $df = 8$). The average magnitude of shortening differed considerably for the pairs. The average shortening for pair (9) was 31.6 msec or 14 percent; for pair (10), 60.5 msec or 23 percent; for pair (11), 18.2 msec or 9 percent; for pair (12), 28.4 msec or 12 percent; and for pair (13), 48.8 msec or 20 percent. In the corresponding pilot experiment, an average effect of 25 percent was obtained for pair (9) and 19 percent for pair (11).

The slightly smaller effect for pair (12) compared with other sentences may indicate that a weak processing juncture exists between phrases that are strictly subcategorized by the main verb. *Strict subcategorization* refers to the notion that a specific phrase can or must co-occur with a particular constituent in order to render a sentence grammatical (Chomsky, 1965). For example, the verb "tell" obligatorily subcategorizes a direct object NP and optionally subcategorizes a complement clause, accounting for the grammatical versus ungrammatical strings: "John told Mary (that it was snowing)," "*John told smaller than a breadbox," "*John told for Bill to wash the car." While obligatory subcategorization may account for the small-magnitude effect in pair (12), it cannot account for the lack of effect observed for pair (7) in experiment 2, which involves only optional subcategorization.

The 20 percent shortening effect obtained for pair (13), containing an NP-VP boundary, should be compared with effects of similar magnitude obtained for a variety of other boundaries in this experiment and in experiments 1 and 2. For this sentence pair, the key word "Chuck(y)" was the final word in the subject NP of the main clause, as indicated by the descriptive label assigned to this sentence. But this word was also the final word of three other constituents, including the relative clause, as well as the VP and NP direct object within the relative clause, as shown in the tree diagram in figure 6.1. Despite the presence of four coinciding syntactic phrase boundaries, the magnitude of effect for this pair was no larger than that observed for sentences containing fewer coinciding boundaries. This finding suggests that the effect of TSR blocking is not cumulative for these sentences, perhaps because the blocking effect is complete for any single major syntactic boundary (representing a ceiling effect on the amount of blocking; see note 3).

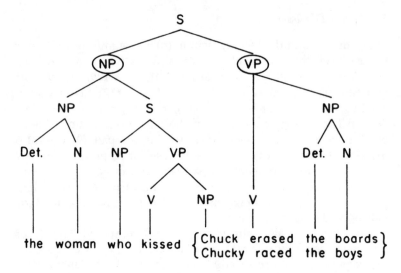

Figure 6.1 *Surface structure tree for the sentences in pair (13) of experiment 3. The circled nodes represent the most inclusive phrases that border the boundary under consideration.*

GENERAL DISCUSSION: BLOCKING OR PHRASE-FINAL LENGTHENING?

Up to this point in the discussion, we have assumed, following Huggins (1974), that the effects observed for syntactic boundaries represent the blocking of TSR across a word boundary. We can propose an alternative explanation, however, which does not rely on the blocking notion at all. According to this alternative account, the effects Huggins and we obtained represent differences in phrase-final lengthening. Two key assumptions underlie this account: (1) phrase-final lengthening occurs exclusively or primarily for the very last syllable of a phrase, assuming the last syllable is stressed, and (2) the amount of phrase-final lengthening varies with the type of syntactic phrase. The first assumption appears warranted but has not been rigorously tested. Klatt (1975) found no major lengthening of the next-to-last syllable of phrases in a connected discourse, although it is possible that minor lengthening occurred but was outweighed by the influence of other, particularly phonetic, factors. Kloker (1975), on the other hand, found cases of lengthening which extended to a few syllables before the end of a phrase in a spontaneous speech corpus. The second assumption, regarding phrase types, is almost certainly true in its general form, as indicated, for example, by the results of chapter 2; the question of immediate interest, however, is whether differences in phrase type can account for the specific trends noted in our experiments. No systematic data on phrase-final lengthening are available on this point. Nonetheless, both the first and second assumptions of the alternative account seem intuitively reasonable, making this alternative a serious contender to the blocking account.

Because the two accounts make equivalent predictions about the effects observed for the Trochaic rule, it was necessary to study a different phonological rule to provide an adequate test of the blocking account. An appropriate experiment was conducted using the phonological rule of Palatalization, mentioned at the outset of this chapter. As it operates across word and morpheme boundaries, the rule palatalizes an alveolar obstruent in the environment of an immediately following palatal. Thus, a /d/ may be palatalized in the environment of a following /y/ in such phrases as "did you" /dɪ̆jyu/, "had yet" /hæ̆jyɛt/ (Oshika et al., 1975). According to the blocking account, cross-word palatalization of this sort should be prohibited at major syntactic boundaries, other factors being equal. To test this prediction, we conducted an experiment using sentence pairs like the following, in which an identical context for palatalization occurred with two different syntactic boundary types.

(14) NP-ADV   (a)   We didn't break the code yet but we intend to break it soon.

S-S   (b)   We didn't break the code yet we intend to break it soon.

In (14) the palatalization context of interest occurs for the /d/ (the /d/ in a few cases was glottalized, in which cases no palatalization context existed) of "code" in "code yet." A trained listener marked this context as palatalization if he perceived an unambiguous /ǰ/ in place of /d/ at the end of "code." The results showed that speakers occasionally palatalized the /d/ in (a) but not in (b), as expected by the blocking account under the assumption that the S-S boundary represents the more major syntactic break. Further experiments, to be described in study 2 below, have been conducted with cross-word palatalization to test a variety of additional, extrasyntactic influences, but it appears that syntactic blocking does constrain the operation of this rule. Some instances exist for which palatalization may cross a syntactic boundary regardless of its strength, but the syntactic boundary strength constrains the probability with which palatalization may occur in any given context.[4]

A THEORY OF BOUNDARY TYPES

An important theoretical consideration arises regardless of whether the results of experiments 1–3 are accounted for in terms of blocking or in terms of differences in phrase-final lengthening. There is presently no theory of syntactic boundary types to provide a framework for testing hypotheses about the relative strengths of various boundaries, even though it appears that many gradations of boundary strength exist. However, based on linguistic intuition, it is possible to outline such a theory and provide an account for the results of experiments 1–3. At present, we shall describe only those aspects of the theory that pertain to the blocking of Trochaic Shortening. Further discussion will be included in a subsequent study of Alveolar Flapping in this chapter, and a full description of the theory will be presented in chapter 7.

In trying to formalize the notion of "strong" versus "weak" syntactic boundaries, a couple of possibilities were considered, all of which may eventually be shown to play some role in capturing boundary strength (see, for example, Bierwisch, 1966; Robinson, 1973). Among these, however, one structural property—branching depth—appeared to provide the best single measure. As defined here, *branching depth* refers to the extent to which a given phrase node branches hierarchically. The relevant index is the depth of branching, not the number of particular branches from a given node. This property may assume any integer value and may be quantified precisely given a syntactic tree diagram. On this account, very strong syntactic boundaries include those which separate phrase nodes having large integer values of branching depth. The boundary between two main clauses will thus be marked as a strong boundary, as will the boundary between the NP and VP of a main clause. Very weak boundaries will include those between an adjective or determiner and a head noun. The notion of branching depth, coupled with a well-defined set of rewrite rules

---

Figure 6.2   *Surface structure trees for the sentences in pair (1) of experiment 1, pair (7) of experiment 2, and pair (8) of experiment 2. The circled nodes represent the most inclusive phrases that border the boundary under consideration. These tree diagrams illustrate a difference in branching depth of the circled nodes. In the top tree diagram, the circled PP branches twice. The total phrase branching of the circled nodes in the middle and bottom tree structures is only one branching. In an elaboration of these tree structures, in terms of Chomsky's X̄ notation, the same approximate strength relations would hold for the boundary types studied here.*

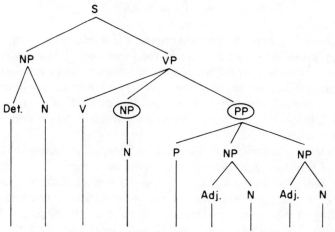

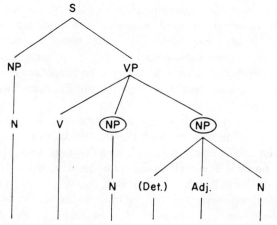

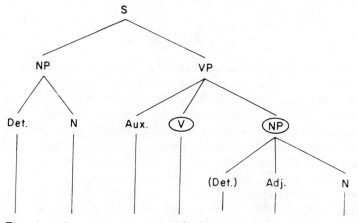

for generating syntactic tree descriptions (for example, Chomsky, 1965), provides a natural account for some basic intuitions concerning boundary strengths, and, in addition, makes a number of specific predictions about the relative strengths of certain boundaries for which intuition is a poor guide. Finally, this metric provides a first-order account of the data obtained in the experiments of this study.

Of the various syntactic boundaries tested in experiments 1–3, two of them—the boundaries between a verb and a direct object NP—failed to show a significant boundary effect. As can be seen in figure 6.2, these two boundaries are structurally weaker, according to the metric of branching depth, than the boundary between an NP and a PP, which did show a significant effect. For the latter boundary, as well as for the other ten boundaries that showed an effect, the branching depth of the phrase node to the right of the boundary was ≥2, whereas the boundaries not showing an effect had a branching depth that never exceeded 1 (for either the left or the right phrase node). It appears, then, that a branching depth of ≥2 for either bordering boundary is sufficient to show a significant blocking effect for the durational rule studied here.

For present purposes, branching depth can account for the relative weakness of the V-NP and NP-NP boundaries in conjunction with almost any type of linguistic tree diagram, including those shown in figure 6.2 as well as diagrams generated by competing linguistic theories. In later work, it will become of interest to utilize the blocking method in testing critical differences in the predictions between such theories. In a linguistic study of French liaison, Selkirk (1974) has provided an illustration of this kind of work.[5]

Study 2: Palatalization

As we noted in the general discussion of the last study, Palatalization is more suitable as a means of studying blocking than Trochaic Shortening, since apparent blocking of the latter may in fact represent phrase-final lengthening. Palatalization offers the additional advantage of being a readily perceptible feature of the speech wave. Because perceptual and acoustic judgments in this case can be shown to coincide, blocking can be studied by a trained phonetician, with less need for acoustic analysis.

As we observed earlier, there is little question that Palatalization is blocked at the sites of major clause boundaries. In study 2 we examined the blocking of this rule in terms of deletion sites (see chapter 4) and in terms of other conditioning factors that may influence the probability of its application.

EXPERIMENT 1: DELETION

The aim of experiment 1 was to determine whether the deletion site produced by Verb Gapping would influence the application of Palatalization, and, if so, whether the effect is attributed to blocking per se or to the influence of a coinciding pause. In chapter 4 it was observed that this deletion site is accompanied by lengthening of both the pause and the preceding word segment for key words whose phonetic environment did not permit Palatalization across the word boundary.

Sentence Materials and Procedure

Eight pairs of sentences were constructed. The sentences of each pair contained two main clauses conjoined by the coordinate conjunction "and." Each pair included one sentence (a) in which no deletion site was present at the key word boundary, and one sentence (b) in which Verb Gapping had occurred. The sentences appear below in sentence groups (15)–(22), with the palatalization context italicized.

(15) (a) The seamstress wove your hat and then *made your* scarf.

    (b) The seamstress wove your hat and the *maid your* scarf.

(16) (a) The porter took your bags and *weighed your* luggage.

    (b) The porter took your bags and *Wade your* luggage.[6]

(17) (a) The chef fixed the soup and then *made your* sandwich.

    (b) The chef fixed the soup and the *maid your* sandwich.

(18) (a) The head teacher will help your daughter and then *aid your* son.

    (b) The head teacher will help your daughter and the *aide your* son.

(19) (a) The bus driver will take your brother and then *guide your* sister.

    (b) The bus driver will take your brother and the *guide your* sister.

(20) (a) The hostess will show your aunt and then Tom will *guide your* uncle.

    (b) The hostess will show your aunt and the touring *guide your* uncle.

(21) (a) Aunt Bessie took your fruit and my uncle *weighed your* vegetables.

(b)   Aunt Bessie took your fruit and my Uncle *Wade your*
       vegetables.

(22)   (a)   The intern will help your father and the nurse will
             aid your mother.

(b)   The intern will help your father and the nurse's *aide*
       your mother.

The members of each sentence pair contained phonetically identical words at the site of the palatalization context. In addition, the phonetic environment surrounding the key words was kept as similar as possible for the members of each pair, and stress contours of the members were approximately matched.

A randomized list of sentences that contained the sixteen test sentences and six filler sentences was presented to each of ten speakers. The speaker was instructed to consider each sentence individually and to utter it (i) in a casual speaking mode, and (ii) at a relatively rapid rate. The speaker was instructed not to place emphatic or contrastive stress on any word of the sentence (see note 6).

The recorded test utterances were analyzed for palatalization by a phonetically trained listener. A key segment was marked as palatalized if and only if a clearly perceptible /ǰ/ (as in "jive") was detected. In most cases, a determination of palatalization could be made unequivocally by listening to the utterances at normal playback speed.[7] In a few unclear cases, the utterances were replayed at half-speed to facilitate the detection of /ǰ/ frication.

The perceptual judgments were normalized to some extent to take into account differences in speaking rate and intensity for the different speakers. Thus the criterion for marking an utterance as palatalized was slightly more stringent for a slower, higher intensity speaker than for a faster, lower intensity speaker.

A subsequent acoustic analysis was conducted to determine the validity of the perceptually based judgments of palatalization. The utterances of four speakers were chosen for this analysis. Their utterances provided the most stringent test of validity for two reasons: first, approximately 50 percent of the utterances for each of these speakers were judged to be palatalized on the basis of the perceptual analysis, and second, the utterances for these speakers included all of the utterances previously considered to be somewhat equivocal with regard to the presence of palatalization. The acoustic analysis was carried out by the same phonetically trained experimenter who conducted the perceptual analysis. To insure independence of the perceptually and acoustically based judgments, a second experimenter first digitized each utterance at a sampling rate of 10 kHz and set a marker on an oscillo-graphic display of the speech segment to the key region of the ut-terance. Good exemplars of a given speaker's palatalized and nonpalatalized utterances were then shown on the oscilloscope display to the observer to permit a degree of normalization for speaking rate and intensity similar to that utilized for the percep-tual judgments. The observer was not aware of which particular speaker or utterance was being presented. The observer could manipulate a computer-controlled cursor (Huggins, 1969) to mea-sure the duration of /ǰ/ frication in each utterance. The remaining fourteen utterances of the speaker were judged for palatalization, based on whether a stretch of /ǰ/ frication (typically lasting more than 20 msec) appeared just prior to the vowel of the /y/-word. Using this procedure, the observer's acoustically based judgments of palatalization matched the perceptually based judgments in fifty-four of fifty-six cases. The close agreement between the two sets of independent judgments establishes the validity of the per-ceptual analysis as a means of providing efficient yet objective judgments of palatalization.

On a separate occasion the utterances were analyzed acousti-cally, using the procedure described in chapter 1, to determine the presence of pauses at the key word boundary.

Results for Palatalization and Pauses

The percentage of occurrence of palatalization for the ten speakers for each sentence appears in table 6.1. In all eight sen-tence pairs, the percentage of palatalization was less for the gapped sentences (b) than for the nondeletion counterparts (a). Overall, Verb Gapping reduced the percentage of palatalization from 56 to 32 percent).[8]

The duration of frication was approximately equal for the pala-talized utterances in the gapped versus nondeletion sentences

Table 6.1 *Percentage of palatalization for the ten speakers in experiment 1*

Sentence group	Nondeleted (a)	Deleted (b)
(15)	70	40
(16)	50	30
(17)	60	50
(18)	60	30
(19)	50	30
(20)	60	30
(21)	40	20
(22)	60	30
Mean	56	32

(43.6 msec versus 40.9 msec), and this duration measure did not differ systematically across speakers or across sentences. Since the duration of frication can be considered a measure of the amount of palatalization, these results indicate that the amount is not graded as a function of the syntactic environment, unlike the probability of palatalization's occurrence.

Pauses occurred in only 8 of the 160 test utterances. The small number of pauses for these sentences as opposed to the similar structures in chapter 4 can be attributed to two factors: first, the phonetic environment at the key boundary for sentences in this experiment was always /d#y/, permitting palatalization, whereas the environment at the key boundary for sentences in the Verb Gapping experiment of chapter 4 was always /t#k/, prohibiting palatalization and necessitating the presence of a silent interval at the word boundary; and second, the speakers in the present experiment were asked to talk at a fairly rapid rate, in order to minimize opportunities for palatalization across word boundaries.

All eight pauses occurred in the gapped sentences (b) of four speakers. Half of the pause-containing utterances were palatalized. It thus appears that the reduction in palatalization was produced by the grammatical structure of the gapped sentences rather than by an intermediary influence of pausing. That is, the results suggest that the speaker's grammatical code exerts a direct influence on palatalization, not indirectly via the route

$$\text{Deletion site} \xrightarrow{\text{produces}} \text{pause} \xrightarrow{\text{blocks}} \text{palatalization.}[9]$$

This conclusion is reinforced by the data in table 6.2, which show the percentage of palatalization for the six speakers who never paused at the key word boundary. As in table 6.1, the percentage of palatalization was reduced for all eight sentence pairs in the gapped versions. The overall reduction in palatalization was from 70 to 41 percent for the six nonpausing speakers. The fact that a reduction in palatalization was maintained for the non-pausing speakers also militates against the possibility that the effect for gapped sentences is attributed to their intrinsic awkwardness.

Discussion

The results of this experiment indicate that a syntactic deletion site serves to reduce the frequency of palatalization across word boundaries. Furthermore, the results show that this effect cannot

Table 6.2 *Percentage of palatalization for the six nonpausing speakers in experiment 2*

Sentence group	Nondeleted (a)	Deleted (b)
(15)	83	67
(16)	67	33
(17)	83	67
(18)	83	33
(19)	67	33
(20)	67	33
(21)	50	33
(22)	67	33
Mean	70	41

be attributed to the presence of pauses at the key word boundaries. As suggested in chapter 4, a deletion site may be specially marked by the speaker's grammatical code as an unfilled element of the surface structure. The present results seem to indicate that the deletion site also marks the boundary of a syntactic domain across which phonological rules typically cannot operate (see also Baker and Brame, 1972).

Experiment 2

In experiment 2 we investigated whether a nonsyntactic factor would reduce the frequency of palatalization. In particular, we tested whether placing emphatic stress on either the /d/-word or the /y/-word would reduce the percentage of palatalization. Such a reduction has been assumed by Hyman (1975). A reduction was predicted here, based on the notion that emphatic stress is accompanied by more careful articulation than the type of casual articulation that is conducive to palatalization.

Sentence Materials and Procedure

Four sentence groups contained identical word strings with (a) no emphatic stress, (b) emphatic stress assigned to the /d/-word, or (c) emphatic stress assigned to the /y/-word. The sentences appear below.

(23)   (a)   Certainly the nurse will *aid your* son.
      (b)   Certainly the nurse will AID *your* son.
      (c)   Certainly the nurse will *aid* YOUR son.
(24)   (a)   Certainly the nurse will *aid you* soon.
      (b)   Certainly the nurse will AID *you* soon.
      (c)   Certainly the nurse will *aid* YOU soon.

(25) (a) Peter said that he *stood your* bottles by the fire.
      (b) Peter said that he STOOD *your* bottles by the fire.
      (c) Peter said that he *stood* YOUR bottles by the fire.
(26) (a) Peter said that he *stood you* in the ring of fire.
      (b) Peter said that he STOOD *you* in the ring of fire.
      (c) Peter said that he *stood* YOU in the ring of fire.

Sentence groups (23) and (25) contain the pronominal adjective "your" for the /y/-word, and respectively matching sentence groups (24) and (26) contain the pronoun "you." With this contrast, a further test of stress was provided, with greater stress naturally assigned to the pronoun "you" than to the adjective "your."

The procedure was similar to the previous experiment. Ten new speakers were instructed to place emphatic stress on a word when it appeared in capitalized letters.

Results

The percentage of palatalization for each sentence is presented in table 6.3. The results show that assigning emphatic stress to either the /d/-word or the /y/-word produced a reduction in the percentage of palatalization. When emphatic stress was placed on the /y/-word, this reduction occurred systematically for each of the four sentence groups. When emphatic stress was placed on the /d/-word, however, the overall reduction was from 60 to 43 percent, and the reduction effect was observed for only three of the four sentence groups. It thus appears that placing emphatic stress on the /y/-word exerts a more substantial and consistent reduction in the frequency of palatalization than does placing emphasis on the /d/-word.

The results in table 6.3 also show a reduced frequency of palatalization when the /y/-word was the pronoun "you" as opposed to the adjective "your." The overall reduction was from 42 to 28 percent. This result indicates that the greater intrinsic stress as-

Table 6.3 *Percentage of palatalization for the ten speakers in experiment 2*

Sentence group	Nonemphatic (a)	/d/ emphatic (b)	/y/ emphatic (c)
(23)	70	50	0
(24)	30	30	10
(25)	80	50	0
(26)	60	40	0
Mean	60	43	3

signed to the pronoun restricts palatalization in a manner similar to the assignment of emphatic stress.[10]

The reduction in palatalization with emphatic stress may be regarded as an indication of the speaker's tendency to maintain fairly precise articulation in the environment of a word bearing a large information load (Lieberman, 1963). Our results indicate that the speaker is particularly careful in articulating the beginning of an emphasized word, as opposed to its ending, since palatalization was blocked to a much greater extent when emphatic stress was placed on the /y/-word as opposed to the /d/-word.

Experiments 3–7

Experiments similar to experiment 2 were conducted to test other nonsyntactic effects on palatalization. One experiment was designed to test for an effect of the frequency of usage of either the /d/-word or the /y/-word (for example, "yarn"-"ukes"), using high- versus low-frequency words as determined by Kučera and Francis (1967). It was predicted that palatalization would be reduced in the environment of low-frequency words, since, as with the emphasized words in experiment 2, such words bear a large information load and are hence apt to be carefully articulated. Umeda (1977), for example, found that the duration of word-initial consonants was longer when they appeared in low-frequency words. Four additional experiments were designed to test phonetic effects for the /d/-word, including the following: long versus short vowel ("bead"-"bed"), monosyllable versus bisyllable ("need"-"needed"), word-initial consonant cluster versus word-initial single consonant ("bread"-"bed"), and word-final consonant cluster versus word-final single consonant ("had"-"hand").

Sentence Materials and Procedure

The method for each of the experiments was, except for the sentence materials, identical to that of previous experiments. Examples of sentence pairs for each experiment appear below, along with the total number of sentence pairs. Ten speakers participated in each experiment.

Experiment 2: high- versus low-frequency word (/d/-word: four sentence pairs; /y/-word: twelve sentence pairs)

(27) (a) The cowboys *rode your* horse into Kansas.
    (b) The cowboys *goad your* horse into kicking.
(28) (a) The scientist *had utensils* in his lab.
    (b) The scientist *had euglena* in his lab.

Experiment 4: long versus short vowel (six sentence pairs)

(29) (a) The children *feed your* chickens every morning.
      (b) The children *fed your* chickens every morning.

Experiment 5: monosyllable versus bisyllable (three sentence pairs)

(30) (a) The children *dread your* arrival.
      (b) The children *dreaded your* arrival.

Experiment 6: word-initial consonant cluster versus single consonant (eight sentence pairs)

(31) (a) Nancy told Tom that she *dried your* coat on the back porch.
      (b) Nancy told Tom that she *dyed your* coat on the back porch.

Experiment 7: word-final consonant clusters versus single consonant (seven sentence pairs)

(32) (a) We *paved your* way through college.
      (b) We *paid your* way through college.

Results

The percentage of palatalization for each experiment was as follows:

Experiment 3:
/d/-word, high frequency, 33%; low frequency, 30%; /y/-word, high frequency, 34%; low frequency, 10%.

Experiment 4:
/d/-word, long vowel, 50%; short vowel, 43%.

Experiment 5:
/d/-word, monosyllable, 33%; bisyllable, 30%.

Experiment 6:
/d/-word, initial cluster, 60%; no cluster 56%.

Experiment 7:
/d/-word, final cluster, 39%; no cluster, 41%.

The results for experiment 3 indicate that the frequency of usage of the /d/-word plays a negligible role in constraining palatalization. On the other hand, the /y/-word's frequency of usage plays a major role, paralleling the dramatic effect of placing emphatic stress on the /y/-word in experiment 2. In both cases, the frequency of palatalization is greatly reduced when the information load of the /y/-word is high. The results for experiments 4–7 indicate that the phonetic structure of the /d/-word does not play a substantial role in constraining palatalization. These results are paralleled by the relatively small effect of placing emphatic stress on the /d/-word in experiment 2.

It appears, then, that extrasyntactic factors of the /y/-word substantially influence the frequency of palatalization, whereas extrasyntactic factors of the /d/-word play at most a minor role. This conclusion would be further strengthened by a demonstration that /y/-word phonetic factors, such as those studied in experiments 4–7 for the /d/-word, also constrain palatalization. However, English does not permit the construction of suitable controlled sentences for such tests, largely because of the scarcity of pairs of /y/-initial words that are controlled for other variables. In the two cases in which a direct comparison between /d/- and /y/-word factors is permitted, the greater reduction in palatalization with the factors of the /y/-word may be attributed to the fact that speakers are more concerned with attaining precise articulation of the first phoneme of a word (in this case, /y/) than of the last phoneme /d/, in accordance with the greater informational load carried by the former. The greater precision in articulating word-initial phonemes is paralleled in perception by listeners' greater ability to detect mispronunciations in word-initial than in word-final phonemes (Cole, Jakimik, and Cooper, 1978).

GENERAL DISCUSSION

The results of this study indicate that palatalization is influenced by syntactic structure, emphatic stress, and frequency of word usage. These findings emphasize the need to consider the application of optional rules of phonology in terms of a model in which numerous factors may operate to constrain the probability of rule application. In effect, the traditional notion of *optional* phonological rules should be replaced by the notion of *probabilistic* ones, with the probability rule application in a given utterance based on well-defined factors such as those identified here (see also Labov, 1969; Bailey and Shuy, 1973; Cedergren and Sankoff, 1974; Robinson, 1975).

Study 3: Alveolar Flapping

The study of blocking was extended to the rule of Alveolar Flapping, because this rule is applied with much higher frequency in casual speech than Palatalization, and could thus be used to examine syntactic influences on blocking in more detail. Alveolar Flapping operates to flap an intervocalic alveolar stop, optionally preceded by /r/ or /n/, when it occurs in a falling stress pattern, as stated in (33).

$$(33) \quad \begin{Bmatrix} t \\ d \end{Bmatrix} \rightarrow [\mathrm{r}] / \begin{bmatrix} V \\ \alpha \ \ \text{stress} \end{bmatrix} \begin{pmatrix} [r] \\ [n] \end{pmatrix} \underline{\hspace{1em}} (\#) \begin{bmatrix} V \\ \beta \ \ \text{stress} \end{bmatrix}$$

where $\alpha > \beta$ or $\alpha = \beta$ = reduced stress or primary stress

As shown by the following examples, this rule may apply both within and across word boundaries.

(34) sanity /sænɪti/ → /sænɪɾi/
(35) party /parti/ → /parɾi/
(36) sort of /sort#əv/ → /sorɾ#əv/[11]

For our purposes, the critical feature of this rule is that, as for Palatalization, its application across word boundaries requires that the phonetic segments on both sides of the boundary be of a specific type. In order for the rule to apply, the phonetic information about both segments must be available to the speaker during the same domain of processing.

EXPERIMENT 1

In experiment 1 we attempted to determine the effects on Alveolar Flapping of strong versus weak syntactic boundaries, as a prerequisite for further experiments. In addition, as with the earlier study of Palatalization, we examined whether any blocking effects could be attributed directly to the syntactic boundary or to the presence of an accompanying pause.

Sentence Materials and Procedure

Four pairs of test sentences, (37)–(40), were used. A flapping environment was included in the key region of each test sentence, at the boundary between the italicized words below. The flapping environment is composed of a postvocalic word-final /t/ followed by a word-initial vowel. In the (a) version of each sentence the key boundary is very weak according to Branching Depth, while in the (b) version the key boundary is strong, constituting the boundary between two clauses. In each pair the sentences are matched as closely as possible for phonetic structure and stress pattern. In addition, the sentences of each pair contain the same number of syllables.

(37) (a) Steven said that *late applications* should be sent to the Dean's office.

       (b) Even if they're *late applications* should be sent to the Dean's office.

(38) (a) If you like to *knit a* lot the store downtown has yarn on sale.

       (b) If you like to *knit a* lot of stores downtown have yarn on sale.

(39) (a) For those of you who'd like to *eat early* lunch will be served.

           (lunch will be served early)

       (b) For those of you who'd like to *eat early* lunch will be served.

           (some people like to eat early)

(40) (a) If you want something *sweet oranges* are a good choice.

           (oranges that are sweet)

       (b) If you want something *sweet oranges* are a good choice.

           (if you want something sweet)

Ten speakers were tested according to the procedure described earlier. The recorded test utterances were analyzed for flapping by a phonetically trained listener. A key segment was marked as flapped only if a perceptible [ɾ] was detected. In most cases, a determination of flapping could be made unequivocally by listening to the utterances at normal playback speed. In a few unclear cases, the utterances were replayed at half-speed to facilitate the detection of flapping. A sample of the utterances was analyzed acoustically in the form of a digitized oscillographic trace, and the results of this analysis were in complete agreement with the independently derived perceptual judgments. Utterances that contained a flapped consonant at the key word boundary showed no silent interval nor any release burst at the boundary, unlike those utterances which contained a word-final /t/ in this region. The unambiguous distinction between flapped and nonflapped consonants in the cross-boundary environments tested here contrasts with the more problematic assignment for flapping in within-word contexts (Laferriere and Zue, 1977; Zue and Laferriere, 1979).

An acoustic analysis was also conducted to measure the pause durations in the (b) sentences, which contained major syntactic boundaries. The duration of the pause was determined with the aid of a computer-controlled cursor (Huggins, 1969). The pause interval was measured from the end of the vowel in the word preceding the boundary to the beginning of the vowel in the word following the boundary. For unflapped utterances, any /t/ release burst was thus included as part of this measurement.

Results

The flapping data for the speakers are shown in table 6.4. Speakers never applied flapping in the four (b) sentences, which contained strong boundaries, whereas they applied flapping an average of 60 percent of the time in the (a) sentences, which contained weak boundaries. The dramatic blocking of flapping at major syntactic boundaries suggests that such boundaries exert a major influence on the operation of this phonological rule across word boundaries. It thus appears that syntactic boundary markers or their equivalents are available at the stage of the speaker's coding at which phonological rules are applied.

The analysis of pauses at the key word boundaries revealed that the blocking of flapping in the (b) sentences could not be attributed to pausing. Of the forty total (b) utterances, none of which were flapped, 55 percent contained silent intervals of less than 150 msec. It is reasonable to assume that breathing pauses cannot occur within such a short silent interval (Grosjean and Collins, 1979) and that the silent intervals in these utterances simply represented the stopgap for the word-final /t/. It thus appears that there is no relation between breathing pauses and the blocking of flapping, similar to the results with palatalization.

Table 6.4 *Percentage of flapping for the ten speakers in experiment 1*

Sentence pair	Weak boundary (a)	Strong boundary (b)
(37)	80	0
(38)	80	0
(39)	40	0
(40)	40	0
Mean	60	0

EXPERIMENT 2

Previous formulations of boundary-strength metrics share the assumption that boundary markers associated with different phrase nodes contribute equally to the total strength of the juncture. However, it is quite possible on a priori grounds that different syntactic nodes may contribute unequally to the strength of a syntactic boundary, especially since a similar situation obtains in morphology. Stanley (1969, 1973) proposes that seven morphological boundaries of varying strength are required to handle the morphological structure of the Navaho verb. Chomsky and Halle (1968) argue that two different morphological boundaries are needed for English. In experiment 2 we attempted to determine whether boundary markers associated with different phrase nodes contribute equally to the total strength of a syntactic juncture.

Sentence Materials

Four pairs of test sentences, (41)–(44), were used in this experiment. The surface structure of the test sentences closely matches their underlying forms, as represented in a current version of transformational grammar (Akmajian and Heny, 1975). This provision was included so that we could restrict our attention to possible effects of syntactic boundaries associated with surface structure. In the first two pairs, the juncture at the key region is identical in strength for both members of each pair according to a strength metric that considers the boundaries associated with different phrase nodes to be of equal strength. However, the (b) version of each sentence pair contains a marker that corresponds to an S node, unlike the key boundary in the (a) version. It is likely that a marker associated with an S node may contribute more to the total strength of the boundary than markers associated with lower phrase nodes. If this hypothesis is correct, the occurrence of flapping should be blocked more often in the (b) version. If, on the other hand, the boundary markers associated with different nodes are equal in strength, the occurrence of flapping should be equal in the (a) and (b) versions.

(41) (a) The little kid with the *cut alarmed* us with all his screaming.
      (b) The little kid who got *cut alarmed* us with all his screaming.
(42) (a) The man with the *net announced* that he was going fishing.

    (b)   The man who had *bet announced* that he was losing
        money.[12]

Of necessity, the (a) and (b) versions of the first two pairs of
sentences also differed in that the word to the immediate left of
the key boundary was a noun in (a) and a verb in (b). Two additional pairs of sentences were thus constructed in which the word
to the left of the key boundary was a noun in both (a) and (b)
sentences. In so doing, one additional boundary marker was introduced at the key region of the (b) sentences of these two pairs.
Intuitively, it would seem that the unequal number of boundary
markers in the (a) and (b) versions would also favor the hypothesis that flapping would be blocked more often in the (b) sentences. However, we will present other data in the discussion of
this experiment which militate against this possibility.

  (43) (a)   The woman with the winning *bet agreed* to give us
           part of the money.
      (b)   The woman who had won the *bet agreed* to give us
           part of the money.
  (44) (a)   Every person with a *pet advised* us to get one our-
           selves.
      (b)   Every kid who had a *pet advised* us to get one our-
           selves.

Results

Of fourteen speakers tested, three flapped in every test utterance and one flapped in none of the utterances. For these four
speakers it appears that syntactic environment did not influence
the production of flapping. As such, evidence is provided neither
for nor against the hypothesis under investigation. The ceiling
and floor effects obtained for these few speakers were also exhibited in additional utterances involving flapping environments.

The flapping data for the remaining ten speakers are shown in
table 6.5. In each of the four sentence pairs, the occurrence of
flapping was much greater for the (a) versions. Overall, the speakers flapped 70 percent of the time in the (a) sentences, but only 30
percent in the (b) sentences. Pilot data using (42a) and (42b)
showed parallel results. Nine out of ten speakers, none of whom
participated in this experiment, flapped (42a) whereas only three
out of ten flapped (42b). These results indicate that boundary
markers associated with different node types do not contribute
equally to the total strength of a syntactic boundary, insofar as the
boundary serves to block the application of flapping. Rather, our

Table 6.5 *Percentage of flapping for the ten speakers in experiment 2*

Sentence pair	No S marker (a)	S marker (b)
(41)	50	20
(42)	80	40
(43)	60	10
(44)	90	50
Mean	70	30

data suggest that a boundary marker associated with the node S contributes to a substantial reduction in occurrence of flapping, whereas markers associated with other nodes do not.

This latter claim is substantiated by a number of additional experiments, designed to test for possible differences in strength among boundaries containing markers associated with phrase nodes other than S. In all of these experiments, speakers produced flapping in virtually all utterances, regardless of the number of boundary markers. For example, in sentences (45) and (46), two more boundary markers are included in the key boundary of the (b) versions, yet speakers flapped both (a) and (b) versions more than 90 percent of the time.

(45) (a) The Wallaces' *cat appeared* from under the canvas tent.
　　 (b) The boy with the *cat appeared* from under the canvas tent.
(46) (a) The little boy's *cat astounded* us with all his tricks.
　　 (b)　The boy with the *cat astounded* us with all his tricks.

As in experiment 1, the analysis of pauses at the key juncture indicated that the blocking of flapping in the (b) sentences was not attributable to pausing. Of the forty total (b) utterances, twenty-eight were not flapped. Of these twenty-eight, only three contained pauses of more than 150 msec.

EXPERIMENT 3

In experiment 3 we sought to determine whether the blocking effects observed at a deletion site for Palatalization in study 2 would generalize to the rule of Alveolar Flapping. As in the experiment with Palatalization, the deletion site was produced by Verb Gapping.

Sentence Materials and Procedure

Four pairs of test sentences, (47)–(50), were used in this experiment. The test pairs included a sentence (a) containing no deletion site at the key boundary, and a closely matched sentence (b) whose derivation involved the rule of Verb Gapping, with the deletion site at the key boundary.

(47) (a) John likes to have both eggplant and veal for dinner and *Pat eats* fish for lunch.
       (b) John wants to try both eggplant and veal for dinner and *Pat each* dish for lunch.
(48) (a) Jake likes to play with Uncle Henry's puppy and *pat Aunt* Mary's kitten.
       (b) Jake likes to play with Uncle Henry's puppy and *Pat Aunt* Mary's kitten.
(49) (a) Jeff had two apples with his coffee and *Pete ate* bananas with his milk.
       (b) Jeff had two apples with his coffee and *Pete eight* bananas with his milk.
(50) (a) I plan to fly into town on Friday and we'll *meet on* Saturday.
       (b) The swimming practice was held on Friday and the *meet on* Saturday.

The testing procedure and methods of analysis were the same as in the previous experiments.

Results

The flapping data for each test sentence are shown in table 6.6. For each of the four sentence pairs, the ten speakers tested produced more occurrences of flapping in the nondeletion (a) sentences. Overall, speakers flapped in 53 percent of the nondeletion (a) sentences and in only 8 percent of the deletion sentences. The results indicate that the occurrence of flapping, like that of auxiliary reduction (King, 1970) and palatalization, is markedly reduced in the environment of a deletion site.

The pause analysis again indicates the lack of a strong relation-

Table 6.6 *Percentage of flapping for the ten speakers in experiment 3*

Sentence pair	Nondeleted (a)	Deleted (b)
(47)	50	10
(48)	40	0
(49)	50	0
(50)	70	20
Mean	52.5	7.5

ship between pausing and blocking. Of the forty total (b) utterances, thirty-seven were not flapped. Of these thirty-seven, only six contained pauses of more than 150 msec at the key boundary.

Conclusion

The experimental studies presented in this chapter indicate that the blocking of cross-word phonetic conditioning rules provides another window into the speaker's syntactic code. In particular, blocking effects have permitted us to make some inferences about the kinds of syntactic domains processed during speech production.

Syntactic information is both available and influential at the processing stage at which phonological rules are applied. The blocking at major syntactic boundaries suggests that such boundaries serve as junctures in the speaker's processing, prohibiting look-ahead. The phonological rule is blocked, in effect, because the speaker cannot look ahead to consider the nature of the word-initial segment contained in the subsequent domain of processing. As noted in the linguistic formulation of the phonological rules themselves, consideration of this latter segment is required for the normal application of such rules.

The results of each study in this chapter suggest that the blocking effect appears to reflect a syntactic influence on look-ahead, not a possible intermediary influence of pausing. The results consistently indicate that pausing is neither a necessary nor a sufficient condition for blocking.

On this account, the blocking effect should be all or none, and for individual utterances this appears to be the case. However, as shown in tables throughout this chapter, the data for speakers as a group do not typically show such a pattern; this may be due to extralinguistic factors. While syntax plays a major role, it is very likely that factors such as speaking rate also influence the operation of phonological rules. In particular, blocking at a strong syntactic boundary may be suspended at fast rates of speech (see chapter 7). In such cases, speakers may process larger domains of segment information. In our experiments no attempt was made to neutralize speaking rate across different speakers because our hypotheses involved comparisons between sentences rather than among speakers.

While blocking seems to reflect the presence of a processing juncture, it is not yet possible to provide a principled account of why blocking occurs at clause boundaries and at deletion sites. One possibility (among many alternatives) is that blocking occurs at these particular sites because a limited-capacity processor must devote its computational machinery to programming special phonetic effects that accompany these locations. At both clause boundaries and deletion sites, speakers typically lengthen the preceding segment and produce a falling fundamental frequency contour for the same segment (chapter 4, and Cooper and Sorensen, 1980). It is quite possible that the programming of such phonetic attributes depletes the processor of its capacity momentarily, prohibiting normal look-ahead to the word immediately following the boundary, and thereby preventing the application of the phonological rule.

Finally, for the sake of clarity, we should distinguish the kind of blocking obtained here in the studies with deletion sites from the blocking of certain phonological rules studied earlier in linguistic circles (for example, King, 1970; Zwicky, 1970; Baker, 1972), mentioned in chapter 1. In the case of Auxiliary Reduction, which converts "Bill has" into "Bill's," for example, King (1970) first observed that the operation of this rule is blocked at certain deletion sites, as in (51b) below:

(51) (a) Joan's taken more from you than Bill's taken from me.
      (b) *Joan's taken more from you than Bill's from me.

Here, the deletion site immediately follows the auxiliary, whereas in our studies of cross-word phonetic conditioning, the deletion site intervened between two words whose phonetic structure satisfied the conditions for applying a certain phonetic conditioning rule. In light of the fact that the deletion site *follows* the auxiliary in cases like (51b), it is somewhat surprising that Selkirk (1972) accounted for such blocking by proposing that the boundary markers originally associated with the deleted constituent remain intact following the deletion, providing a surplus of boundary markers at the deletion site (see also Baker and Brame, 1972). In actuality, this kind of account seems more plausible for explaining the results of our studies, where blocking occurs at the deletion site per se.

The blocking notion has also been invoked to account for a constraint on the reduction of phrases like "want to" to "wanna" (Lakoff, 1969; Baker and Brame, 1972). In these cases, blocking presumably results because of the intervening presence of a movement site (that is, the location occupied by a moved constituent in underlying structure). For example, consider the ambiguous string below.

(52)   Who do you want to visit?

This string can mean either (a) Who do you want for you to visit? or (b) Who do you want to visit you? On the (b) reading, WH-Fronting has applied to move the WH word from its underlying position between "want" and "to" (Chomsky, 1977). Lakoff (1969) first observed that the string is disambiguated when "want to" is phonologically reduced to "wanna," in favor of the (a) reading. It has been argued that disambiguation takes place because phonemic reduction is blocked at the movement site for the (b) reading. If this account is correct, it would provide direct evidence for the notion that speakers code more than a single level of syntactic structure. In more recent experimentation, Danly (1980) has conducted a study to determine whether WH traces in questions are marked by differences in segmental timing in comparison to nontrace locations that are not accompanied by phonemic reduction. Ambiguous sentences similar to (52) were preceded by disambiguating paragraph contexts. For example, the sentence "Who did Peg want to drive to Vermont?" was embedded in each of the following contexts:

(53)   (a)   Bob and Jack decided to take Peg to the Green Mountains to go hiking. On Friday afternoon, when they arrived in their car to pick her up, Bob looked to Peg as though he had been drinking heavily. Peg wasn't sure whether she should insist that Jack drive or whether it was safe enough to allow Bob to drive.

   Who did Peg want to drive to Vermont? She decided that she would risk telling Bob that he was too drunk to drive and insist that Jack drive.

   (b)   Peg belongs to the Harvard Outing Club, and last week she drove a carload of members up to the Green Mountains to go hiking. Since there were so many people in need of rides, Peg had to decide whether to drive a bunch of her friends or some new club members.

   Who did Peg want to drive to Vermont? She decided to drive her friends because it had been several months since she had last spent time with them.

The results for twenty speakers showed that the duration of the segment span including "want to" in phonemically nonreduced utterances was significantly longer, by an average of about 25 msec, for the (a) reading in which the trace appeared immediately after "want" (that is, for the reading "Peg wants WH to drive" versus the reading "Peg wants to drive WH"). The effect observed here for WH subjects appeared systematically for the group of twenty speakers in each of four other structurally ambiguous sentences embedded in similar paragraphs. The results indicate that the trace sites of WH subjects are accompanied by longer duration than a comparable nontrace location even when the latter location is not accompanied by phonemic reduction of the sort described by Lakoff (1969) and Baker and Brame (1972). However, a similar effect was not observed for the trace sites of WH objects—for example, the duration of "drive" in (53b) was not longer than its duration in (53a)—which suggests that the durational effects are either limited to WH traces involving subjects or restricted to traces that happen to be located near the middle of the string. Further work is needed to clarify the constraints, but the evidence obtained for subject traces does provide a measure of support for the notion that speakers compute more than a single level of syntactic representation for some sentence structures.

7 | Theory and Further Experimentation

THE THEORY of speech production presented in this chapter contains two major components, concerning the speaker's representations of syntactic structures and the processing of these representations. The structural component is the better understood of the two, in terms of its basis in the available data. However, because the present studies have focused on the speech wave, a real-time phenomenon, it is also possible to make some initial inferences about constraints on processing; these will be presented alongside new experiments designed to examine the speaker's orchestration of speech planning and execution.

The first important step in constructing any theory involves deciding precisely what the theory should account for—that is, defining the theory's scope. In the present case, we believe that the theory should account for three general characteristics of syntactic effects on speech properties: their location, direction, and magnitude.

In the case of segmental duration, for example, the theory should account for why durational effects are observed at particular clause and phrase boundaries (location), why the effects involve lengthening rather than shortening of segments (direction), and why the lengthening effects are of a particular magnitude. Regarding magnitude, the theory is primarily concerned with the rank order of magnitude at various locations rather than with absolute magnitude, since the latter appears to be determined by a variety of situational and speaker-dependent factors.

In section 1, a general model of information flow will be reviewed to provide a general context for the theory. Section 2 contains a detailed discussion of the structural component of the theory, while section 3 focuses on aspects of real-time processing. Attempts at developing a theoretical account in these sections will, in many cases, be interwoven with presentation of intuitions and new experiments bearing on theoretical choice points.

Section 1: General Framework

In chapter 1 a general model was presented to characterize information flow during speech production. We now revisit this model in light of experimental evidence and observations that have emerged during this project (see figure 7.1).

First, let us ask whether each of the stages of coding included in this model can be identified in terms of its ability to influence speech timing. At the first stage, there is little question that the planning of ideas has a direct influence on the occurrence of lengthy hesitation pauses (for example, Goldman-Eisler, 1968), although we have not focused on such pauses here. It is extremely

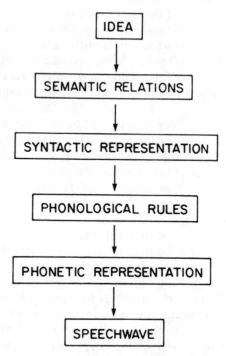

Figure 7.1   *Information flow model of speech production, including only those stages that seem to influence the speech wave properties studied in this project.*

difficult, however, to determine whether these hesitation pauses are primarily a by-product of the planning of ideas, as coded nonlinguistically, or a by-product of planning semantic propositions (see, for example, Ford, 1978).

SEMANTICS

Although we have not undertaken a systematic experimental study of semantic influences on speech timing, certain intuitions seem sufficiently well founded to incorporate in a model of information flow. Considering traditional semantic factors, only a few seem to influence speech timing. Intuition suggests that timing is not affected by semantic features of lexical items or by logical attributes assigned to entire utterances. By *semantic features* we refer to dimensions that distinguish such properties as concrete versus abstract ("box" versus "joy") and superordinate versus subordinate ("animal" versus "cat"). By *logical attributes* we mean properties such as presupposition, entailment, and opacity (see Katz, 1974, and Fodor, 1977, for extended discussions).

There does exist at least one semantic factor—negation—which seems to influence speech timing, however. With conjoined adjectives, for example, it is more likely that pausing will occur immediately before a negative conjunction ("yet," "but") than before a positive one ("and"), as in (1) below:

(1) (a) The tall yet frail student flunked chemistry.
    (b) The tall and frail student flunked chemistry.

Posner (1973) has suggested that pausing with negation may reflect the speaker's need for an extra interval of processing time, necessary to access lexical information that is more distant from the lexical information just spoken. This view thus relies on a theory of nonrandom lexical access. Yet pausing seems more likely before the conjunction in (1a) than in (1b) even though the lexical material on both sides of the conjunction has been held constant. Rather, it appears that the pausing represents an influence of negation per se. Perhaps pausing in this case is intentionally used by the speaker as a signal to the listener of an upcoming semantic change.

Pausing also seems to accompany negation even when the surface conjunction is deleted, as in (2a):

(2) (a) The speedy careful driver rode into town.
    (b) The speedy reckless driver rode into town.

It is possible that Posner's account is applicable here, since the only way we have of knowing whether the deleted conjunction is positive or negative is by varying the similarity of the lexical information of the two adjectives. But if negation itself produces the pausing, then the effect must be programmed at a stage of coding that precedes the deletion of the negative conjunction.

The need for more processing time is probably not restricted to lexical access but is also present for access to changes in syntactic structure between the two clauses, as shown by the following contrast:

(3) (a) I punched John and then Pete was cornered by Harry.
     (b) I punched John and then Harry cornered Pete.

Pausing seems more likely in (a) than (b); the two clauses in (a) are syntactically distant due to a change from active to passive. At present, we suggest that pausing may well be controlled both by negation per se and by syntactic similarity (and possibly also by sentence stress).

Aside from negation and syntactic similarity, a functional semantic factor seems to influence speech timing. This factor is termed *functional completeness* and refers to the degree to which a given constituent may be interpreted independent of context. Consider, for example, the contrast in (4):

(4) (a) If John comes home, the party will be a disaster.
     (b) I went into town, and I bought new shoes.

In (4a), the semantic interpretation of the first clause is incomplete, depending to some extent on the information provided in the second clause. In contrast, the first clause in (4b) is semantically complete, capable of standing in isolation as a well-formed utterance. Carroll and Tanenhaus (1978) have shown that the distinction drawn here plays a role in perceptual segmentation, and we believe it is likely that this notion also plays some role in production. In particular, it is expected that semantically incomplete clauses will be terminated with more clause-final lengthening than semantically complete ones. The reason for the extra lengthening in cases like (5a) may represent the speaker's effort to cue the listener about the lack of completion. A marked continuation rise in F_0 also typically accompanies this boundary.

The role of completeness is pointed out more clearly in two-clause sentences like the following, in which we observe a greater likelihood of pausing at the end of a clause when conditional or causal clauses precede the material they modify, as in the (a) versions:

(5) (a)   If Harry goes to the store, Joan will be upset.
    (b)   Joan will be upset if Harry goes to the store.
(6) (a)   Because Harry left early, Joan was ecstatic.
    (b)   Joan was ecstatic because Harry left early.

In these cases, the functional interpretation of the first clause is incomplete in the (a) versions but is complete in the corresponding (b) versions, where the order of the two clauses is reversed. Although pausing is possible at the clause boundaries in both (a) and (b), the likelihood of pausing seems greater in (a) (as is the appearance of a comma in writing), and this asymmetry is captured by the same functional notion required to account for (5).

In summary, it seems that there exist at least three new general factors—negation, syntactic similarity, and functional completeness—which are candidates for controllers of speech timing. As noted earlier, most semantic factors appear to play no such role, however, and our theory must be capable of handling this distinction. In general, semantic factors apparently influence speech timing only if they express relationships between two or more constituents. This property holds for each of the three factors mentioned above. In all three cases, lengthening seems to be exhibited when the canonical relation between constituents is broken, either by negation, syntactic dissimilarity, or semantic incompleteness. This view may lead to an account for why most semantic factors do *not* influence speech timing, since semantic features of lexical items (such as concrete-abstract) and logical relationships (such as presupposition-entailment) do not exhibit canonical values.

SYNTAX

In the original model of chapter 1, a distinction was drawn between underlying and surface levels of syntactic representation, analogous to the distinction commonly depicted in transformational grammars. In chapters 4, 5, and 6, we tried to determine whether speech timing might be influenced by more than a single syntactic level, but evidence favoring the influence of more than one level was not compelling. We have adopted in figure 7.1 a framework containing a single stage of syntactic coding, since this surface structure stage certainly seems to bear the *primary* syntactic influence on speech timing. The experimental research reported in previous chapters leads to a fairly detailed characterization of the syntactic influence; this characterization will be presented in section 2.

PHONOLOGY

Before leaving the subject of general information flow, we must also examine the phonological component more closely. In this study a variety of phonetic effects have been observed, including segmental lengthening, pausing, blocking of cross-word conditioning, and changes in fundamental frequency contours. Are these diverse effects programmed serially or in parallel during the production process? Furthermore, are the precise syntactic variables that control one phonetic effect the same as those that control another? We have no definite answers here, but it is worthwhile to mention some previous proposals, their drawbacks, and a plausible alternative.

First, let us consider the effects of lengthening and pausing. At an early point in our thinking, we tested whether these two effects might reflect distinct types of processing. It seemed possible that segmental lengthening, as it occurs at the end of a constituent, might represent the speaker's relaxation response to executing the end of a constituent, whereas the following pause might be programmed to allow the speaker extra time to plan the upcoming constituent. We tested for this distinction in experiments using a method of one-sided variation, to be presented in a later subsection; however, the results failed to support this dichotomy. The available evidence suggests that lengthening and pausing are usually by-products of the same underlying source which, for a particular utterance, may be either relaxation or planning.

A possible relationship between segmental lengthening and F_0 inflections was mentioned by Klatt (1975), who observed that lengthening might be produced in order to allow the speaker more time to convey an overlaid F_0 inflection (see also Lyberg, 1979). To test this hypothesis, Cooper and Sorensen (1977) examined correlations between the amount of F_0 inflection and the duration of the word on which the inflection was superimposed. No relationship was found, suggesting that F_0 and segmental lengthening are not very intimately related. At a more general level, it does seem that the speaker must lay down some general grid for timing so that F_0 inflections can be programmed satisfactorily. However, at the level of timing studied here, there is reason to believe that F_0 and timing inflections produced at syntactic boundaries are influenced by the same sorts of syntactic factors and are, for the most part, programmed in parallel (see also Cooper and Sorensen, 1980).

The blocking of cross-word conditioning effects also seems to be influenced by most of the same syntactic factors that control segmental lengthening, pausing, and F_0 inflections; yet there is a logical basis for assuming that blocking is influenced more by the nature of upcoming material than are the other phonetic effects. With cross-word conditioning, the speaker must have simultaneous access to phonetic segments on both sides of a syntactic boundary, but this degree of look-ahead is not necessary for other phonetic effects that occur before the beginning of the next constituent (Danly and Cooper, 1979).

Section 2: Structural Representation

This component of the theory specifies the characteristics of syntactic structures that exert an influence on speech properties. A major aim here is to formulate a metric of syntactic boundary strengths, discussed preliminarily in chapter 6. Ideally, this metric should be applicable to each of the major phenomena with which we dealt in our experimental studies, including pausing, segmental lengthening, blocking of phonological conditioning, and fundamental frequency contours. Despite their differences, all of these phenomena share the property of occurring most vividly at major syntactic boundaries; yet we have not specified a very elaborate theory of what constitutes "major" versus "minor" boundaries. Such a theory should be helpful in accounting for the location and rank magnitude of the experimental effects.

BACKGROUND

A theory of how speakers represent phrase structures is an essential prerequisite to specifying syntactic boundary strengths, since metrics of boundary strength are valid only insofar as they take as input a correct representation of constituent structure. In chapter 2 we conducted experiments to answer the following questions about the speaker's syntactic representation: (a) Are syntactic constituents such as sentence, noun phrase, and verb phrase processed as units? (b) Are constituents related to one another hierarchically in a manner specified by linguistic theory? (For example, does the constituent verb phrase dominate the constituents verb and noun phrase?)

First, let us review the evidence for whether constituents such as S, NP, and VP are processed as units in speech production. For the constituent S, the evidence is abundant. Clause boundaries are favored locations for breathing (Henderson, Goldman-Eisler, and Skarbek, 1965; Webb, Williams, and Minifie, 1967). In addition, such boundaries are typically accompanied by systematic changes in the prosodic structure of the speech wave, as we have observed throughout this study. These changes include pausing, segmental lengthening, fall-rise patterns of F_0, and the blocking of phonological rules.

Clausal units are also implicated by the analysis of speech errors. Exchange errors of phonemes ("tay drip" for "day trip") almost never span clause boundaries (Garrett, 1975), suggesting that the clausal unit is the largest domain over which a speaker can compute a phonemic representation. The evidence from speech errors dovetails with our observations of the blocking of phonetic conditioning in chapter 6. The speaker must simultaneously represent two phonemes in order either to exchange them in speech errors or to apply a phonological rule, and in both cases clause boundaries serve to block these possibilities. We can conclude, then, that the speaker does not typically have simultaneous access to phonemic representations that span a major clause boundary.

When we begin to examine constituents smaller than the clause, the study of speech wave properties becomes particularly important. In chapter 2, we presented evidence in favor of NP and VP constituents as units of processing on the basis of a detailed examination of speech timing effects for structural ambiguities. The evidence in favor of the VP constituent was especially useful because of a linguistic controversy concerning the existence of this constituent. Based on our findings, we have adopted a theoretical framework for syntactic coding that includes the representation of units S, NP, and VP, along with the units they dominate, such as adjective, noun, and verb.

The hierarchical arrangement of constituents is more difficult to assess. We have, however, obtained evidence for a type of hierarchical representation in chapter 2; this representation is adopted in the theory of syntactic coding. The issue of hierarchical coding will be discussed in more detail when we consider the information processing of constituents.

Lastly, we shall assume that, at the stage of syntactic coding relevant to effects on speech wave properties, the speaker computes a representation of constituents in a left-to-right fashion, as these are elaborated in a phrase structure grammar. At earlier stages of processing, it is quite likely that this ordering is not obeyed; that is, a speaker may perform grammar-lexical recycling as described in chapter 1. For present purposes, however, we adopt a strict left-to-right ordering of constituents in syntactic coding.

With this framework of constituent coding, it is now possible to formulate aspects of a metric of syntactic boundary strengths. The metric has a number of identifiable subparts, and we will discuss each of these in turn.

STARTING POINT NODES

At a given boundary, the question arises as to whether there is ever a need to refer to syntactic information beyond what is provided by the grammatical category type of the words bordering the boundary. In traditional phonology, word boundary markers were associated with words of major grammatical categories, and the boundaries between any two words were considered in terms of either one or two boundary markers. Chomsky and Halle (1968) state their convention as follows: "The boundary # is automatically inserted at the beginning and end of every string dominated by a major category, i.e., by one of the lexical categories 'noun', 'verb', 'adjective', or by a category such as 'sentence', 'noun phrase', 'verb phrase' which dominates a lexical category" (p. 366). This convention was accompanied by a principle of erasure, whereby the total number of word boundaries appearing in sequence was reduced to a maximum of two. The erasure principle implied that the distinction between one and two boundary markers is sufficient to represent the phrase phonology of English (see also Selkirk, 1972).

However, as shown in earlier chapters, there appears to be a need to retain the boundary markers associated with the dominating phrases that coincide with the word bordering the boundary, for the purposes of predicting the application of cross-word phonetic conditioning effects as well as segmental lengthening and pausing. To take just one example, consider the string in (7) below:

(7) If John leaves, Sue will resign.

According to traditional phonology, the boundary between "John" and "leaves" contains two boundary markers, as does the boundary between "leaves" and "Sue." Yet clearly we want the theory of boundary strengths to reflect the fact that the latter boundary is the stronger of the two. This fact can only be captured by assuming that the word boundary makes reference to the notion that "leaves" and "Sue" coincide with the border of the syntactic boundary separating two clauses. Thus, the starting point for any viable theory of boundary strengths must be the dominating phrase nodes that coincide with the key word boundary. The dominating phrase node for each side of the boundary may be determined by locating the highest node in the structural representation that dominates the word lying to either the immediate left or right of the boundary but does not dominate both such words. For example, in figure 7.2, the dominating phrase nodes for the boundary between "leaves" and "Sue" include the two S nodes which are themselves dominated by the highest S node in the tree.

NODE HEIGHT VERSUS BRANCHING DEPTH

Having resolved the issue of where to start the counting of nodes, one can now ask whether the metric should calculate strength in terms of nodes lying above or below the dominating nodes that border a given boundary. We know that the theory should consider the boundary between the two main clauses in (7) a very strong one—certainly the strongest boundary within this particular utterance. Examining the tree diagram in figure 7.2, we see two major alternatives for achieving this aim. One possibility is to utilize a metric that calculates boundary strength by counting *upward* from the bordering phrases to the highest S node in the utterance. According to this general type of metric, which we have termed *Node Height*, a boundary is strong to the extent that a small number of nodes intervene between the bordering phrase nodes and the highest node in the tree. This type of metric would cap-

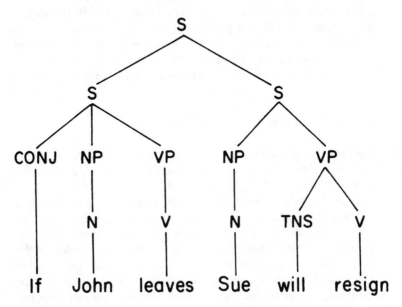

Figure 7.2 *Structural representation for the sentence "If John leaves, Sue will resign."*

ture the notion that the boundary between the two clauses in (7) is the strongest one within the utterance.

Another possibility involves a metric that counts *downward* from the bordering phrases to the lowest nodes in the utterance flanking the boundary. According to this metric, termed *Branching Depth*, a boundary is strong to the extent that a large number of nodes intervene between the most inclusive nodes bordering the boundary and the lowest flanking nodes in the tree. This type of metric also captures the notion that the boundary between the two clauses in (7) is strongest.

There are a number of subsidiary and orthogonal issues concerning the precise form taken by either Node Height or Branching Depth metrics, to be discussed in later subsections. For the moment let us simplify the problem by assuming that the metric calculates a total strength integer by adding together the strengths of each bordering phrase. In addition, let us assume that non-flanking nodes play no role in determining the strength of the boundary according to Branching Depth and that conjunctions are ignored for the purpose of computing strength.

With these assumptions in hand, it is now possible to select between the Node Height and Branching Depth types of metric. A first piece of experimental evidence in favor of Branching Depth was provided in chapter 6, in the study on Trochaic Shortening. In that study, differences in blocking were observed for boundaries in which the Branching Depth differed while the Node Height was equalized. However, the structures were not perfectly matched for other factors that may have influenced the blocking phenomenon. We now present a more elaborate justification of the Branching Depth metric.

Consider the sentence "Old men eat many apples near tall trees," diagrammed in figure 7.3. According to the Node Height hypothesis, the boundary between "old" and "men" in the subject NP is stronger than the boundary between "many" and "apples" in the object NP, by virtue of the existence of an extra intervening node—the VP node—at the latter boundary. According to Branching Depth, these two boundaries are equal in strength, since the bordering nodes of both boundaries do not branch further downward. Intuition tells us that the two boundaries are, in fact, of equal strength, in accordance with the Branching Depth metric.

To test for positive effects of Node Height, we conducted an experiment to compare the strengths of boundaries in conjoined clauses that were either immediately attached to the highest S or

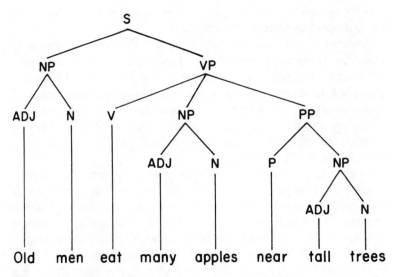

Figure 7.3 *Structural representation for the sentence "Old men eat many apples near tall trees."*

embedded within a complement clause. Example sentences appear below.

(8) (a) At the party Sue danced with *Clark* and Jill danced with Pete.

(b) We thought that Sue danced with *Clark* and Jill danced with Pete.

(9) (a) On Thursday Sue walked to the *park* and Pete walked to the store.

(b) I knew that Sue walked to the *park* and Pete walked to the store.

As shown in figure 7.4, the Node Height metric predicts that the boundary in (a) will be stronger than in (b), since two extra nodes, S and VP, intervene between the second of the conjoined clauses at the highest S in (b). The Branching Depth metric, however, predicts no difference. Downing (1970) has argued on subjective perceptual grounds that the clause boundary in (a) is in fact stronger than in (b). In our experiment, ten speakers read the example sentences, and an acoustic analysis was carried out to measure the durations of the underlined key word and the following pause in each sentence. The results showed no significant differences in the durations of either the key word or following pause

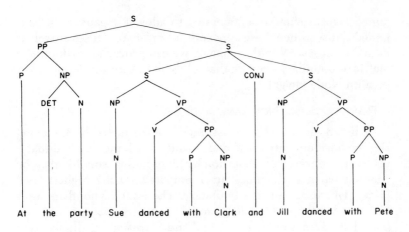

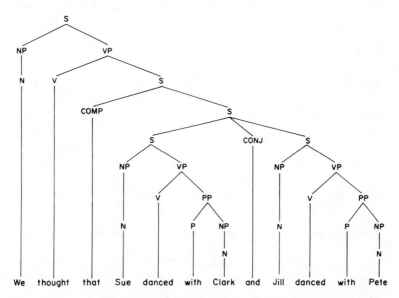

Figure 7.4 *Structural representations for sentences (8a) (top) and (8b) (bottom).*

for the (a) versus (b) versions of each sentence pair (sentence pair (8): word duration, $p > 0.20$, $t = .134$, $df = 9$; pause duration, $p > 0.20$, $t = -0.03$, $df = 9$; sentence pair (9): word duration, $p > 0.20$, $t = 0.78$, $df = 9$, pause duration, $p > 0.20$, $t = 0.33$, $df = 9$). The mean word durations were slightly longer in the (b) sentences, disconfirming the notion that the Node Height produces an increase in boundary strength.

Returning to chapter 1, we note that the pause rule for con-

joined clauses should be amended to allow for pausing in conjoined clauses when these appear in subordinate clauses as well as
in main clauses. With this change, we can proceed by adopting a
metric of boundary strength that relies on Branching Depth rather
than on Node Height.

FLANKING VERSUS NONFLANKING NODES

As noted earlier, we have assumed that the metric of Branching
Depth considers only those nodes which flank the key boundary;
yet it is conceivable that nonflanking nodes should also be
counted when such nodes are dominated by the highest-level
phrase which borders the boundary. The issue of nonflanking is
illustrated in figure 7.5. The (a) and (b) sentences possess the same
boundary strength between "cop" and "arrested" if the flanking
nodes are considered, but (a) is much stronger than (b) if the non-

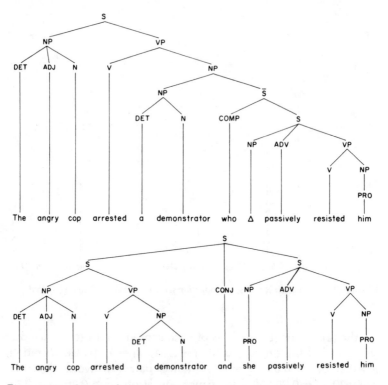

Figure 7.5 *Structural representations for sentences (10a) (top) and (10b) (bottom). According to the flanking metric of computing boundary
strength, the strength at the key boundary is 2-2 in both (a) and (b).
According to the nonflanking metric, however, the strength at this
boundary is 2-7 in (a) and 2-3 in (b).*

flanking nodes are also counted. An experiment with ten speakers was conducted by Danly and Cooper (1978) to test whether greater segmental lengthening would be produced in the following (a) versus (b) sentences.

(10) (a) The angry *cop* arrested a demonstrator who passively resisted him.
      (b) The angry *cop* arrested a demonstrator and she passively resisted him.

The results showed no significant difference in the duration of the key word either for these two sentences or for another similar pair.

Another experiment was designed to provide a positive test of the notion that flanking nodes are considered in the strength metric but that nonflanking nodes are not. The role of flanking nodes is considered in sentence pairs such as (11), illustrated in figure 7.6.

(11) (a) The assistant that worked for the *cook* fried the chicken and everyone liked it.
      (b) The assistant left work and the *cook* fried the chicken that everyone liked.

In this case, the results were highly significant. Greater segmental lengthening was produced for the key word in the (a) version of this pair ($p < 0.001$, $t = 5.53$, $df = 9$) and in another similar pair ($p < 0.001$, $t = 6.45$, $df = 9$). In combination with the previous experiment, these results indicate that the metric of boundary strength should consider only nodes that flank the key boundary.

LEFT VERSUS RIGHT PHRASES

To this point we have tested various properties of boundary strength by varying the phrase located either to the immediate left or right of the boundary, while holding the other bordering phrase constant. We must now ask whether the weight accorded to phrases on both sides of the boundary is computed in the same fashion. A related question arises as to whether the total strength of a given boundary is measured only in terms of the stronger of the two bordering phrases or whether the weights assigned to each phrase are combined. We will adopt the terms *collapsing* and *combination* to refer to these two respective possibilities.

A series of experiments have been conducted to test both of these questions (Danly and Cooper, 1979). The first set of experiments was designed to test the issue of collapsing versus combi-

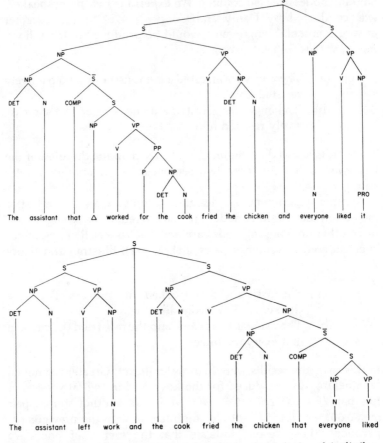

Figure 7.6 *Structural representations for sentences (11a) (top) and (11b) (bottom). According to the flanking metric, the strength at the key boundary is 7-2 in (a) and 2-2 in (b).*

nation, using the blocking of alveolar flapping as a dependent measure. Sentence triplets were designed so that their left and right bordering phrases contained strength values of 3-1, 1-3, 3-3, or, in other triplets, 5-1, 1-5, 5-5. By the notation N_L-N_R, we may refer to the strength value as measured by the number of flanking nodes for the left phrase L and the right phrase R. If total strength at the boundary is determined by collapsing, no difference would be expected in the total strength among the members of each triplet. On the other hand, if total strength is determined by combination, the 3-3 and 5-5 boundaries should be the strongest. In addition, comparisons of mirror-image pairs such as 3-1 and 1-3 would be expected to show equal strength if the left and right phrases contribute equally to the total strength value.

The results of these experiments revealed a strong tendency for the left phrase to be counted more heavily in determining the strength of the boundary, as measured in terms of the blocking of alveolar flapping. For example, the percentage of flapping was lower at a 3-1 boundary than at a 1-3 boundary, despite the fact that the total number of nodes was equal in the two cases.

From this finding, it appeared that the most appropriate test of collapsing versus combination was a comparison between boundaries such as 3-1 and 3-3, for which branching depth on the left side was held constant. The percentage of flapping should be equal if collapsing was in operation, since the left phrase is equally strong at both boundaries. However, if combination prevailed, flapping should be blocked more in the 3-3 sentence, since the right phrase is stronger here than in the 3-1 sentence. The results showed a consistent tendency favoring the combinatorial option, and now we adopt this characteristic as part of our overall theory of boundary strength.

However, because the differences in strength between left and right phrases dominated the results for alveolar flapping, it was decided to conduct additional experiments on this asymmetry with segmental duration as the dependent variable. We hoped by doing this to obtain a more precise assessment of this factor. In these experiments the contribution of the left phrase was determined in sentences for which the strength of the right phrase was held constant, and vice versa. In addition, the relative contributions of the left and right phrases were further examined in mirror-image pairs like the 3-1 and 1-3 boundaries discussed above. An example group of sentences involved either 1- or 2-valued phrases on each side of the boundary, as shown below.

(12) (a) 1-1 The head of the Little League wanted to *coach* a good team and he picked a successful one.

(b) 2-2 The head of the Little League gave the new *coach* a good team and three less successful ones.

(c) 1-2 The head of the Little League wanted to *coach* a good team and three less successful ones.

(d) 2-1 The head of the Little League gave the new *coach* a good team and he also managed one.

The results showed that adding one unit of strength concurrently to both sides of the boundary—comparison of (a) with (b)—produced significant lengthening of the key word. Comparisons of (a) with (d) and (b) with (c) provided tests of whether strength is increased by adding a single unit of strength to the left side only; in both cases significant lengthening was obtained. Comparisons of (a) with (c) and (b) with (d) provided corresponding tests of whether strength is increased by adding a single unit of strength to the right side only; in these cases no significant lengthening was found. The results for segmental lengthening were replicated in another experiment for sentences in which the key words were matched for grammatical category (Danly and Cooper, 1979). Taken together, the results provide a strong confirmation of the earlier findings obtained with alveolar flapping, showing that the left side of the boundary is weighted more heavily than the right side in determining the overall strength of the boundary.

In addition, these data point to the acute sensitivity of segmental lengthening as an acoustic variable whose magnitude varies systematically with very fine gradations in boundary strength. In (12), for example, a single node unit of strength distinguished versions (a) and (d), yet a significantly greater amount of lengthening was observed at the stronger boundary in (d).

NODE TYPES

Another potential source of elaboration of the theory concerns the weights assigned to different node types—for example, S, NP, VP. Specifically, we would like to know whether or not all nodes should be weighted equally. Findings reported in chapter 6 (study 3, experiment 2) suggested that more weight should be assigned to nodes such as S which are structurally more dominant in the hierarchical representation attributed to the speaker. However, more systematic work must be conducted before any firm conclusions on this issue can be reached.

CONTROVERSIAL NODES

Having specified major aspects of a metric of boundary strengths, it should be possible to use the metric as a foundation for testing the effects of nodes whose very existence is controversial. Thus far, we have limited our focus on boundary strengths primarily to phrase nodes whose existence is well established both in linguistic theory and in studies on speech production units. However, when we extend our view to consider a wider range of syntactic constructions, there are many nodes whose existence is in doubt.

Danly and Cooper (1978) have conducted a number of experiments to determine whether controversial nodes add strength to a syntactic boundary. In one experiment, they studied the issue of whether an extra NP node is included in the boundary strength when an NP branches into a noun and a following prepositional phrase, as shown in figure 7.7. According to one version of linguistic theory (for example, Chomsky, 1965), a prepositional phrase is Chomsky-adjoined to a noun phrase. To determine if the extra NP node introduced by Chomsky-adjunction figures into the strength of the boundary, sentence pairs such as the following were designed in which the right-hand phrase contained the extra NP node.

(13) (a) Since I had a little extra money to spend I *bought a vase* for Florence.
(b) Since I had a little extra money to spend I *bought a vase* of flowers.

In (a) the nodes at the key boundary purportedly include $]_V[_{NP}[_{DET}$, whereas in (b) the nodes include $]_V[_{NP}[_{NP}[_{DET}$. However, the results failed to show any significant differences in the occurrence of flapping for the (a) and (b) versions, suggesting that the extra NP node in (b) either is not computed during speech production or is somehow not strong enough to produce a difference when included in the phrase following the key boundary. For this particular construction, it is not possible to include a test in which the extra NP appears in the phrase preceding the key boundary.

In other experiments Danly and Cooper investigated additional controversial NP nodes, including nodes produced by phrasal conjunction and by relativization. In each case no significant effects of the nodes were obtained; yet, as with the previous test, the differences in structure were of necessity contained in the phrase

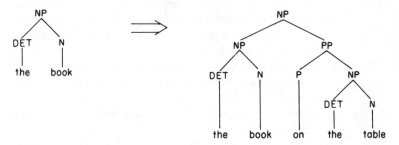

Figure 7.7 *Structural representation illustrating Chomsky-adjunction of a prepositional phrase.*

following the key boundary. Thus it is not certain whether the NP nodes themselves are not computed during speech production or whether their effect is simply barred because they occur in right-hand rather than relatively strong left-hand phrases.

THE METRIC OF BOUNDARY STRENGTHS: A CONSOLIDATION

In the preceding sections we have attempted to answer a fundamental question: What constitutes the difference between major and minor syntactic boundaries from the standpoint of their influence on speech properties? In dealing with this question it was possible to identify and test a number of individual factors that may contribute to the strength of a particular boundary. On the basis of available evidence we offer the following algorithm as a first-order approximation for determining the strength of any syntactic boundary within an utterance.

Algorithm I for Determining Boundary Strength

Step 1. Define the structural representation of the utterance, using rewrite rules of phrase structure grammar such as those presented in chapter 2.

Step 2. Locate the key boundary.

Step 3. Locate the dominating phrase structure nodes by finding the highest nodes which dominate the word to the immediate left or right of the key boundary but which do not dominate both of these words.

Step 4. Determine the number of flanking nodes between the dominating phrase structure nodes and the nodes immediately dominating the words to the immediate left and right of the key boundary, assigning a value of 0 to (a) any nodes referring to minor category terms (including conjunctions, determiners, and nonlexical prepositions) and (b), when considering the left side of the boundary, any nonterminal nodes that do not branch. Such nodes include those that do not branch into at least two nodes, each of which dominates a major category item.

Step 5. Add one unit of strength to any branching S node.

Step 6. Multiply by two the number of nodes listed for the left side of the boundary.

Step 7. Combine the number of nodes for both left and right sides of the boundary.

With this metric it is possible to predict the rank magnitude of syntactic influences on speech properties at various locations in an utterance. These predictions apply to the magnitude of segmental lengthening, pausing, and fall-rise patterns of fundamental frequency, and as a first approximation to the percentage of blocking cross-word phonetic conditioning. As Danly and Cooper (1979) observed, the phrase to the right of the boundary seems to be weighted somewhat more heavily in the case of cross-word conditioning than is specified by step 6 here.

Ideally, this algorithm is intended to apply to rank magnitudes of syntactic influences at various locations within an individual utterance (although location per se may also influence the magnitude of prosodic effects, as discussed in the next subsection). Thus, cross-sentence comparisons of the type examined in previous chapters, in which the key word appeared at the same location in different sentences, provide only an indirect means of evaluating the present algorithm. For experiments in which such cross-sentence comparisons seem to deal with purely surface structure effects, such as those in chapter 2 involving structural ambiguities, the results for rank magnitude are in agreement with the metric for paired readings of each sentence. It is not possible, however, to make a large-scale comparison of magnitudes of effect across different sentence pairs because of the confounding influence of phonetic and other extrasyntactic variables. The problem of interpretation in such cases may be illustrated by the study of trochaic shortening presented in chapter 6. According to the present metric, the boundary strength at the key location in each of the three sentences presented in figure 6.2 should be equivalent; yet trochaic shortening was blocked significantly in only the first of these sentences. According to one possibility, this discrepancy could be used as partial motivation for a refinement in the algorithm for determining boundary strengths. The suggested refinement would involve ignoring altogether the presence of minor category words in calculating the boundary strength, allowing a consideration of the strength associated with the nodes corresponding to the major grammatical category words closest to the boundary. In the first sentence of figure 6.2, for example, this refinement would permit skipping the preposition node at the key boundary site in order to take into consideration the following NP, which includes two units of strength—one associated with the NP and the other with the ADJ dominated by this NP. While such a refinement offers one means of accounting for the results, it is also possible that an extrasyntactic difference among these sentences contributed to the presence or absence of an effect. For example, a greater number of words follows the key boundary location in the first of these sentences, and data in a later subsection of this chapter indicate that upcoming constituent length may influence segmental lengthening in the direction consistent with the present results. Clearly, systematic testing of the metric presented here will indicate the need for at least some refinement.

COMPREHENSIVE ALGORITHM FOR PROSODIC EFFECTS

The preceding metric is based on purely syntactic factors, and, as we have pointed out, predictions about rank magnitude are valid only when extrasyntactic influences on the speech properties are either negligible or held constant. This syntactic metric must therefore be incorporated into a more comprehensive one that specifies the absolute magnitude of phonetic effects based on a joint consideration of syntactic strength and extrasyntactic factors such as speaking rate, length of constituent, stress, and internal phonetic structure (for example, Bierwisch, 1966; Robinson, 1973; Grosjean, Grosjean, and Lane, 1979).

The goal of such a comprehensive model is to predict both the probability of occurrence and absolute magnitude of prosodic effects for individual utterances, a task far more ambitious than the one attempted above for the metric of boundary strengths. Although a considerable amount of empirical work remains to be conducted before an adequate model of this scope can be developed, we present below our first best guess, stated in the form of a general algorithm for determining the probability of occurrence of the three prosodic effects considered in our empirical work—segmental lengthening, pausing, and blocking of cross-word phonetic rules—as well as the absolute magnitude of the first two of these effects. In developing this algorithm, the primary aim was to provide a quantifiable method of predicting these prosodic effects in individual utterances without regard to whether steps included in the algorithm or their order of application might be analogous to human processing operations involved in programming such attributes. Later, however, we will discuss some aspects of the algorithm in light of their possible psychological relevance.

Comprehensive Algorithm II for Determining the Probability of Occurrence of Prosodic Effects in Individual Utterances in the Region of a Given Word Boundary

Step 1. *Syntactic Boundary Strength*—Determine the boundary strength using the seven-step metric discussed in algorithm I. The output of this step is an integer value from 1 to *n*. Example: Sentence (14), diagrammed in figure 7.8, appears below with the syntactic strength of each word boundary indicated.

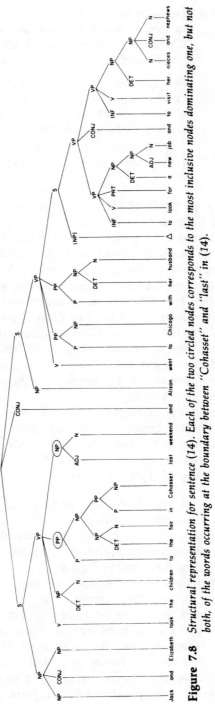

Figure 7.8 Structural representation for sentence (14). Each of the two circled nodes corresponds to the most inclusive nodes dominating one, but not both, of the words occurring at the boundary between "Cohasset" and "last" in (14).

(14)   Jack and Elizabeth took the children to the fair
in Cohasset last weekend and Alison went to
Chicago with her husband to look for a new job
and to visit her nieces and nephews.

Jack (2) and (1) Elizabeth (6) took (3) the (1)
children (3) to (2) the (1) fair (3) in (1) Cohasset
(6) last (3) weekend (10) and (3) Alison (4) went
(3) to (1) Chicago (3) with (1) her (1) husband
(4) to (1) look (2) for (1) a (2) new (3) job (6) and
(1) to (1) visit (3) her (2) nieces (2) and (1) nephews.

For purposes of illustration, the strength of the syntactic boundary between "Cohasset" and "last" is
derived via algorithm I as follows. First locate the
highest phrase structure nodes dominating each of
these words (step 3 of algorithm I). Next, list the appropriate flanking nodes, following step 4 of algorithm I. In this case, the relevant nodes include two
NPs to the left of the key boundary and an NP and
ADJ to the right; the PPs immediately dominating the
NPs are not included in the calculation, since these
PPs become nonbranching nodes when nodes corresponding to minor category items (here P) are ignored
(see step 4 of algorithm I).

Finally, derive the index of the strength of the
boundary between "Cohasset" and "last" by multi-
plying the number of left-hand nodes by the output
of step 6 of algorithm I and adding to this product the
number of right-hand nodes $[(2 \times 2) + 2 = 6]$.

Step 2.   *Bisection* (modified from Grosjean et al., 1979)—Compute an index for the point of bisection by counting
up the number of major grammatical words in the
most inclusive constituent being analyzed and then
dividing this number by two. Determine the proximity of the key word boundary to the point of bisection
by counting the number of major category words
from either the beginning or end of the constituent to
the boundary (whichever is less), divided by the point
of bisection. Example: In sentence (14) the boundary between "Cohasset" and "last" is six major category words from the beginning of an eighteen-word
string, so its proximity to the point of bisection is

$6 \div (18/2) = .67$. The proximity of each word boundary in (14) to the point of bisection for the full string appears in (14a) below.

(14a)   Jack (.11) and (.11) Elizabeth (.22) took (.33) the (.33) children (.44) to (.44) the (.44) fair (.56) in (.56) Cohasset (.67) last (.78) weekend (.89) and (.89) Alison (1.00) went (.89) to (.89) Chicago (.78) with (.78) her (.78) husband (.67) to (.67) look (.56) for (.56) a (.56) new (.44) job (.33) and (.33) to (.33) visit (.22) her (.22) nieces (.11) and (.11) nephews.

Step 3.   (Adapted from Grosjean et al., 1979)—Multiply the outputs of steps 1 and 2 for each word boundary. The boundary exhibiting the largest product represents the major constituent break (in the event of a tie, a major constituent break would occur at each relevant boundary). Any such boundary retains its product. The output of this step for the full string (14) appears in (14b) below.

(14b)   Jack (.22) and (.11) Elizabeth (1.32) took (.99) the (.33) children (1.32) to (.88) the (.44) fair (1.68) in (.56) Cohasset (4.02) last (2.34) weekend (8.90) and (2.67) Alison (4.00) went (2.67) to (.89) Chicago (2.34) with (.78) her (.78) husband (2.68) to (.67) look (1.12) for (.56) a (1.12) new (1.32) job (1.98) and (.33) to (.33) visit (.66) her (.44) nieces (.22) and (.11) nephews.

Step 4.   If both constituents demarcated by the major constituent break obtained in step 3 contain more than seven major category words, repeat steps 2 and 3. Thus, in the example sentence, step 4 applies within each of the two constituents "Jack and Elizabeth took the children to the fair in Cohasset last weekend" and "and Alison went to Chicago with her husband to look for a new job and to visit her nieces and nephews." The final values obtained with this procedure appear in (14c) below.

(14c)   Jack (.50) and (.25) Elizabeth (3.00) took (2.25) the (.75) children (3.00) to (2.00) the (1.00) fair

(2.25) in (.75) Cohasset (3.00) last (.75) weekend (8.90) and (0.00) Alison (.80) went (1.20) to
(.40) Chicago (1.80) with (.60) her (.60) husband (3.20) to (.80) look (2.00) for (1.00) a
(2.00) new (2.40) job (3.60) and (.60) to (.60)
visit (1.20) her (.80) nieces (.40) and (.20) nephews.

Step 5.   *Constituent Length*—If the most major constituent
boundary marks the beginning or end of a constituent
that contains more or less than a certain number of
words belonging to major grammatical categories,
add or subtract a percentage amount to the output of
step 4 for that boundary. As a first approximation, if
the boundary marks the beginning or end of a sen-
tence-internal constituent containing more than seven
major category words, increase the output of step 4 by
5 percent for each such additional word. On the other
hand, if the most inclusive constituent bordering the
boundary contains less than four major category
words, then decrease the output of step 4 by 5 percent
for each fewer word.

Step 6.   *Speaking Rate*—Assume a predetermined speaking rate
in percent, ranging from extremely fast (0 percent) to
extremely slow (100 percent), as discussed later.

Step 7.   Multiply the output of steps 4, 5, and 6. For example,
assuming a speaking rate of 50 percent, application of
this step for sentence (14) yields the values presented
in (14d) below.

(14d)   Jack (.25) and (.13) Elizabeth (1.50) took (1.13)
the (.38) children (1.50) to (1.00) the (.50) fair
(1.13) in (.38) Cohasset (1.50) last (.38) weekend (5.12) and (0.00) Alison (.40) went (.60) to
(.20) Chicago (.90) with (.30) her (.30) husband
(1.60) to (.40) look (1.00) for (.50) a (1.00) new
(1.20) job (1.80) and (.30) to (.30) visit (.60) her
(.40) nieces (.20) and (.10) nephews.

Step 8.   Divide the output of step 7 by 10, and express as percent.

Step 9.   *Individual Prosodic Effect Adjustments*—Multiply the output of step 8 by a factor of 2.5 for the prosodic effects
of pausing and blocking of cross-word phonetic con-

ditioning and by a factor of 3 for segmental lengthening. No product may exceed 100 percent. Example:
For sentence (14) the word boundary values for pausing and blocking derived via this final step are shown
in (14e) below, and the values for segmental lengthening appear in (14f).

(14e) Probability of Pausing, Blocking:
       Jack (6%) and (3%) Elizabeth (38%) took (28%)
       the (10%) children (38%) to (25%) the (13%)
       fair (28%) in (10%) Cohasset (38%) last (10%)
       weekend (100%) and (0%) Alison (10%) went
       (15%) to (5%) Chicago (23%) with (8%) her
       (8%) husband (40%) to (10%) look (25%) for
       (13%) a (25%) new (30%) job (45%) and (8%) to
       (8%) visit (15%) her (10%) nieces (5%) and (3%)
       nephews.

(14f) Probability of Segmental Lengthening:
       Jack (8%) and (10%) Elizabeth (45%) took (34%)
       the (11%) children (45%) to (30%) the (15%) fair
       (34%) in (11%) Cohasset (45%) last (11%) week-
       end (100%) and (0%) Alison (12%) went (18%)
       to (6%) Chicago (27%) with (9%) her (9%) hus-
       band (48%) to (12%) look (30%) for (15%) a
       (30%) new (36%) job (54%) and (9%) to (9%)
       visit (18%) her (12%) nieces (6%) and (3%)
       nephews.

The output of step 9 states the probability of occurrence for
each of the three prosodic effects examined experimentally in previous chapters. The predicted probabilities are intended to provide only a first-order approximation. Most of the probabilities
for both word segments and pauses in this hypothetical example
seem reasonable in light of previous findings and intuition. At a
few locations, however, the algorithm appears to make improper
predictions that will probably necessitate further refinements in
the algorithm. For example, the values specified for the words and
following pauses toward the middle of the second clause seem
somewhat larger than intuition suggests. Apparently this situation
represents a case in which the bisection principle is weighted too
heavily at the expense of syntactic boundary strength, the latter of
which should undoubtedly play the more important role. At this
and similar locations, the predicted effects could be better aligned
with intuition by including a provision that reduces the weighting

of bisection, by reducing the range of values obtained by the proximity index.

In addition, certain factors known to play a role in speech prosody have been omitted here for the sake of simplicity. One factor involves the interactive nature of at least some extrasyntactic variables. For example, speaking rate is known to interact with a variety of variables, including length (Fonagy and Magdics, 1960), emphatic stress (Weismer and Ingrisano, 1979) and the probability of occurrence for pausing versus segmental lengthening (Goldman-Eisler, 1968). In the first study, it was shown that shorter constituents are typically spoken at a slower rate. In regard to the second study of the relation between speaking rate and stress, the authors asked three speakers to utter a number of different versions of the sentence "Bob hit the big dog," at two different speaking rates (conversational and fast) and with emphatic stress on one of the four content words. Their results indicate that the inclusion of emphatic stress not only increases the duration of the emphasized word but also exerts some influence on the duration of other words in the sentence. In particular, emphasis near the beginning of the utterance produced shortening of word durations toward the end of the utterance. In addition, the effects of emphasis on neighboring word durations were both qualitatively and quantitatively different for the two different speaking rates (see also Folkins, Miller, and Minifie, 1975). In the third study mentioned above, Goldman-Eisler observed that the probability of occurrence for pausing increases by a much greater amount than for segmental lengthening at increasingly slow rates of speech. Taken together, these three studies suggest that certain extrasyntactic variables cannot be merely superimposed on the theory of boundary strengths developed in this chapter; this fact should be reflected in further refinements.

As for the steps included in the algorithm, let us encapsulate the rationale for each of these. Step 1 represents the metric of syntactic boundary strengths discussed in detail earlier in this chapter. Step 2 is intended to reflect the intuition that prosodic effects are most likely to occur near the middle of a string, other things being equal. The bisection rule seems to represent a special case of a more general work principle, by which a period of work is typically subdivided into two work intervals separated by a rest, with the rest occurring about halfway through the entire work period. For speech, a lengthy constituent is typically subdivided into two subordinate domains, and, in cases where the syntactic structure does not demarcate the two domains, the speaker tends to insert a break about halfway through the long constituent. The break serves as a very short but timely rest period for the speaker. By viewing the bisection rule as a special case of a general work principle, we can also provide a basis for the intuition that bisection probably does not apply at all in very short utterances, since the total work interval is too brief to warrant a rest period.

The bisection rule has received empirical support in the case of pausing from the work of Grosjean et al. (1979), who studied the magnitude of pausing between words in sentences spoken at very slow rates. They found, for example, that pausing tends to be greater in magnitude at the boundary between an NP and a VP in a relatively long single-clause utterance when this boundary occurs near the middle of the string, as in "My sister and her friend Joan/left for Atlanta in the morning" rather than when this boundary was displaced toward one end of the string, as in "Joan/left for Atlanta in the morning rather than at night." Further empirical work is necessary to specify this "string center of gravity" more precisely. It may be, for example, that the actual center of gravity is displaced somewhat toward the end of the constituent. This possibility is compatible with our impression that, in many human activities, a lengthy period of labor is divided by a rest period into two unequal segments, the second being slightly shorter than the first.

The principle of bisection employed in the present algorithm is similar to that included in the algorithm developed by Grosjean et al. The two procedures differ, however, in that our algorithm counts only words that belong to major grammatical categories, in accordance with the belief that words belonging to minor categories do not contribute significantly to the weighting. In addition, the present rule is intended to characterize prosodic effects of segment duration, fall-rise patterns of F_0, and blocking, in addition to pausing.

Steps 3 and 4 represent arithmetical procedures to combine the effects of syntactic boundary strength provided in step 1 with the bisection influence computed in step 2. In the case of step 4, bisection may be repeated within the major constituents demarcated by the primary boundary obtained in step 3. This step reflects the intuition that the influence of bisection may operate over a domain smaller than the entire utterance when, as in our example, the utterance contains lengthy subparts. The procedure adopted here is constrained by the number of major category words, again differing from the procedure of Grosjean et al. Following these steps, it is possible to derive a measure of boundary strength for each word boundary in any given string.

Step 5, involving constituent length, is adapted from the work of Bierwisch (1966), Martin, Kolodziej, and Genay (1971), and others, who suggest that pausing in particular is more likely to accompany a boundary between long constituents. Since little is yet known about the details of this influence, here we limit its application to the most major constituent break in a string. Step 5 seems to represent a special case of a very general work principle—the longer the work, the more time needed to rest. According to this view, the lengthening effects of segmental lengthening and pausing in particular are viewed as rest stops during which the speaker need not execute new segmental information. Apparently, elongation of these prosodic effects at the boundary of a very long constituent is carried out in order to allow the speaker extra time for relaxation and/or planning of upcoming material (see later section for further discussion).

Step 6, concerning speaking rate, represents a very important filter through which the potential prosodic effects must pass, and in step 7 this influence is combined with an index of boundary strength. In the present algorithm, the rate of speech is provided as input, reflecting the belief that this information is typically determined by the speaker before the utterance begins.

We consider speaking rate and syntactic boundary strength the two most important factors in determining the probability of occurrence for each of the four prosodic effects under consideration. As observed in chapter 6, faster speaking rates are believed to be accompanied by longer processing domains for phrase structures, such that two or more phrases that mark distinct processing domains at normal or slow rates of speech are now included within a single large domain. Consequently, for a given boundary location, the blocking of cross-word phonetic effects as well as the other prosodic effects discussed here will decline in probability at faster rates.

Steps 8 and 9 represent arithmetical procedures to derive an indication of the probability of occurrence at a given word boundary of each of the prosodic effects studied here, expressed as percent.

Having determined the probability of occurrence, the algorithm can now be extended to determine the magnitude of the prosodic effects of segmental lengthening and pausing in cases where the effects actually occur. Again, our schema represents only a first-order approximation but leads to some interesting questions.

Throughout this research we have noticed that the probability of occurrence for a prosodic effect is closely related to its magnitude for individual utterances; this relationship can be incorporated into the algorithm by stating that the probability of occurrence is the major factor upon which percent magnitude is based. For each of the two prosodic effects discussed here, however, the absolute relation between probability and percent magnitude differs greatly, creating the need for the following individual adjustment rules.

Step 10. *Individual Prosodic Effect Adjustments (Magnitude)*—For each boundary at which prosodic effects occur, multiply the output of step 9 by the following:
0.25 for segmental lengthening
2.00 for pausing

These adjustments for segmental lengthening and pausing magnitudes reflect one of the most abiding generalities of this study: that although the probability of occurrence is greater for segmental lengthening than for pausing in an individual utterance, the magnitude is greater for pausing.

A final step in the algorithm is required to incorporate the magnitude of prosodic effects into the speech wave itself. For segmental lengthening, this step simply involves the following:

Step 11A. *Speech Output* (for segmental lengthening)—For each boundary, multiply the output of step 10 by the inherent phonetic value for the duration of the word comprising the left of the boundary and then add this product to the word's inherent phonetic value in the speech output. The inherent phonetic value is considered to be the inherent phonetic segment duration (Klatt, 1973), representing the duration of the word segment when spoken in phrase-medial position, plus any durational effects contributed by factors such as stress and focus, phonetic conditioning, or hesitation not included explicitly in this algorithm. For lack of information, we rely here on two simplifying assumptions: first, that lengthening applies to the entire word segment, and second, that lengthening effects are added linearly to inherent word durations, regardless of the particular phonetic structure of the word segment. Empirical investigation of these assumptions is currently under way (Danly and Cooper, forthcoming); the outcome of this work should permit further refinement of the present algorithm.

Step 11B. *Speech Output* (for pausing)—Convert the percent magnitude to an integer value and add this value (in msec) to the speech output.

The dichotomy between substeps A and B of 11 reflects the intuition that segmental lengthening is a percent effect applied to inherent phonetic values for segment duration, whereas pauses are absolute integer effects. For many word boundaries, the "inherent" pause duration is zero, whereas segments always have non-zero inherent values of segment duration. Thus, pause effects could not be readily applied in terms of percent, and for this reason we have adopted the integer adding of pause effects in step 11B. It should be emphasized that the pause durations predicted by this algorithm do not include additional pause time for hesitation, breathing, or for silent intervals associated with stop consonants. It remains an interesting question to determine how the durations of two or more different types of pauses might be added together when these coincide at the same location.

In (14g) below, we present a hypothetical example of the algorithm's predictions for the segment and pause durations (in msec) of (14), spoken at an average rate. For purposes of illustration with this example, we shall assume that prosodic effects of lengthening and pausing occur at all word boundaries for which the output of step 9 (probability of occurrence) is 40 percent or greater. For each word in (14g), a hypothetical inherent phonetic value is indicated by the upper number and the predicted segment duration by the lower number. No predicted value is inserted for the duration of the utterance-final word, "nephew," since a separate factor of utterance-final lengthening, not computed by this algorithm, is assumed to apply to this word. The numbers between words represent the predicted pause duration at each given word boundary.

```
            (200)     (100)      (500)       (200)      (100)
(14g)   Jack (0) and (0) Elizabeth (0) took (0)  the (0)
            (200)     (100)      (555)       (200)      (100)


             (250)     (100)    (100)     (200)      (100)
       children (0)  to  (0)  the (0)  fair (0)   in  (0)
             (278)     (100)    (100)     (200)      (100)


             (300)       (200)        (300)            (100)
       Cohasset (0) last (0) weekend (200) and (0)
             (334)       (200)        (375)            (100)
```

```
 (300)      (200)     (100)       (300)
Alison (0) went (0)   to   (0) Chicago (0)
 (300)      (200)     (100)       (300)
```

```
 (100)     (100)       (250)        (100)      (200)
with (0)  her (0)  husband (80)   to  (0)  look (0)
 (100)     (100)       (280)        (100)      (200)
```

```
 (100)     (100)     (200)      (200)     (100)      (100)
 for (0)   a  (0)  new  (0)  job (90) and (0)   to  (0)
 (100)     (100)     (200)      (227)     (100)      (100)
```

```
 (250)     (100)      (250)      (100)       (250)
visit (0)  her (0) nieces (0)  and (0) nephews.
 (250)     (100)      (250)      (100)
```

CONCLUSION

We began this section by discussing a number of issues that led to the formulation of a metric of syntactic boundary strengths, aimed at predicting the rank magnitude of prosodic effects at various word boundary locations in a sentence, other things being equal. This metric was then incorporated into a more comprehensive algorithm for determining the probability of occurrence of prosodic·effects in individual utterances as well as the absolute magnitude of these effects. This algorithm may serve as a first-order approximation to the implementation of prosodic effects in a program to synthesize speech by rule. In constructing the comprehensive algorithm, it was necessary to consider extrasyntactic influences on prosody, including bisection, constituent length, and speaking rate. In so doing, it was also necessary to make assumptions that go well beyond the available data, and a considerable amount of further empirical testing must be conducted to determine the algorithm's predictive adequacy on a large scale.

Section 3: Processing Issues

Having examined the speaker's structural representation of syntactic units, we turn now to a consideration of how these structures might be processed by the speaker. Three major questions arise. First, are constituents planned in a top-down manner? Next, are constituents planned from left to right? And finally, how does the speaker's orchestration of the operations involved in planning and execution of speech influence speech wave properties?

TOP-DOWN PROCESSING

Evidence for the existence of a hierarchical type of syntactic representation was obtained in chapter 2; we now ask whether syntactic constituents are processed serially from largest to smallest, following the top-down method of applying rewrite rules in formal grammar. This question is a difficult one to deal with, both theoretically and experimentally.

At first glance, top-down coding of constituents seems to be a logical necessity, but this intuition is not well founded. It is possible, for example, that the speaker plans a subject NP and simultaneously begins planning a clause. It is certain on logical grounds that he cannot begin planning a clause later than the planning of its subject NP. However, it is not necessary that he begin planning the clause beforehand. The same situation holds for other hierarchically related constituents. Thus, the serial versus parallel issue of information processing is a real one.

How can this question be put to an experimental test? We will present one plausible approach based on real-time speech output, reaching the conclusion that even this test cannot provide the required information. It is instructive to work through this example, nonetheless, since this issue is usually accorded much importance in models of information flow despite recent attempts to show that it is unresolvable on general grounds (for example, Townsend, 1972).

The test for speech involves phrase-final lengthening. It was noted in chapter 2 that this lengthening effect is cumulative when two hierarchically related phrases end with the same word, such as when a word marks the termination of both an NP direct object and the VP that dominates it. Assuming that lengthening for each constituent involves some percentage increase to the key word's inherent duration, the prediction concerning the total amount of lengthening produced for a word marking the simultaneous end of more than one phrase will differ depending on whether the effects are applied in series or in parallel.[1] In particular, the word should be lengthened by a greater amount if the effects are programmed serially. To illustrate why this is so, let us consider a hypothetical example involving the duration of the noun-verb homophone "coach." Let us assume, following the discussion in chapter 3, that the inherent duration of a word corresponds to its duration when it occurs in non-phrase-final position, as in (15).

(15)   If Ann and Martha *coach* Andrew's teammates we'll quit.

Let us assume further that the duration of "coach" in this environment is 200 msec. Suppose that "coach" is lengthened by 10 percent when it occurs at the end of an NP, as measured in (16), and that the same word is lengthened by 30 percent when it occurs at the end of the two constituents VP and S, as in (17). The corresponding tree diagrams for these sentences appear in figure 7.9.

(16)   Diane will meet the *coach* at the squash courts tonight.
(17)   If Ann and Martha *coach* Andrew's teammates will quit.

Under the assumption that lengthening effects are cumulative, one can predict the total duration of "coach" when it marks the end of all three of the constituents NP, VP, and S, as in (18). This sentence is diagrammed in figure 7.10.

18)   If the owner fires the *coach* Andrew's teammates will quit.

If the lengthening effects are applied serially, the total duration of "coach" in (18) should average 286 msec. Assuming a top-down application of the lengthening effects, this total duration is obtained by the calculation in (19).[2]

(19)   Total duration of "coach" in (18) assuming top-down serial application of the VP/S and NP lengthening effects:
       (i)   200 msec
              (inherent word duration)
       (ii) $200 + (200 \times 30\%) = 260$ msec
              (duration after VP/S lengthening applied)
       (iii) $260 + (260 \times 10\%) = 286$ msec
              (duration after NP lengthening applied)

On the other hand, the total duration of "coach" should average only 280 msec if the lengthening effects are added in parallel, assuming that the additivity is linear. This calculation is shown in (20).

(20)   Total duration of "coach" in (18) assuming parallel linear application of the VP/S and NP lengthening effects:
       (i)   200 msec
              (inherent word duration)

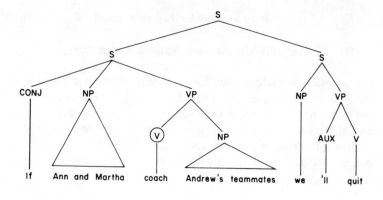

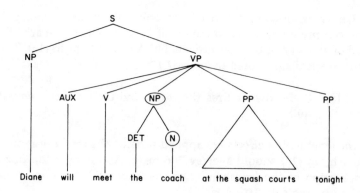

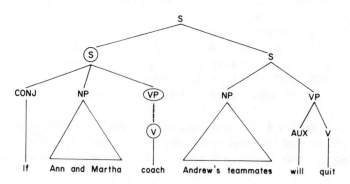

Figure 7.9 *Structural representation of sentences (15)–(17). In the top diagram, the key word "coach" occurs in non-phrase-final position. In the middle diagram, the same key word occurs at the end of an NP. In the bottom diagram, the key word appears at the end of a VP and an S. In each case the nodes ending with the key word are circled.*

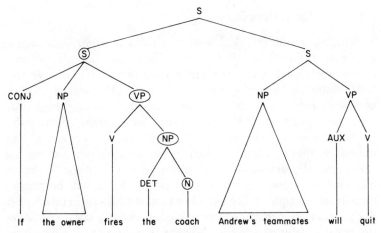

Figure 7.10 *Structural representation of sentence (18). Here the key word "coach" marks the end of four constituents, N, NP, VP, and S, as circled in the tree diagram.*

(ii) 200 + (200 × 30%) + (200) × 10%) = 280 msec
(duration after VP/S lengthening and NP lengthening applied)

In this case, the predicted difference in total duration for the two models is a mere 6 msec. Such a small effect could easily be obscured by normal variations in speech rate. The effect could be magnified somewhat by measuring a word with a larger inherent duration, such as a polysyllabic word; but, in any event, the predicted difference would remain relatively small, since the magnitude of the effect critically depends on the percentage difference in lengthening between VP/S and NP, which is probably not more than 20 percent. But even surmounting this drawback would not permit a conclusive demonstration that lengthening effects are applied either in series or in parallel. Evidence in favor of a serial model could alternatively be accounted for by a parallel model in which the effects are added in a nonlinear fashion. Conversely, a nonlinear serial model could handle results otherwise attributed to a linear parallel model. In short, while the serial versus parallel models of applying phrase-final lengthening can be distinguished mathematically under the assumption of linear additivity, the models cannot be adequately tested at present because (a) the predicted difference is very small, and (b) any obtainable difference could be attributed to nonlinear additivity, pending an independent test of linearity.

LEFT-TO-RIGHT PROCESSING

Within each hierarchical level, the rules in a phrase structure grammar are applied left to right. Thus, for example, when a clause is elaborated into the major constituents NP and VP, the NP is elaborated in turn before the VP during the next application of rewrite rules. As with the issue of top-down processing, intuitions run strong about the question of left-to-right versus right-to-left processing. The output of speech occurs left to right by definition; that is, words spoken before or after one another are conventionally described as occurring to the "left" or "right" of one another. However, it is not necessary that words be considered in left-to-right fashion at all computational stages involved in the planning of speech. For example, at an early stage of coding, the speaker may decide on a particular noun phrase without regard to its linear position in the speech output.

Yngve (1960) proposed a model of sentence production which included the assumption that the speaker elaborates phrase structures in a top-down, left-to-right manner. His theory embodied the prediction that a speaker's processing load is directly proportional to the number of nodes yet to be elaborated in an utterance. Forster (1966, 1967) attempted to test this prediction by presenting subjects with sentence fragments such as those appearing in (21) below.

(21)   (a)   On his return to the house he found ————.
     (b)   ———— the woman in a state of great agitation.

The subjects were asked to complete each sentence fragment by adding material on either the right (21a) or left (21b) to compose a grammatical string. Forster reasoned that if syntactic constituents are elaborated from left to right in speech production, then subjects in this completion task should be more adept at completing a sentence fragment when its left-hand portion is provided, as in (21a), than when its right-hand portion is given, as in (21b). Not surprisingly, the results showed that subjects were indeed able to complete fragments like (21a) faster than (21b). Forster (1967) went on to argue that the effect was attributable to processing of phrase structures that correspond to a surface level of syntactic analysis.

Forster's results confirm our intuition that speakers are more capable of completing sentence fragments from left to right than from right to left. However, the experiments do not provide a satisfactory answer to the question of whether left-to-right processing accompanies syntactic stages in *ongoing* speech production. In short, while the phonetic output of speech proceeds in left-to-right fashion by definition, there is still no assurance that left-to-right processing accompanies all of the syntactic stages of coding which occur internally.

PLANNING AND EXECUTION

Three distinct types of processing seem to be active simultaneously during a typical speech act. These include planning of upcoming speech, execution of current speech, and short-term storage of recent speech and recently formulated plans for upcoming material (for a general discussion, see Clark and Clark, 1977). In this section we will focus primarily on the two activities of planning and execution.

Consider the phenomena of segmental lengthening and pausing at major syntactic boundaries. A priori, it is quite possible that the direction of these effects (that is, lengthening, not shortening) can be attributed to either planning, execution, or a combination of both. According to a planning account, these lengthening effects are produced in order to allow the speaker an extra fraction of time for planning upcoming material in the next phrase. This planning may involve not only semantic and syntactic computations but also the resetting of laryngeal and articulatory postures. One immediate limitation of this account is that it does not explain the existence of segmental lengthening at the end of an entire utterance, where no following material exists to be planned.[3] It is conceivable, of course, that utterance-final lengthening is attributable to an independent factor while utterance-internal lengthening at clause and phrase boundaries is attributable to planning.

Both utterance-final and utterance-internal lengthening effects could be attributable to execution rather than planning. According to this account, the lengthening effects represent a general relaxation response of that component of the speech processor responsible for timing computations. The internal clock, in effect, runs more slowly at the ends of major constituents, presumably due to processing fatigue brought on by the activity associated with computing time intervals for all the previous segments within the constituent. The temporary slowdown at the end of a constituent could account for both segmental lengthening and pausing, as well as for the fall in fundamental frequency that typically accompanies the end of a major constituent (Cooper and Sorensen, 1977).

In addition to accounting for the direction of lengthening effects, the operations of planning and/or execution provide a psychological rationale for the close relationship noted earlier in this chapter between a prosodic effect's probability of occurrence and its magnitude, as captured by the comprehensive algorithm for determining prosodic effects. This relationship is certainly not a logical necessity. For many events, the probability of occurrence and magnitude are in fact inversely related; consider earthquakes, for example. For speech prosody, however, the direct relationship between probability and magnitude of the effects studied here can be explained in terms of the requirements of planning and/or execution operations. For a location in the speech stream at which relaxation and/or planning are at a premium, prosodic effects are most likely to occur, and, furthermore, these effects will exhibit their highest magnitudes, since larger lengthening effects for segments and pauses are assumed to allow the speaker more time to relax and/or plan. Thus the processing notions introduced here seem to aid in explaining at least one major property of the algorithm for determining the probability and magnitude of prosodic effects.

Before dealing with planning and execution in more detail, we should note two other candidate accounts of segmental lengthening and/or pausing. According to one account, these lengthening effects are produced not as a by-product of an automatic, internalized aspect of the production system, but rather are intended to cue the presence of a major syntactic boundary to the listener. While it is likely that listeners can utilize large-magnitude lengthening effects as cues to syntactic structure, it is by no means clear that speakers typically produce lengthening with this intention. As a working principle, it seems that the first place to search for a proper account of the lengthening effects resides with the internal computations of the speaker (see chapter 8).

Finally, it is conceivable that segmental lengthening may be produced at syntactic boundaries in order to allow the speaker a larger portion of speech over which to execute a sizable fall in fundamental frequency. However, as noted earlier, we have found no correlation between the magnitude of segmental lengthening and the magnitude of F_0 fall in individual utterances, suggesting that this hypothesis is incorrect (Cooper and Sorensen, 1977).

The Method of One-Sided Variation

Because planning and execution probably operate simultaneously during the production of speech, it is particularly difficult to isolate them. However, their relative contributions can be determined by a straightforward method, which we have termed the *method of one-sided variation.* The method involves holding the material on one side of a given boundary constant while systematically varying the material on the other side of the boundary. Under these conditions the contributions from one source of segmental lengthening at the boundary are controlled for, so that any observed effect may be attributed to the additional influence of the alternative source. In formal terms, let X denote material to the left of a constituent boundary and let Y refer to material to the right of that boundary. By holding Y constant while varying the complexity of X, we may determine the extent to which X-final timing effects are attributable to the execution of constituent(s) X.[4] Alternatively, one may evaluate any role that the planning of Y plays in determining the duration of the X-final segment by systematically varying the complexity of Y while holding X constant.

The influence of upcoming material has already been indicated in some of the findings of previous chapters, including the results for preposing and raising in chapter 5 as well as for trochaic shortening in chapter 6. In addition, an influence of preceding material has been suggested by results of cumulative phrase-final lengthening in chapter 2 and by the effects of postposing in chapter 5.

To investigate the relative contributions of planning and execution, we tested whether the magnitude of timing effects that occur at the juncture between two major clauses is affected by overall clause length and complexity. These tests are described below. Following this, we will consider the results of additional experiments that provide some indications about the role of both planning and execution.

The investigation of speech planning involves determining whether the overall length and complexity of an upcoming clause exerts an influence on segmental timing at the end of the preceding clause. The test sentence pair appears in (22) below. The first clause for both sentences is identical, while the second clause varies in length and complexity. Any differences in the duration of the key material between the two sentences may thus be directly attributed to a difference in the upcoming clause.

(22) (a) Tom and I will reprimand Sue and *Clark* and Jane will talk to Steven.

      (b) Tom and I will reprimand Sue and *Clark* and Jane plans to talk to Steven's brother and send Jeffrey to the principal.

The results for twenty speakers showed that the duration of the key word "Clark" was significantly longer in the (b) sentence, which contained the longer second clause ($p > 0.001$, $t = 3.97$, $df = 19$; two-tailed t test for matched pairs). The duration of "Clark" averaged 6 percent longer in this sentence. Speakers did not produce long pauses in either sentence, and there was no significant effect of pause duration. The lengthening obtained for the key word "Clark" indicates that the timing of clause-final speech segments is influenced by the length and complexity of upcoming material. This finding provides inferential support for the notion that segmental lengthening may be programmed as an aid to the speaker in planning at least some aspects of an upcoming constituent. The effect observed here cannot, incidentally, be attributed to a more global effect of lengthening all words in longer utterances (see Fonagy and Magdics, 1960).

Having found that the phenomenon of clause-final lengthening is partially controlled by speech planning, at least in terms of the general feature of the length/complexity of upcoming material, we now consider the corresponding contribution of execution-based processing operations. More specifically, one would like to know whether the length/complexity of a clause affects the magnitude of the speech timing effects occurring at the end of that clause. To test this, an experiment was designed involving the sentence pair in (23) below. We varied the overall length and complexity of the first clause in each sentence while holding constant the second clause. Thus any difference in either the key word "Jake" or the following pause between the two sentences can be directly attributed to the length and complexity of material already spoken.

(23)   (a)   Bob went to visit *Jake* while Mary went on a picnic.
       (b)   Bob went to the hospital in Atlanta to visit *Jake* while Mary went on a picnic.

The results for ten speakers showed no significant effect of lengthening for the segment marking the end of the longer clause ($p > 0.20$, $t = 0.77$, $df = 9$). Likewise, there was no significant difference in the duration of the following pause for the two sentences ($p > 0.20$, $t = -0.44$, $df = 9$). Taken together, the results for these two sentence pairs suggest that utterance-internal lengthening at a clause boundary is influenced by the overall length and complexity of upcoming material but not by the length/complexity of preceding material. Alternatively, however, it seems that the different results obtained for sentence pairs (22) and (23) may be due to the fact that constituent Y in (22b) was four major category words longer than in (22a), whereas constituent X in (23b) was only lengthened by two major category words relative to (23a). In an experiment with quite different sentence structures involving preposing (chapter 5, study 1, experiment 2), an increase in the length of the preposed material by three major category words did produce an increase in segment and pause durations. Clearly, we need to know much more about the variations in constituent length and/or complexity necessary to produce timing effects before any firm conclusions can be reached regarding the relative contributions of planning and execution operations to speech timing effects occurring at any given constituent boundary.

Planning: Clauses versus Phrases

We have reviewed evidence showing that material yet to be spoken in an utterance may exert an influence on the timing of speech segments. It is now possible to take a somewhat closer look at the nature of the speaker's planning and its influence on timing. The main question to be addressed concerns exactly what it is that the speaker plans at the point in the utterance at which segmental lengthening is applied. Does the speaker simply note that an upcoming clause is to be uttered and consider a general estimate of its length? Or does the speaker instead look ahead to consider the length of the first major phrase within the clause?

To test this latter possibility we conducted an experiment in which the length of the upcoming NP in a new clause was varied while the total length of the clause was held constant. An example sentence pair appears in (24) below.

(24) (a) Kim has decided to take the dog that she bought to the *park* and Ed and the boys who work with my nephew went to the racetrack. (upcoming long NP)
(b) Kim has decided to take the dog that she bought to the *park* and Erika plans to visit the museum that Amy works at. (upcoming long VP)

If the speaker's planning is in any way limited by phrase boundaries, one would expect that the duration of "park" would be longer in (a) than in (b), since the long NP phrase in (a) immediately follows the key segment whereas the long VP in (b) does not. The results for ten speakers showed no significant differences, however. These data suggest that, at the time when segmental lengthening at the clause boundary is programmed, the speaker considers the general length of the upcoming clause but not the separate lengths of its component phrases.

It remains to be determined whether the speaker's representation of upcoming material is computed in terms of number of syllables, number of words, or number of syntactic constituents, or whether it is simply a visual representation of the general length of the typewritten utterances used in this particular task. If the preceding experiment had revealed significant differences, we could have disposed of this latter task-dependent possibility.

We have conducted an additional experiment which indicates that upcoming material plays some role in speech timing. In this experiment we compared segmental lengthening for sentence pairs in which the key sites both marked the end of a clause but in which only one site simultaneously marked the beginning of a new clause. An example sentence pair appears below.

(25) (a) The workers who could *type* decided to purchase a typewriter.
      (b) If Winnifred could *type* Delores would buy her a typewriter.

In (25a) a subordinate clause ends with "type," and after "type" the main clause, which began at the start of the utterance, is resumed. In (25b), however, a conditional clause ends with "type," and immediately thereafter an entirely new main clause begins.

The results for ten speakers showed that the duration of "type" was significantly longer in (25b) ($p < 0.05$, $t = 2.54$, $df = 9$). These data are consistent with the notion that segmental lengthening at clause boundaries is partly attributed to the beginning of a new clause after the key word. Unlike the results cited earlier, however, this particular result is open to an alternative ad hoc account that would explain the lengthening in terms of the difference in the precise type of clause ending at the key site—relative clause in (a), conditional clause in (b).

Evidence from Fundamental Frequency

The examination of the F_0 contour of an utterance provides a particularly clear example of the speaker's planning activity. As noted in chapter 1, the F_0 contour represents the frequency of quasi-periodic vibration of the vocal folds during voiced portions of speech. Perceptually, this frequency information plays a major role in judgments of pitch. Like segment and pause durations, fundamental frequency is an attribute of the speech wave that can provide useful information about the nature of the speaker's internal processing scheme (for example, Maeda, 1976; Sorensen and Cooper, 1980). A salient feature of F_0 contours in single-clause declarative sentences consists of a general decline in F_0 throughout the sentence. Although many local rises in F_0 may be superimposed on this falling contour, the presence of the F_0 declination occurs with considerable regularity in both oral reading (Maeda, 1976; O'Shaughnessy, 1976) and in spontaneous speech (M. Liberman, personal communication, May 1978). This decline in F_0 is generally attributed to a decrease in lung and/or intraoral pressure during the utterances (Maeda, 1976). The declination appears in most languages (Bolinger, 1964), although it is not universal. C. Grimes (personal communication, May 1978) cites an example of a Brazilian language in which F_0 contours of declarative utterances are generally rising. Thus, while declination is a general feature of F_0 contours and seems to represent a physiological running-down of the speech system, this effect is at least partially controlled by higher-level commands of the speaker.

This latter point is supported by the observation that long utterances are generally accompanied by a higher F_0 at the beginning of the utterance than shorter utterances are (McAllister, 1971; O'Shaughnessy, 1976). This observation indicates that speakers must consider the general length of the sentence prior to the initiation of speech, a clear example of look-ahead. In order to provide a rigorous test of this possibility, Sorensen and Cooper (1980) asked speakers to read pairs of sentences which varied in length but which contained the same words at the beginning of the utterance, as in (26) below.

(26)　(a)　The *deer* could be seen from the car.
　　　(b)　The *deer* by the canyon could be seen from the window of the car.

The results showed that the peak F_0 of the first key in the utterance was indeed significantly higher in long than in short utterances, by an average of 13.5 Hz. The effect demonstrates that speakers perform some very general planning for utterance length and that this planning exerts a systematic influence on the F_0 peak of the first key word of the utterance. Since the effect is present at the very beginning of the sentence, there can be no question that we have here a demonstration of an effect critically dependent on the nature of material yet to be spoken.

While this experiment indicates the existence of speech planning for oral reading, there is no assurance that the effect will also hold for spontaneous speech. In general, there may be a greater likelihood of long-range planning in oral reading, especially since speakers have already familiarized themselves with the material to be read; yet this familiarization does not render a foregone conclusion about the influence of planning on the programming of F_0. The speakers in this experiment had no awareness of the F_0 effect, and it is plausible that the look-ahead exhibited here is also present in spontaneous speech.

Beyond demonstrating the existence of long-range planning and its effect on F_0, we would like to know why the speaker begins at a higher F_0 when producing longer sentences. One possibility is that speakers start higher in order to allow more of a frequency range for F_0 fall during the longer utterances. This latter requirement may stem from a need to keep the ending values of F_0 above a certain frequency. Our experimental results indicate that speakers tend to produce a relatively fixed value for the F_0 peak of the last stressed syllable in the utterance, regardless of sentence length (see Sorensen and Cooper, 1980, for a more detailed presentation of these and other F_0 effects for long versus short utterances). For present purposes, however, the F_0 effect at the beginning of long versus short utterances serves as a demonstration of long-range planning and its role in determining speech wave values.

Evidence from Spontaneous Speech

A recent study based on spontaneous speech provides further evidence about planning during ongoing speech production. While interviewing speakers, Ford and Holmes (1978) randomly presented tones as the interviewees talked. The speakers were asked to respond to each tone by pressing a button. Reaction times (RTs) were measured and analyzed in an attempt to determine whether they would vary as a function of the tone's occurrence at various locations within an utterance. Ford and Holmes found that RTs were slower for tones placed at ends of clauses, compared with RTs for tones placed at the beginnings of clauses. The slower RTs were accounted for in terms of an increase in the speaker's processing load at clause endings. In addition, Ford and Holmes were able to attribute this increase in processing load to planning-based as opposed to execution-based operations, since the effect on RT was restricted to clause boundaries that did not coincide with the ends of entire sentences.

Taken together, the tone-monitoring task of Ford and Holmes and our own analyses of speech timing and F_0 contours provide effective means of obtaining information about the planning operations engaged in during the ongoing production of speech. The results suggest that a variety of different types of planning units may play a role in production; future work might be directed at examining what specific processing operations are performed with each type (see McNeill, 1979). It seems possible, in particular, that the tone-monitoring task taps a stage of planning that involves the programming of propositions, possibly corresponding to underlying syntactic clauses (Ford and Holmes, 1978), whereas acoustic analysis of practiced sentence reading taps a subsequent stage of planning in which surface length (and possibly surface complexity) of upcoming material is programmed.

While the effects of planning observed here typically involve global features such as constituent length, the preliminary evidence presented here suggests that, with the possible exception of very long constituents (see step 5 of the comprehensive algorithm described earlier), the effects of execution seem more sensitive to the fine structure of the speaker's syntactic representation. This asymmetry was brought out clearly in the testing of left-right differences of structural complexity during the investigation of a metric of syntactic boundary strengths in the previous section. The structural complexity of preceding material also provided the most plausible account of the findings of cumulative phrase-final lengthening in chapter 2.

We regard these effects in terms of execution-based operations rather than short-term memory (STM) because the load on STM at the end of a major constituent should be very light, at least according to the model proposed by Yngve (1960). Thus there would be no basis for the speaker's need to lengthen the last segment of a constituent or to insert a following pause for the sake of relieving the load on STM. Rather, the lengthening effects at major boundaries attributed to the structural complexity of preceding material appear to represent a general relaxation response of the speaker upon execution of the ending of the constituent, as discussed at the outset of this section on planning and execution.

The predominance of structural effects for the left versus right side of the key boundary is understandable in view of the fact that a speaker must have computed a detailed structural representation of the material currently being executed, whereas the speaker need not have planned upcoming material in such detail. As shown in the foregoing experiments, it seems that planning at this juncture primarily involves extrasyntactic factors, such as the general length of the upcoming material. These extrasyntactic factors need not be retained for information already spoken, and so may not contribute as substantially to the effects of execution-related operations.

Conclusion

We have shown that the activities of both planning and execution contribute to segmental lengthening and pausing at major syntactic boundaries within utterances.[5] On the basis of preliminary evidence, it appears that the effects of planning are revealed primarily for global features of upcoming material, such as general length and complexity, whereas the effects of execution seem to be more closely linked to the syntactic structure of the constituent currently being spoken. The method of one-sided variation has proved valuable in isolating the contributions of planning and execution, but a great deal of further systematic investigation needs to be conducted with this method before a clear picture will emerge.

At present, our understanding of processing activities is minimal. For one thing, we know nothing about the possible interplay between planning and execution. Is each type of activity carried out by a separate processor with independent resources, or are the two activities dependent on the same processor to at least some extent? Investigation of the combined effect of articulatory and syntactic features of speech on prosody may shed some light on this question. For example, one could examine whether the planning of an upcoming clause (as reflected in speech timing) is impaired (or postponed) when the speaker is confronted with the immediate need to execute a difficult consonant cluster. In addition to this issue concerning the independence of planning- versus execution-based processing operations, we know nothing about whether planning is performed at discrete intervals, presumably just at major syntactic boundaries, or whether this activity is performed continuously throughout an utterance. Our intuition favors the former alternative, but the question has not been subjected to empirical testing.

A plethora of additional unanswered questions exist concerning planning, execution, and the manner in which these activities are monitored by the speaker (for discussion, see, for example, Clark and Clark, 1977; Rosenberg, 1977; Schlesinger, 1977; McNeill, 1979). For example, as noted in chapter 1, the speaker seems to have a fair amount of flexibility in his initial choice of a major linguistic unit to be processed, and in some cases the speaker may begin executing a phrase before the planning of a superordinate constituent has been completed. Meanwhile, the speaker may also be monitoring the speech output and revising the planning of the superordinate constituent. Further work on this topic should lead not only to a more elaborate theory of processing operations but also to refinements in the algorithm for determining the probability and magnitude of prosodic effects.

Summary

In this chapter a theory of syntactic-to-phonetic coding has been developed to account for the major phenomena studied in this project. The theory contains two components, one involving structural representation, the other, real-time processing of these representations. The structural component of the theory includes the representation of syntactic constituents as well as a metric of syntactic boundary strengths. These aspects of the theory, coupled with the influence of various extragrammatical factors, enable one to provide a general account for the location and magnitude of the speech effects examined in experimental studies. The processing component of the theory includes a partial characterization of the speaker's planning- and execution-related activities. This component provides an account of the direction of the speech timing effects—that is, lengthening rather than shortening. Although many questions about processing remain to be answered, the experimental method of one-sided variation seems to provide a particularly direct means of disentangling the activities of planning and execution.

While many aspects of the theory seem applicable to spontaneous speech, such behavior also involves somewhat different processing operations than those tapped in experiments with practiced oral reading. Processing operations in spontaneous speech are influenced by a variety of additional factors, including whether the speech requires detailed on-line planning or merely involves regeneration of prefabricated material that can be retrieved from long-term memory. A surprisingly large percentage of spontaneous speech appears to be comprised of prefabricated routines, but we do not know the extent to which the detailed phonetic form of such routines is stored in long-term memory or requires the same on-line processing as for non-prefabricated phrases. Most speech includes a mixture of prefabricated and newly generated phrases, and any theory of planning and execution in spontaneous speech must specify how these phrases are processed alongside one another.

8 | Ramifications

THE RESULTS of this study can be brought to bear on related areas of basic research as well as finding application in language pathology and engineering. Our organization for the broad range of topics to be discussed in this chapter is guided in part by a research strategy outlined in figure 8.1. This strategy is based on the idea that the outcome of studies on one topic often provides useful input to the design of studies on another. For example, the results of studies on speech production are vital to the design of studies on speech perception, since the human perceptual system must deal with the restricted range of acoustic signals that are actually produced by speakers. Studies of production thus permit one to focus on issues in perception that are most likely to be important to normal listening. In turn, research on perception provides guidelines for the implementation of rules in engineering programs for speech synthesis, since these rules are only useful insofar as they aid listeners in decoding the synthetic signal. Other information flow guidelines in figure 8.1 are more a matter of efficiency than necessity. For example, we decided to conduct studies on speech timing prior to studies on fundamental frequency because the former acoustic variable is easier to measure yet can be used as a tool to address many issues common to both. Similarly, research with normal adults is conducted before work with either normal children or clinical populations because normal adults are easier to test.

Although the diagram in figure 8.1 represents one plan for extending this research project, as more studies are conducted on each topic there will no doubt exist opportunities for feedback as well as for the type of feedforward specified in this figure. For example, aspects of studies on language pathology may provide inferences about mental coding that lead to new predictions about

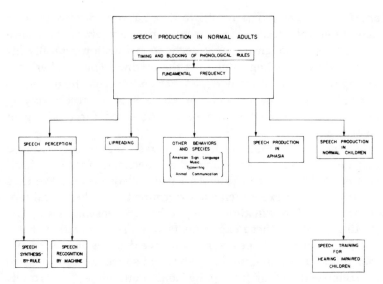

Figure 8.1 *Flow diagram for a research strategy on syntax and speech.*

speech processing in normals. And studies of speech synthesis may provide a valuable tool for guiding studies of human speech insofar as synthesis programs provide a testing ground for complex information flow hypotheses, the implications of which cannot be discerned informally.

Fundamental Frequency

We have focused throughout this study on duration as a dependent measure in examining the speaker's syntactic code. As observed in chapters 1 and 7, another major speech wave property that can be measured for the same purpose is F_0. We have recently begun to examine F_0 using the same experimental method employed in this book. In some cases our findings closely parallel the results obtained with duration; yet because of its complexity F_0 promises to convey even more information about the syntactic code.

DECLINATION AND RESETTING

In declarative sentences of English and many other languages, a general fall in F_0 has been observed from the beginning to the end of the utterance (Bolinger, 1964; Cohen and 't Hart, 1967). This declination effect is presumably applied by the speaker over some specified domain, and experiments have been undertaken to determine whether this domain corresponds to a major clause unit or to an entire utterance (Cooper and Sorensen, 1980; Sorensen and Cooper, 1980). The results to date suggest that the speaker may reset the declination attribute partially at major clause boundaries, although the new declination function typically includes a lower starting value than the original. The speaker's resetting seems to be directly dependent on the syntactic boundary strength, not on the presence or absence of an accompanying breath pause, paralleling the results obtained for blocking in chapter 6.

In attempting to examine declination resetting, we soon realized that a more precise description of the F_0 declination attribute itself was needed in order to provide a truly adequate test. We thus began a series of experiments to determine the mathematical representation of declination (Cooper and Sorensen, 1980). The starting point for these experiments was the observation that a line connecting the F_0 peaks in a sentence declines at a faster rate than a line connecting the F_0 valleys, and so we decided to try to characterize the separate "topline" and "bottomline." Our results for the topline indicate that, except for the first peak in a sentence, the peaks lie along a fairly straight line, with the slope determined jointly by the F_0 value and the time of occurrence of the first and last peaks in the utterance. The abstract mathematical expression that captures this relation has been termed the *Topline Rule*. In English the first peak typically lies well above this imaginary line; yet this peak plays a key role in determining the slope of the line itself. The Topline Rule appears to adequately predict the F_0 values of intermediate F_0 peaks in a manner that is unchanging across variables such as sentence length, number of F_0 peaks, major grammatical category type, and sex of speaker.

FALL-RISE PATTERNS

Within the domain of a single declination, the influence of syntax is more readily apparent, and a number of parallels have been noted between F_0 fall-rise patterns and the major effects studied in previous chapters, including segmental lengthening, pausing, and the blocking of phonological rules. Fall-rise patterns of F_0 have been shown to accompany word boundaries that coincide with both strong surface syntactic boundaries and deletion sites, including many of the boundaries marked by segmental lengthening, pausing, and blocking in chapters 2, 4, and 6 (for an extended presentation, see Cooper and Sorensen, 1980). In addition, the magnitude of the fall-rise patterns appears to vary directly with the strength of the boundaries, consistent with the theory of boundary strengths developed in chapter 7.

CONCLUSION

Studies of F_0 patterns in sentence production have indicated that syntactic coding influences these patterns in much the same way that it influences duration. The results with F_0 thus provide a converging source of evidence in favor of the general framework developed in chapter 7. Because of the inherent complexity of F_0 patterns, however, it is possible that further examination of F_0 will provide more detailed information about both the speaker's structural representations and processing operations than could be inferred from an examination of speech timing alone.

Perception

One question frequently asked about this work is whether prosody might be used by the listener as an aid to decoding structural relations. Before discussing relevant theoretical and experimental work, however, let us hasten to point out that the present study of speech production should be judged primarily for what it tells us about speech production activity itself. Historically, experimental psychology has paid far more attention to issues of perception than production, largely because the stimulus can be quantified more precisely in perceptual experiments. What we have tried to show here, however, is that a large portion of the speech production process can also be studied with well-specified stimulus materials. To be sure, the research to date bypasses the early stages of idea formation involved in speaking, but we are able to study the subsequent stages in a manner that is no less rigorous than experimental work in perception.

Thus far, almost nothing is known about listeners' ability to utilize prosodic cues, although we do know something about the ability to detect their presence (for example, Huggins, 1972; Nooteboom, 1973; Klatt and Cooper, 1975; Nooteboom and Doodeman, 1980). Klatt and Cooper (1975) conducted experiments in which judgments of segment duration were required of listeners for a given word in different sentence contexts. In one experiment, the sentences were constructed by electronically deleting or reduplicating individual glottal cycles of the central portion of a vowel. Listeners could detect differences in vowel duration that were on the order of one or two glottal cycles (roughly 8–16 msec for a male voice). This result suggests that lengthening effects such as those that occur at the boundary between two conjoined clauses may be readily detected. However, work is only beginning to be directed at the more important question of whether listeners *typically use* this information in decoding constituents.

Lehiste, Olive, and Streeter (1976) have made an attempt to test this latter question, using structurally ambiguous sentences such as "The hostess greeted the girl with a smile," in which the prepositional phrase modifies either "the girl" or the entire verb phrase, analogous to sentences for which we reported speech timing effects in experiment 3 of chapter 2. Lehiste et al. found that listeners were more likely to perceive the latter reading of this sentence when the interstress interval spanning the boundary between "girl" and "with" was lengthened, by virtue of expanding each segment of the string "girl with a smile." Although Lehiste (1977) claims that the increase in the interstress interval is the relevant factor, it is possible that the listeners' judgments were determined by the absolute lengthening of a particular segment within the manipulated string.

In the remainder of this section we outline experiments on perception that are yet to be conducted. These proposals provide a focal point for discussing some issues concerning both theory and experimental design in perceptual research.

RECOVERY AND PREDICTION

A major distinction in perceptual processing can be drawn between a listener's recovery of information already presented in the speech wave and the prediction of information yet to be heard. Just as the speaker presumably performs the processing operations of planning and execution simultaneously during much of speech production, it seems that the listener is often similarly engaged in recovering and predicting information simultaneously.

To assess whether listeners are capable of utilizing durational information to recover and predict structure, one could systematically vary the durations of key word segments from naturally spoken utterances (see Klatt and Cooper, 1975) and then test whether listeners can determine the character of the preceding or upcoming structure when a portion of the sentence not containing lexical cues to structure is presented. It would be useful to include many different sentences in each experiment to avoid incurring a perceptual set for certain speech rhythms (a main drawback in previous perception studies—see Huggins, 1972a,b). In one experiment, testing the ability of listeners to recover structural information could include the presentation of subject-predicate strings such as "whenever we pay," in which the duration of /e/ in "pay" is systematically varied. The listener's task would be to determine whether "pay" is the last word of a clause (as in "whenever we pay, John is thankful") or not (as in "whenever we pay John, he is thankful"). It might be useful to test two different versions of this task. In one version, the task could be to categorize the last word of the string as clause-final (CF) or non-clause-final (NCF). In the other version, the task would involve categorizing the string in terms of two possible endings, using example endings such as those mentioned above ("John is thankful" versus "John, he is thankful").

The ability of listeners to recognize the ends of clauses is important in light of the notion that some processing is delayed until an entire clause has been heard (Fodor, Bever, and Garrett, 1974). The results of this type of experiment should indicate whether listeners are capable of utilizing acoustic information contained in the vowel duration to determine the presence of a clause boundary. If so, listeners should judge "pay" to be at the end of a clause as a direct function of the length of the vowel /e/, in accordance with the occurrence of clause-final lengthening in speech production.

In a related type of test, it should be possible to determine whether listeners can utilize variations in duration to predict the occurrence of deletion sites such as Verb Gapping. Given the sentence portion "Jane eats peas and Kate," in which the duration of /e/ in "Kate" is varied, listeners would be asked to judge whether this sentence portion is more likely to be followed by "eats chicken" (no deletion) or simply "chicken" (Verb Gapping). Given the fact that speakers typically show segmental lengthening prior to a Gapping deletion site, listeners should judge the sentences to contain a gapped structure as a direct function of the vowel duration, if they are capable of utilizing this acoustic information.

While experiments such as the above would enable one to determine whether listeners are at all capable of utilizing durational information to recover and predict structural relations, the experiments involve an unnatural task that may not reflect the performance of listeners during normal sentence processing. Listeners do not consciously judge the presence of clause endings or of deletion sites in sentence processing, as seems to be required by the procedure described above. This drawback is shared by a number of tasks currently in use to test on-line processing in sentence perception, including phoneme monitoring (Foss, 1969; Cutler, 1976), listening for mispronunciations (Cole, 1973), speech shadowing at fast rates (Marslen-Wilson, 1975), and studies of click detection and reaction time (Bever and Hurtig, 1975). Listeners do not normally listen for the presence of a particular phoneme, a mispronunciation, or an extraneous click, although certain results with phoneme monitoring, listening for mispronunciations, and click detection indicate that the methods do reflect at least some aspects of perception in its typical form.

In the case of speech shadowing at fast rates, only a small proportion of prospective subjects are capable of performing the task, and here the difficulties of interpretation are compounded by the fact that this task necessarily includes both perception and production. Yet, as with the other tasks, the shadowing technique has proven fruitful for studying certain issues of speech information processing.

The heart of the problem is to devise a task that is simultaneously natural for the listener and capable of providing the experimenter with information about the listener's internal processing. One possibility is a task in which listeners are asked semantically appropriate questions about sentence materials. The questions must be specially constructed so that the listeners' answers will provide an indication of their processing of the sentence material.

We will present two examples of this type of test, since the paradigm seems to provide one possible means of assessing the normal use of prosody. The test involves reaction time and so is not a fully natural task, but the artificiality is minimized. Consider the sentence "My Uncle Abraham presented his talk naturally." In chapter 2 we found that speakers lengthened the duration of "talk" and inserted a pause after this word when they intended to convey the meaning "Of course my Uncle Abraham presented his talk," as opposed to the other possible reading, "My Uncle Abraham presented his talk in a natural manner." Now, consider a perceptual task in which the listener is asked, prior to presentation of a disambiguating paragraph containing this sentence, to press a key as soon as he knows from the paragraph whether it was obvious or not to the narrator that Uncle Abraham presented his talk. For one group of listeners, the prosodic information for duration that is appropriate for the "of course" reading would be included in the critical sentence. For this group, it is expected that correct responses occur during or immediately after the occurrence of "naturally." Because the prosody is appropriate for the "of course" reading, listeners might well be able to press the key as soon as several syllables of "naturally" had been presented, since other evidence on sentence perception suggests that listeners utilize information in each syllable to constrain word choice (for example, Cole, Jakimik, and Cooper, 1980). On the other hand, when the prosodic information for the sentence is neutral, favoring neither the "of course" reading nor the "in a natural manner" reading, listeners would not be able to respond as quickly. As they hear the first syllable of the key word "naturally," they constrain word choice to some extent, but the prosodic information is not appropriate for signaling the presence of an adverbial that modifies the entire sentence. Rather strong support would be obtained for the notion that listeners normally use prosodic information in predicting structural relations if the results of this experiment confirmed our prediction. Since the paragraph contexts would disambiguate the sentence in such a manner that listeners would not detect the presence of an ambiguity, the listeners would not have to depend on prosody as an aid to disambiguation in this task. Furthermore, since their task is meaning-dependent, in line with the normal goal of sentence comprehension, listeners should not be conscious of the experimental hypothesis or even of the fact that prosodic information is the critical variable under study.

The general test procedure introduced here can also be applied to unambiguous sentences. Consider the sentence "I gave some oranges to Max." In this case, listeners could be asked beforehand to press a key as soon as they know whether the narrator gave oranges to Max or to Harry. In the paragraph preceding the key sentence, Max and Harry are introduced as persons who are receiving gifts from the narrator. The basic structure of the critical sentence could be used in some of the preceding sentences, in which a prepositional use of "to" occurs prior to the key information. In addition, sentences would be included in which an adverbial use of "too" occurs, as in "I gave some apples, too, and I gave them to Susan instead of Max or Harry." By including both "to" and "too," the listener is prevented from forming a definite set for guessing that the word following /tu/ provides critical information about the receiver of the gift. In the key sentence, prosodic information on /tu/ can be appropriate for the prepositional reading when /tu/ is short, or it can be appropriate for the adverbial reading when /tu/ is much longer (see chapter 2). By varying the critical prosodic information, it should be possible to influence listeners' reaction time to answering the question about who received the oranges. When the prosodic information is appropriate for the prepositional reading, listeners are cued that the next word will contain the critical information, and their response times should be very short compared with sentences in which the prosodic information is more appropriate for the adverbial form "too."

The same testing paradigm can also be used to determine whether listeners utilize prosodic information to close off constituents for detailed perceptual processing. It is generally believed that, during on-line perception, listeners perform initial processing of each syllable as it is presented. In some cases the initial processing is actually quite sophisticated (Marslen-Wilson and Welsh, 1978; Cole, Jakimik, and Cooper, 1980). However, there also appears to be a second stage of processing during which deeper analysis is performed on the input; this stage of processing typically occurs at major syntactic boundaries (Fodor, Bever, and Garrett, 1974; Bever and Townsend, 1979). The question addressed here is whether listeners use prosodic information to determine where a major constituent ends, in order to activate this second stage of processing.

Pauses seem to be important in this regard, allowing the listener to close off a domain of information and clear the immediate storage for new information. Experiments could be designed to test the role of pausing in aiding the listener to terminate processing domains. In such experiments the dependent variable would be the subject's reaction time to make an inference judgment similar to the one required above. The experiments might manipulate pause duration in a fixed syntactic environment to disentangle the role of pausing and surface syntactic boundaries in determining when the listener will close off a processing domain (see Fodor, Bever, and Garrett, 1974). The notion that pausing enables a listener to terminate a domain of input might account for the disambiguating effect of pausing in simple surface ambiguities of the type "old men and women," as discussed in chapter 2 (Lehiste, 1973; Lehiste, Olive, and Streeter, 1976). Insertion of a pause after "men" encourages the listener to process "old men" as a self-contained noun phrase, blocking the possible modifying relation between "old" and "women." This line of reasoning could account for the perceptual results obtained by Lehiste, Olive, and Streeter (1976), described at the beginning of this section.

BLOCKING

As in the case of speech production, there exist certain attributes of speech perception that require processing over a relatively large domain. An example is the computation of speaking rate, important for the correct perception of individual phonemes (for example, Lisker and Abramson, 1967; Summerfield and Haggard, 1972). Summerfield and Haggard showed that the perception of a bilabial stop consonant as /b/ or /p/ is dependent on the rate of a phrase preceding the target phoneme. They showed, furthermore, that manipulation of the rate of this phrase affects the perception of the target stop consonant only when the linear distance between the last word of the manipulated phrase and the target is less than or equal to six syllables. This latter result suggests that listeners recompute speaking rate across a domain covering about six syllables. Our work with speech production suggests that the correct characterization of this domain may not be in terms of a number of syllables, but rather in terms of major clause or phrase units. If speaking rate is computed within such domains, it should be possible to block the effects of the rate of the carrier phrase if the target phoneme is separated from the manipulated phrase by a certain strong syntactic boundary, such as that of a major clause, regardless of how small the number of intervening syllables between the end of the manipulated phrase and the target.

Experiments could be conducted to examine independently (a) the strength of the syntactic boundary between the manipulated phrase and the target phoneme necessary to block the perception effect, and (b) the distance between the last word of the carrier phrase and the target phoneme which must be present for blocking. The outcome of these experiments should provide information about the domains of the listener's computation of speaking rate. In particular, the results should indicate whether these domains are syntactically defined, or perhaps better defined simply in terms of the number of words or phonemes. Similar experiments could be conducted to test the blocking of other interdependencies between nonadjacent words in sentence perception (for example, Meltzer et al., 1976).

PERCEPTION OF FUNDAMENTAL FREQUENCY

The method of perceptual blocking can also be applied to the study of F_0. Two experiments will be proposed, both utilizing natural speech stimuli with selectively altered F_0 contours and speaking rates. The first experiment is designed to investigate the domain over which listeners normalize for the average height of F_0 peaks. Let us assume, in line with an effect of perceptual compensation obtained by Pierrehumbert (1979), that listeners will perceive a given peak F_0 value as higher in pitch to the extent that the average value of the F_0 peaks in the utterance is low. As in the case of work on speech rate normalization, one could vary the position of a phrase whose F_0 peaks heavily influence this average peak value, to determine whether listeners normalize for average F_0 peaks over a syntactically specified domain, such as the main clause. If so, it is predicted that the carrier phrase will influence perceptual judgments of F_0 peaks in words belonging only to the same clause, regardless of the number of intervening syllables between the end of the manipulated phrase and the target.

In a related study the blocking method could be applied to the perception of F_0 at different rates of speech. Work on speech production reveals that mean F_0 values increase as a function of faster speaking rates (Cooper and Sorensen, 1980), and one could test whether perceived pitch will be normalized for speaking rate. If so, listeners should perceive a given F_0 peak as being higher in pitch as a function of slower speaking rates. By varying the position of the manipulated phrase, one could also test whether the listener's normalization for pitch in relation to speaking rate is computed over the domain of a main clause.

Finally, it would be interesting to learn whether listeners are capable of using variations in F_0 fall-rise patterns to recover and predict structural relations. For example, we would expect listeners to judge a word as ending a major clause if the word contains a major F_0 fall. This issue could be investigated using procedures analogous to those outlined earlier for testing whether listeners utilize durational information as an aid in recovering and predicting syntactic structure.

CORRELATIONS OF INDIVIDUAL DIFFERENCES IN SPEECH PERCEPTION AND PRODUCTION

In a previous study of speech timing, Klatt and Cooper (1975) obtained a preliminary result which provided support for the notion that some component of the speech processing machinery serves both production and perception. They found that individual differences in the magnitude of a just-detectable durational difference were positively correlated with the magnitude of individual durational differences in speech production for the same subjects. This finding suggests that a common control process serves both production and perception for individual subjects. It would be interesting to extend this type of correlational testing to some of the experiments described above, involving timing and F_0. By asking subjects to make perceptual judgments and productions of the same sentence materials in separate test sessions, and then by looking at the correlation between a given effect in production and perception, one could determine whether a common control process exists in speech processing. A study of individual differences in verbal learning by Suci (1967) is relevant to this issue. In the study, subjects were asked to learn and relearn material from spoken stories or word lists. Subjects were first asked to repeat the material verbatim, and their locations of pausing were marked. In a subsequent session, the subjects were asked to re-learn the material in a different order. In one condition, the reordering was accomplished by moving units bounded by pauses of the subject; in another, the reordering was accomplished by moving units bounded by the pauses of another subject which occurred in different locations. Learning was found to be more difficult when the units did not correspond to those originally segmented by the subjects' own pauses. The results suggest that individual differences in speech pausing represent part of an overall schema of individual differences in the organization of verbal material for perception and learning as well as for production.

PERCEPTION IN NOISE

It is quite possible that the listener's reliance on prosodic cues in speech perception is heightened when the acoustic environment is noisy, as in a hectic office. In such an environment, short, often unexpected noises may be particularly disruptive of the perception of individual segments or words, yet the listener is normally capable of recovering such segments with the help of prior speech contexts. By conducting some of the aforementioned experiments in settings with environmental background noises, it should be possible to determine whether listeners rely more heavily on long-term prosody in such contexts to help recover segmental information.

CONCLUSION ON PERCEPTION

In summary, there exist many issues concerning the perception of timing and F_0 that have arisen, in part, from a consideration of the present work on production. The main challenge facing perceptual research concerns the need to blend a natural listening task with means of obtaining precise information about the listener's internal processing operations. Forthcoming research of this kind should enable one to make inferences about the extent to which listeners normally utilize prosodic information in the recovery and prediction of structural relations. At the same time, such studies will provide a means of determining the extent to which many of the present findings bear task-independent relevance to normal processing by the speaker-hearer.

Lipreading

Although emphasis has been placed on normal auditory perception of speech, perception can also be aided visually by lipreading, utilized by many deaf individuals. Recently Geers (1978) has suggested that advanced deaf lipreaders make use of durational cues that are provided by lip position in segmenting speech into major syntactic units, in much the same way that normal adult listeners may utilize durational cues such as phrase-final lengthening and pausing. This conclusion was reached in a study showing that lipreaders misplace the location of a visual flash that has been superimposed on a videotape of an individual talking. The extraneous signal is typically misplaced toward the location of durational cues that normally mark major syntactic boundaries in a manner similar to normal listeners' misplacement of the location of a superimposed auditory clock (Fodor, Bever, and Garrett, 1974). In auditory speech perception, the misplacement is reduced when, by means of tapesplicing or other manipulation of the speech wave, the intonational break does not coincide with the major syntactic boundary (Wingfield and Klein, 1971; Wingfield, 1975). In analogous fashion, the misplacement effect for lipreading vanished when the visual durational cues to segmentation were displaced from the major syntactic boundary. The results suggest that advanced lipreaders normally utilize visual cues of duration to segment the speech into major syntactic units, just as normal listeners utilize auditory cues of duration provided in the speech wave.

Speech Synthesis

A major goal for communications engineering is the automatic conversion of printed text into speech. The applications of such a system are staggering, including a reading machine for the blind (Allen, 1973) and computer readout in the form of speech. The latter application would be useful in virtually all areas of business, government, medicine, and education, all of which are increasingly dependent on quick access to information stored in computer files.

A reading machine for the blind must take printed text as input, and the conversion of text to speech is hampered by the fact that printed text does not contain much information about phrase structure necessary for the implementation of syntactic-to-phonetic rules, which, in turn, appear to be necessary for easily intelligible speech. Printed commas and periods aid in marking off the most major syntactic boundaries, but these printed symbols are not sufficient cues for the implementation of the set of syntactic-to-phonetic rules required for proper intelligibility. Phenomena such as phrase-final lengthening, pausing, and fall-rise patterns of F_0 sometimes occur with considerable magnitude and consistency within major clauses as well as at the boundaries marked off in print by commas. A syntactic parser (Marcus, 1980) has been implemented as one of the early stages of the reading machine for the blind in order to provide the basis for a more complete inventory of syntactic-to-phonetic rules. However, the work on this parser has not proceeded to the stage at which one could implement the full range of effects that might improve intelligibility.

The lack of a good parser need not hinder efforts to synthesize speech by rule (Mattingly, 1968; Klatt, 1976). Such programs take as input a phonetic transcription of the intended utterance plus a well-defined syntactic parse, avoiding printed text. Although synthesis-by-rule programs are not as ambitious as programs to convert text into speech, the former satisfy the requirements for the application of computer readout in a speech format. There is an increasing use of phonetic transcription in computer files, and such files could be read out as speech by a synthesis-by-rule program.

Klatt (1975) has implemented a number of syntactic-to-phonetic rules, including rules for F_0 declination, phrase-final lengthening, and the blocking of common phonological rules such as Alveolar Flapping and Glottal Stop Insertion. Rules like Flapping must be applied across very weak syntactic boundaries and blocked at strong boundaries in order to avoid a stilted speech quality that impedes intelligibility.

According to Klatt (personal communication), one of the problems with the current system of rules involves conjoined adjectives that require different parsings, as in "very big" versus "big red," where the first adjective modifies the second adjective in the phrase "very big" but does not in the phrase "big red." Speakers produce very short durations for adjectives that modify succeeding adjectives, whereas they produce longer durations for adjectives that modify succeeding nouns. As noted in chapters 1 and 4, speakers may also insert pauses between conjoined adjectives as in "tall handsome." A simple parsing strategy cannot account for these timing effects, especially in the latter case, where the pausing is determined by the semantic relation between the two adjectives. However, because this problem is so widespread, it might be worthwhile to implement a pausing rule for conjoined adjectives of this latter type by simply inserting a comma between these adjectives in the input to the synthesis-by-rule program.

Another type of problem in synthesis is posed by parenthetical expressions, which, like conjoined adjectives, occur quite frequently in running discourse. As noted in chapter 1, parentheticals are typically set off from the sentence by pauses. In addition, such expressions are usually produced at a lower amplitude and F_0 than the main clause of the sentence. By marking parentheticals as such in the input to the program for synthesis, it would be possible to implement appropriate rules for pausing, amplitude, and F_0.

In further developments the role of emphatic stress will probably play a major role. Speakers utilize emphasis quite liberally in normal conversation; this feature lends much of the "color" to speech required to maintain a listener's attention. For long-term applications of speech synthesis, in which machine operators will be required to listen to lengthy stretches of synthetic material, the proper use of emphatic stress could make a big difference in listeners' long-term retention. More subtle variations in stress also seem important for quality synthesis, even when these are not associated with syntactic or semantic factors (see Coker, Umeda, and Browman, 1973).

When faced with the job of programming a synthesizer, one is often confronted with questions that might not arise in a purely armchair approach to the problem of syntactic-to-phonetic coding. How, for example, should phrase-final lengthening effects be applied to different segments in a word? Should all segments in the word be lengthened, and, if so, are they to be lengthened by the same percentage of their inherent duration? (See the comprehensive algorithm in chapter 7.) Interactive synthesis programming will provide a testing ground for such issues.

Programs to synthesize speech by rule are also being designed for languages other than English, and many of these programs strive to implement syntactic-to-phonetic rules, as in French (Choppy, 1978), Swedish (Lindblom and Rapp, 1973; Carlson et al., 1975), and Dutch ('t Hart and Cohen, 1973). As these efforts continue, it should be possible to determine the extent to which the rules implemented are universal versus language-particular.

Speech Recognition

Speech synthesis represents half of the total engineering goal of man-machine communication by natural language. The other half is speech recognition by machine (for example, Reddy, 1974), in which programs are designed to permit computer understanding of spoken language. This application is even more problematic than speech synthesis by rule, but there have been some remarkable advances in recent years (for a review, see Klatt, 1978).

We will discuss here one aspect of a speech recognition program that derives some justification from the results of this study. Lea (1973) observed that it is possible for a recognition program to detect major syntactic boundaries on the basis of prosodic information, particularly fundamental frequency contours. He devised a program that could correctly locate more than 80 percent of major syntactic boundaries by relying on fall-rise patterns of F_0. This syntactic representation was then used as a guide for phonetic recognition. The rationale for such top-down processing was based on the notion that the phonetic segments immediately bordering the sites of major boundaries are the most reliably represented in the speech wave; that is, their acoustic representation is relatively invariant. This observation is supported by our own studies on blocking reported in chapter 6. Recall that in this work we found that phonetic conditioning effects operate across word boundaries most frequently when such boundaries do not coincide with major syntactic boundaries. Since these conditioning effects blur the phonemic identity of the segments involved, they produce machine errors in recognition (see also Wolf and Woods, 1976). By directing the initial stages of phonetic recognition to the stressed syllables lying closest to major syntactic boundaries, Lea was able to optimize the likelihood of correct phonetic identification, and this information was then used in constraining the possible set of choices encountered in phonetic recognition of other segments. This schema does not mimic human perception, as the latter is undoubtedly guided more by immediate temporal constraints, but it does provide a way of minimizing machine errors in recognition.

Generalization to Other Behaviors and Species

American Sign Language

It is quite likely that at least some of the major phenomena discussed throughout this study are exhibited not only in speech but in other behaviors, particularly those representing other forms of communication. One of the first places to look for analogues to speech phenomena is American Sign Language (ASL), used primarily by deaf individuals. Hold patterns, in which the terminal position of a given gesture is maintained by the signer, are analogous to segmental lengthening and pausing in speech. Grosjean and Lane (1977) examined these patterns from a syntactic standpoint and found that they typically occur at major syntactic boundaries, as with lengthening and pausing in speech. In addition, Grosjean and Lane report one case in which a hold is inserted at the site of a deleted conjunction (p. 114), suggesting a generalization of the findings for speech timing in chapter 4. In future work it would be interesting to find out whether the pattern of holding at syntactic boundaries for ASL closely matches that for speech found in this study, with respect to issues such as theory of boundary strengths and the processing operations of planning and execution. If a close match does exist, then the results obtained here would reflect the operation of a cognitive system that is common to both verbal and manual modes of language production (see also Grosjean, 1979; Klima and Bellugi, 1979; Wilbur, 1979).

MUSIC

Parallels appear to exist between speech and other communicative behaviors besides American Sign Language. A good example is Western musical composition, for which, like speech, we have some idea on independent grounds about the domains of processing, including movements, stanzas, phrases, and the like. The independent grounds for boundaries in music are provided by the theory of musical composition (for example, Cooper and Meyer, 1960; Lerdahl and Jackendoff, 1977), just as independent motivation for boundaries in speech processing is provided by the theory of grammar. The unaided ear tells us that musical notes are generally longer at the ends of phrases than the average duration of notes within such phrases. This lengthening effect seems to occur with greater than chance regularity in classical and modern music of the Western world. Although a number of other factors may influence the durations of individual musical notes (as with speech segments), the phrase-final lengthening effect appears consistently throughout many compositions.

One of the more famous examples of the principle is taken from the score of Beethoven's Fifth Symphony, containing a phrase of four notes—three short followed by one long. If the ordering of the short and long notes were reversed, the phrase would sound not only unfamiliar, but, we would argue, less natural as well, other factors being equal.

In a recent article, Lindblom (1978) discusses the parallels between phrase-final lengthening in speech and Western music. Phrase-final lengthening in both poetry and music is often accomplished by catalexis, the omission of the final syllable of a metrical unit. For example, the repetition of trochaic feet, involving stressed-unstressed syllable pairs, may be subjected to catalexis so that the final syllable of a phrase is stressed (and hence durationally long). Lindblom notes that catalexis is used commonly in Western music, including folk melodies and nursery rhymes in both Swedish and English.

At the end of this chapter we will suggest that phrase-final lengthening is built into the structure of English, as reflected by words in frozen conjuncts (for example, "hem and haw"). Lindblom notes that phrase-final lengthening is also built into the structure of Western music, by notational devices such as the *fermata* and *ritardando.* The *fermata,* or hold, represents a structural indication to prolong a note beyond its nominal value. The *ritardando,* on the other hand, indicates a gradual slowing of tempo beyond that specified by the nominal metrical form. It is observed that both of these devices occur primarily in phrase-final position, paralleling the structural lengthening for frozen conjuncts in English.

TYPEWRITING

In considering other forms of human communication, skilled typewriting seems to be a likely candidate as a source of effects related to speech. Informal observations suggest that pausing in typing normally coincides with major syntactic boundaries. In a recent study, Sternberg et al. (1978) examined another parallel between speech and typing, bearing implications for motor planning. In their task, subjects were asked to begin speaking or typing on signal, and their reaction times to the initiation of speech or typing were measured as a function of variations in the number of prespecified syllables to be spoken or typed. Sternberg et al. found that the response times to initiate speech and typing lengthened with increases in the number of stress groups (speech) or keystrokes (typing) to be produced. The results suggest that the initiation of both speech and typing requires planning time to organize an overall motor program for the sequence to be produced. It would be interesting to determine whether response times to initiate meaningful sentences in both speech and typing are influenced by syntactic and semantic variables.

As for other types of skilled motor behavior in humans, very little is known about the control of timing (Stelmach, 1976; Welford, 1976). Eventually, one would like to determine whether some of the commonalities among speech and other communicative behaviors are present in noncommunicative motor skills as well.

ANIMAL COMMUNICATION

The communication systems of other species provide a few examples of phrase-final lengthening. In acoustic traces of the song phrases of the chaffinch (*Fringilla coelebs*), for example, phrase-final segments are typically longer than segments at the beginning or middle of a phrase. This claim is based on an examination of the acoustic traces published by Thorpe (1961) and Nottebohm

(1970). Unfortunately for present purposes, these and other researchers of birdsong have been generally concerned with analyzing acoustic traces in terms of the frequency domain rather than in terms of duration, and no highly systematic treatment of segment durations in birdsong has yet been published.

If the spectographic traces published by Nottebohm (1970) are representative of the durational characteristics of chaffinch song, a second major point about birdsong duration is worth noting. Phrase-final lengthening is found not only in traces of the adult song but in the earliest stage of song development as well—even for birds reared in the absence of an auditory model. If the latter condition generally applies to phrase-final lengthening, it would provide evidence that the lengthening effect is an inherent characteristic of motor programming.

In preparing this section we asked researchers of birdsong to comment on possible parallels between speech and birdsong.[1] Most respondents were quick to point out that this topic remains largely unexplored at present. They generally agreed, however, that birdsong traces show parallels to pausing and phrase-final lengthening at major syntactic boundaries. Hall-Craggs (1962; personal communication, 1978), for example, noted hints of phrase-final lengthening in the blackbird. Observations of other types of birds, however, indicate that this tendency is by no means universal.

A better documented example of phrase-final lengthening in animal communication involves chirps emitted by the insect *Amblycorypha oblongifolia*, a member of the family Orthoptera (DuMortier, 1963, p. 359). This insect produces chirp phrases consisting of four segments with successive durations averaging 8, 13, 21, and 38 msec.

In addition to birdsong and insect chirps, one might expect to find examples of phrase-final lengthening in other types of animal communication, particularly those that have been studied with some acoustic detail, including the sound emissions of the dolphin (Lilly, 1963, 1965), squirrel monkey (Winter, Ploog, and Latta, 1966), and bullfrog (Capranica, 1965), among others (see Busnel, 1963, for a review). Yet, as in the case of birdsong, research on these species has not treated segment timing systematically, but has primarily been concerned with frequency information. The results of this study on speech timing suggest, however, that a more detailed investigation of the durational parameters of animal communication systems may contribute to the understanding of the structures and processes of complex animal behavior patterns.

BLOCKING

The phenomenon of blocking, examined in chapter 6, seems intuitively to generalize to human activities ranging from American Sign Language to music, yet to our knowledge there exists no published work on blocking in these activities. Blocking may well be exhibited in many forms of animal communication also. Detailed studies of these forms of behavior may eventually permit us to determine whether the theory of boundary strengths proposed in chapter 7 includes properties common to all complex motor behaviors.

Aphasia

The very different concern to which we now turn involves the implications of this work for adult individuals with aphasia, a centralized language impairment. A few major types of aphasia can be distinguished, the most apparent occurring between patients having a primary lesion in the anterior (Broca's) or posterior (Wernicke's) regions of the language-dominant hemisphere, typically the left. Broca's aphasics have a major deficit in speech production; Wernicke's aphasics have a primary disorder in comprehension. This clinical distinction is far from absolute, however (for example, Zurif and Caramazza, 1976; Zurif and Blumstein, 1978; Blumstein et al., 1980).

For Broca's aphasics, studies of speech production suggest the presence of impairments in both syntactic and phonological processing (Zurif and Caramazza, 1976). Consequently, it is likely that such patients have impairments in the application of syntactic-to-phonetic rules of the type studied throughout this project.

This question has recently been investigated empirically. In a preliminary study, Danly, de Villiers, and Cooper (1979) examined segmental timing and F_0 in the speech of Broca's aphasics. Analyses were based on two-word utterances containing semantically related words that were selected from a corpus of spontaneous speech for three patients. Measurements of F_0 showed that a substantial fall in F_0 accompanied the end of the second word only, as would be expected if speakers had planned the two-word utterance as a unit. This effect was obtained despite the fact that the speakers occasionally produced very long pauses between the two words of an utterance—intervals up to five seconds. The results suggest that, like normals, Broca's speakers are capable of programming F_0 over domains larger than one word. In contrast to the findings for normal adults reported throughout this study, measurements of segment durations in the two-word utterances of Broca's aphasics revealed no effect of phrase-final lengthening; rather, words in utterance-initial position were actually longer in duration than their utterance-final counterparts. Similar results for both F_0 and timing were obtained when Broca's patients were asked to read short sentences containing phonetically matched key words. It is possible that the results Danly, de Villiers, and Cooper obtained for speech timing are reflective of a particular difficulty of Broca's patients associated with speech initiation. Further study of temporal control in longer utterances is necessary in order to determine whether phrase-final segments in Broca's speech are lengthened relative to phrase-medial rather than phrase-initial segments.

Prosodic features of the speech of Broca's aphasics are also of interest from a more practical standpoint—that of rehabilitation. Generally speaking, severely impaired Broca's patients seldom regain their normal language faculty, but therapy can often lead to some improvement in functioning. One type of treatment, termed Melodic Intonation Therapy (Albert, Sparks, and Helm, 1973), bears particular relevance to speech prosody. In the treatment procedure, the patient first learns to repeat short commands that bear an exaggerated intonational contour. Some patients eventually learn to utter commands and declarative sentences with nearly normal intonation. So far, this type of therapy has been systematically applied to about thirty patients over a five-year period at the Boston Veterans Administration Hospital (Sparks, Helm, and Albert, 1974; Sparks and Holland, 1976), and significant improvements have been obtained in the speech of many patients.

Wernicke's aphasics exhibit nearly normal speech prosody in comparison with Broca's aphasics (Goodglass and Geschwind, 1976), but recent experimentation with the sentence-reading procedure has revealed that the speech of Wernicke's patients is marked by abnormalities in sentential aspects of F_0 (Cooper, Danly, and Hamby, 1979). Although Wernicke's patients exhibit F_0 declination, the precise form of declination departs from the Topline Rule, and Wernicke's do not begin a longer sentence with a higher F_0 peak as normals do. On the other hand, the form of Wernicke's declination is not seriously perturbed by the presence of errors of phoneme substitution (*literal paraphasias*), which suggests that the programming of declination proceeds largely independently of the selection of proper phonemes. Further studies of both Broca's and Wernicke's patients are being conducted to determine the extent to which other aspects of their speech disorders are independent of their prosodic abnormalities. Such testing may improve our understanding of the information flow of processing operations that accompany both aphasic and normal speech.

Speech Development

The child's earliest syntactic and phonetic representations are rule-governed, yet these representations change with development throughout childhood. From the time children begin to combine words, they rely on certain syntactic rules to express semantic relations. The acquisition of most of the basic features of an adult grammar is complete by about the age of five (see Dale, 1972, and Brown, 1973, for reviews), although more subtle aspects of a mature syntactic system continue to develop well into late childhood (Chomsky, 1969; Roeper, 1978). Likewise, children's earliest utterances obey various phonetic rules, including those that govern the duration of speech segments (for reviews, see Kent, 1976, and Cooper, 1977). Infant babbling (Oller and Smith, 1977) and the one-word utterances produced by very young children (Smith, 1978) both reveal a tendency toward utterance-final lengthening in a manner similar to domain-final lengthening produced by adults, which implies that this phenomenon may be an inherent feature of speech production. Age-related differences in the temporal control of speech also exist, however. For example, the variability in speech timing (Eguchi and Hirsh, 1969; Tingley and Allen, 1975) decreases with age, as does the mean duration of segments (Smith, 1978). However, developmental studies have not yet been conducted on the relationships between children's syntactic and phonetic representations. Investigation of the syntactic-to-phonetic rules employed by children at varying levels of linguistic competence should provide a means of studying the developmental course of syntactic processing.

The sentence-reading paradigm that we have relied on for studying adult speech is inappropriate for use with young children. However, an imitation paradigm has been successfully employed by Smith (1978) to study the effects of syllable position on duration for nonsense productions of two- and four-year-old children. No significant differences in the magnitude of syllable-final lengthening were found between adults and children. However, this result may be an artifact of Smith's test materials; it is possible that the children imitated the timing pattern of the adult model by rote rather than employing their own durational rules. By presenting children instead with resynthesized versions of natural adult speech (Gold, 1977) in which the key material could be neutralized, one could insure that any timing effects produced by children are attributable to rules that comprise their own speech systems. A potential drawback of presenting tape-recorded stimuli to children involves the limiting child-experimenter interaction, often resulting in a loss of interest in the task by the child (Smith, 1978). This motivational problem could be overcome through the use of a "talking" intermediary such as a clown doll, within which a loudspeaker is concealed. With this type of test, in combination with simplified sentence materials, it should be possible to examine syntactic-to-phonetic coding in young children.

A number of specific issues seem ripe for testing. For example, Tavakolian (1978) has suggested that three- and five-year-old children tend to interpret relative clauses as if they were conjoined. A similar conclusion is reached in Matthei's (1978) study of prenominal adjectives, in which younger children preferred to analyze two prenominal adjectives conjunctively, while older children could also comprehend nonconjunctive readings. When the phrase "the second brown bear" and a series of animals are presented, children's comprehension is not impaired if a bear that is located second from the start of the array is also brown (conjunctive reading). However, when two bears in the array are brown but neither one is located in the second position, younger children have difficulty with a comprehension task in which they are to choose "the second brown bear" in the array. The two readings are shown schematically in figure 8.2 below. The findings of both Tavakolian and Matthei suggest that younger children prefer "flatter" structures—that is, conjunction as opposed to recursion. Other, nonsyntactic interpretations are of course possible here, so it becomes of special interest to examine children's production of these structures, to determine whether their produced speech reflects conjoined treatment of recursive structures.

Danly (1978) has observed the appropriateness of a speech timing analysis of children's relative and conjoined clauses in order to determine whether younger children's processing is limited to conjunction. In chapter 7 we noted that adult speakers exhibit greater lengthening at the boundary of two conjoined clauses than at the boundary between the end of an embedded relative clause and the resumption of the main clause. The absence of this difference from the productions of young children would indicate that recursive and conjoined structures are interpreted by young children as conjoined. Children's ability to distinguish the two structures could then be assessed longitudinally

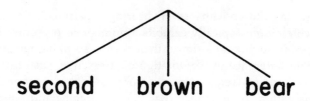

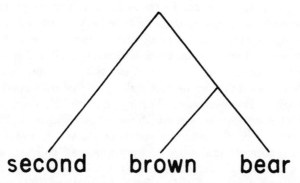

Figure 8.2 *Structural descriptions for two readings of the phrase "the second brown bear." The upper tree displays the conjunctive reading; the lower tree shows the embedded reading.*

by determining when they begin to show relatively greater segmental lengthening at the boundary between the two conjoined clauses.

Finally, it seems that children's use of syntactic-to-phonetic rules in oral reading may provide a good measure of their early reading abilities (Clay and Imlach, 1971). Children beginning to read in phrasal units would probably exhibit phrase-final lengthening when reading aloud, whereas children continuing to read word by word would not. The existence of phrase-final lengthening in oral reading may provide a good index of whether readers are learning to chunk material into appropriate phrases.

Speech Training for Hearing-Impaired Children

The study of the syntactic control of speech may also be useful in guiding efforts to train the production of appropriate prosodic features in children with a severe hearing impairment. The speech of such children typically exhibits a number of prosodic abnormalities, including (a) a slower than normal speaking rate, (b) little or no difference in the duration of stressed versus unstressed syllables, and (c) frequent insertion of pauses at inappropriate locations within the utterance (Bell, 1916; Hudgins and Numbers, 1942; John and Howarth, 1965; Hood, 1966; Houde, 1973; Stratton, 1973; Forner and Hixon, 1977). In addition, the patterns of fundamental frequency produced by hearing-impaired children may include an inappropriate range (usually too high, often in a falsetto register) and either too little or too much variation in F_0 within an utterance (for a review, see Nickerson et al., 1974).

These abnormalities can be traced in part to training programs that emphasize the production of individual words in isolation, neglecting prosodic attributes of phrase and clause units (John and Howarth, 1965; Boone, 1966; Nickerson et al., 1974). A focus on producing individual phonemes, syllables, and words is usually required during the first major phase of any speech training program; however, some hearing-impaired children proceed to a level of performance at which training on prosodic attributes in sentence contexts would be beneficial (Haycock, 1933). Fortunately, speech programs for hearing-impaired children are becoming increasingly concerned with the training of fluent speech, with an attendant emphasis on prosodic attributes (for example, Pollack, 1970; Calvert and Silverman, 1976; Ling, 1976). Further improvements in these programs are expected to yield more highly intelligible speech among advanced hearing-impaired students.

The training of proper timing and fundamental frequency at clause boundaries and other locations can be accomplished with the aid of visual feedback displays, currently in use at some schools for the deaf (Boothroyd and Decker, 1972; Houde, 1973; Osberger, 1977). In one type of display, the fundamental frequency of the child's voice can be tracked on a screen so that the child can see how this attribute varies with his own speech. With this display format, the teacher can design a game that reinforces the child for producing an utterance in which the F_0 contour falls within a given range, represented on the screen as a roadway, for example. The F_0 value may be represented visually as a car, and the child can learn to make the car stay on the road by producing an F_0 contour that is appropriate for the utterance. With this type of game the child can produce such attributes as F_0 declination that typically accompany normal speech. Similar display formats can be constructed to represent speech properties such as duration and intensity.

The intelligibility of deaf speech would certainly be improved by the elimination of pauses at inappropriate locations (Huggins, 1978). In normal speech there exist a variety of locations within phrases where pausing is typically prohibited. For example, according to the algorithm elaborated in chapter 7, pauses should not typically be inserted between a prenominal modifier and the head noun, or after a determiner, conjunction, or preposition; yet deaf children often insert long pauses at these locations as well as at the appropriate locations of major syntactic boundaries. Major improvement in intelligibility would be produced from training designed to reduce the number of pauses at inappropriate locations.

In oral reading, the elimination of pauses within major constituents might be accomplished with a training procedure that relies on explicit underlining of text (Gregory, 1979). According to this method the trainer would underline the phrase groupings in children's standard reading material and instruct the children to pause only at junctures between underlinings. The method offers the advantages of simplicity and adaptability to reading materials already present in the school.

The results of studying normal children's speech should indicate which syntactically governed features of speech should be taught to hearing-impaired children at a given developmental level. By focusing on the attributes that most improve speech intelligibility, it should be possible to teach some basic prosodic characteristics that would enable the hearing-impaired child to communicate more effectively (for example, Huggins, 1978; Osberger, 1978). The training may also serve to aid the child in becoming more aware of basic phrase structures that are useful in reading and writing.

Conclusion

In this chapter we have discussed a general program for further research on syntax and speech coding. In addition, specific topics in basic and applied research were presented for which some preliminary findings have already emerged. Despite the relatively broad scope of this chapter, many other related topics have not been included. Examples are the study of different dialects of English, other languages, and the possible interaction of syntax and prosody with extragrammatical factors, including emotional and situational factors normally studied within the province of social and personality psychology. Evidence suggests that speech timing and fundamental frequency are often influenced by such factors (for example, Williams and Stevens, 1972; Scherer et al., 1973), and further work may uncover interactions with syntactic structure. Work on this topic may in turn establish further links between cognition and social-personal aspects of behavior (for example, Carroll and Payne, 1976).

As for dialects, no studies have yet been conducted in which different dialects of English are examined systematically with respect to syntactic influences on speech timing, but future comparisons of American and British English, northern and southern American dialects, and white and black dialects should prove fruitful. It is expected, for example, that a phonological rule such as Palatalization will be blocked more readily by weak syntactic boundaries in American versus British English, and that segmental lengthening may be employed more prominently than pausing in southern versus northern dialects of American English. Within each dialect, however, a general pattern of syntactic influences is expected to conform to the system of boundary strengths adopted in chapter 7. While the absolute magnitudes of effect are expected to differ widely among the dialects, the rank magnitudes of effect across different boundary strengths is expected to remain invariant.

A number of interesting projects have appeared involving languages other than English, including French (Selkirk, 1974; Rotenberg, 1975), Italian (Napoli and Nespor, 1979), Swedish (Lindblom and Rapp, 1973), Japanese (Fujisaki and Omura, 1971), and African tone languages (Clements, 1977). In most cases, however, the relation between the design of these and other studies and our own work is not strong enough to permit inferences about the extent to which our findings represent universal features of speech.

We do observe, however, that constituent-final lengthening seems to be present not only in on-line production activity, but also in the very structure of languages. In cases where the ordering of words within a conjoined phrase is fixed, the longer word typically appears in phrase-final position, other factors being equal. In particular, conjuncts containing vowels of an inherently longer duration are frozen at the end of the conjoined phrase; examples in English are "stress and strain" and "hem and haw." The lengthening effect for frozen conjuncts appears to operate in terms of structural factors as well. Conjuncts frozen in phrase-final position also have more consonants and more syllables than conjuncts in phrase-initial position (Cooper and Ross, 1975; Pinker and Birdsong, 1979). This structural lengthening appears not only in English but also in a variety of other languages. In effect, then, elongation of phrase-final words is observed both within the structure of natural languages and during real-time speech production, paralleling the circumstances observed for Western music.

Notes

References

Index

Notes

1. Introduction

1. It is conceivable that the coding of ideas and their translation into a semantic representation do not exist as separate levels of processing, but we shall not pursue this possibility because it has no critical bearing on the discussion to follow.

2. This aspect of the model bears a resemblance to the proposal of Yngve (1960). However, Yngve's model is primarily concerned with constraints on short-term memory during the output phase of a planned utterance, whereas our model is primarily concerned with the stages of planning that begin before the onset of speech itself. In a fully elaborated model, planning operations overlap the output of speech in time to a considerable extent (see chapter 7).

3. As Downing notes, (11) must be slightly amended, however, to rule out pausing at the beginning of extraposed clauses (see also Stockwell, 1972).

4. Emonds (1976) advances the intuition that pauses (included in his term "comma intonation") accompany left and right dislocation but not topicalization and PP preposing. Our experimental data (chapter 5), however, indicate that pausing accompanies topicalization and PP preposing as well, when other factors are controlled.

5. Although we have confined the present study to oral reading, the same sentence materials could also be examined with a delayed imitation task, and comparisons of the reading and imitation tasks might provide more clues about the speaker's task-dependent planning operations (see Ingrisano and Weismer, 1979).

2. Hierarchical Coding of Major Phrases

1. The large and diverse standard deviations for the pause data suggest that nonparametric statistics would provide a better test of pause differences. We will continue to report parametric t tests for the pause data, however, since the results of such tests were comparable to the results of nonparametric tests and can be compared more easily with the

parametric statistics applied to the data for syllable segments. This choice has no bearing on the main conclusions.

2. In the original report of this experiment (Cooper, Paccia, and Lapointe, 1978), we mistakenly described the use of the proper noun in this reading as being an *appositive*. Rather, in accord with the representation in figure 2.3, speakers read "Duke James" and "Pope Carl" as nominal compounds.

3. T. G. Bever (personal communication, June 1978) has pointed out to us that the mean durations of the segments and pauses are typically longer in the paragraph contexts (table 2.1) than in the corresponding isolated sentences of earlier experiments. This trend is observed primarily for the pauses, where seven of the eight mean pause durations are longer in the paragraph contexts. For the word durations, five of the eight mean durations are longer in the paragraphs. We have no explanation for this trend, but it can conceivably be attributed to the possibility that the speakers' rate was generally faster in the experiments with isolated sentences, because these experiments always followed the experiment with paragraphs in the test session. (It will be recalled that this ordering was adopted to avoid speakers' awareness of ambiguity in the paragraph contexts.) Because of the ordering factor, the trend observed for mean durations in paragraphs versus isolated sentences is not necessarily attributable to the paragraph contexts per se.

4. According to a slightly different type of linear hypothesis, lengthening would be applied when constituent z modifies or is associated with one of two possible constituents (w of w,x) when the first word contained in w is farther away from z in the linear string than is the first word contained in x. Like the linear hypothesis discussed in the text, this hypothesis falters for cases such as (20), in which the first word of w coincides with the first word of x. In addition, both linear accounts do not lead to an explanation of the disambiguation effects of preposing constituent z, noted earlier in the text. For these reasons, among others, a hierarchical account of the experimental effects observed in this chapter seems preferable over both of these linear alternatives.

5. We thank Robert Grass for discussion of this issue.

6. Susumu Kuno (personal communication, November 29, 1978) has noted that, in addition to the effects studied here, the two readings of each of these structural ambiguities are different in the stress level of the material following the key word. In each (a) reading, this material is accompanied by lowered stress. The systematic nature of this stress difference provides another peg of support for the general notion that each of the structural ambiguities studied here belongs to the same major class. However, the observation about stress also raises the question, unanswerable at present, of whether the proper account of the speech timing effects should be formulated in terms of stress assignment or in terms of cumulative phrase-final lengthening, as proposed here. This issue could be tested by asking speakers to place varying levels of stress on the material following the key word.

3. Phrase Structures and Grammatical Categories

1. We must also assume that there is no interaction effect between grammatical category type and constituent position. This assumption is reconsidered briefly in the discussion of this experiment.

2. For present purposes, it is important to note that the effects run counter to the notion that nouns are inherently longer than verbs. In addition, the lack of systematic effects across all four sentence pairs indicates that the duration of the key word is not influenced primarily by the nature of the grammatical category of the immediately preceding word. In each sentence pair the key word was preceded by a determiner in the (a) reading and by a noun in the (b) reading. Despite the fact that minor categories such as determiner are not bounded by word boundaries, as major categories are (Chomsky and Halle, 1968), this difference does not appear to influence the duration of the immediately following word.

3. Sentences (12a) and (12b) are identical in their surface structure. Subjects were explicitly directed to consider one particular meaning when (12a) or (12b) appeared on the utterance list. In (12a) they were instructed that "the tailor passed away during the summer," and in (12b) that "the sale of the dead tailor's shop will occur during the summer."

4. The selection of verbs in this experiment included criteria in addition to the monosyllabicity required in all experiments to facilitate identification and segmentation of the waveform. Verbs in this experiment were required to either (i) take a direct or indirect object depending on the subject, or (ii) be a member of a homophonous verb pair in which one verb is transitive and the other is intransitive.

5. As pointed out by Chomsky and Halle (1968), some prepositions belong to major grammatical categories, but the preposition "to" as used in this experiment belongs to a minor category.

6. Sentence pairs (19), (21), and (22) contain ambiguous sentences. Sentence (22a), for example, can take either the reading "Ted watched the couple walk a distance of two blocks down the street" or "Ted watched the couple walk and they were two blocks down the street at the moment he watched." In general, however, it has been shown (Cooper, 1976a) that ambiguities involving semantic relations do not influence speech timing, and it is reasonable to assume that any effect due to this ambiguity is minuscule in comparison with the large effect on duration due to type of grammatical category.

4. Deletion Rules

1. The sentences used in this follow-up experiment are presented in Cooper and Sorensen (1980), appearing as sentences (31) and (32) in chapter 3. The same utterances were examined for F_0 fall-rise patterns by Cooper and Sorensen, and it was observed that the F_0 valley was lower for the key word preceding the deletion site.

5. Movement Rules

1. This rule was originally included under the rule It-Replacement (Rosenbaum, 1967). The rule must be kept distinct from a similar rule proposed to raise a subordinate subject into superordinate subject position. The latter rule converts the underlying structure of sentences like "It appeared that John was sick" into "John appeared to be sick," with "John" as the raised element.

2. Under an alternative possibility, (25′) would contain a single surface clause, with the sentence node dominating "be at breakfast" deleted by the convention of S node pruning (Ross, 1969; Hankamer, 1971; Reis, 1973). However, it appears that a Raising analysis, which preserves a two-clause structure by selectively raising the subordinate subject, is sufficient without pruning in English (see Reis, 1973). If, conversely, S node pruning is assumed, then the major result of experiment 1 to be discussed seems to have occurred at a level of processing prior to the level at which pruning occurs.

3. An alternative to the Equi-NP analysis has been proposed by Postal (1974). However, the location of the major clause boundary under his analysis remains the same as in the Equi analysis.

4. Although this analysis is assumed throughout the rest of the study, the linguistic evidence favoring at least one aspect of the analysis is less than compelling. John Robert Ross (personal communication) has pointed out that while the underlying representation of (30) may in fact take an underlying complement (the critical assumption for present purposes), the underlying complement verb may be a verb of motion rather than "to be." A main verb such as "want," used in experiment 3, does appear to require an underlying "to be" in sentences like (30), however. Ross cites as syntactic evidence of an underlying "to be" for "want" complements the existence of idioms such as "I want headway made on this by Friday" and "I want tabs kept on John." The argument applied to "headway" goes as follows: (a) terms like "headway" can occur in underlying object position but not underlying subject position ("Headway is fun"); (b) in order to derive a sentence like "I want headway made on this by Friday," it is necessary to postulate a rule moving "headway" to the left of "make"; (c) the relevant rule, Passive, requires "to be"; (d) thus, the structure of "I want headway made on this by Friday" must include an underlying "to be" which is present when Passive applies. For our speech, the same argument applies to the main verb "expect," lending support for an underlying "to be" for the complement of this main verb also.

5. Although speakers did not place contrastive stress on any syllables in the sentences, some difference in stress pattern existed between the simple sentences (c) and (e) and the other sentences because of the presence of the adjective "big" in the simple sentences. This adjective was inserted to control the total number of words across sentences. An account of the present results in terms of rhythmic groupings of stressed

syllables, however, would run counter to the stress timing prediction needed to account for the results of another experiment (Cooper, 1976a, chap. 2, experiment 2). Thus, in the absence of a more refined theory of stress timing, the syntactic account to be proposed here should be favored.

6. This and similar locations in the waveform differed to some extent depending on the recorded amplitude of the speaker's voice. An effort was made to keep the overall amplitude the same across speakers, but in cases where the amplitude was perceptibly lower for a given speaker, the amplitude display of each of the speaker's waveforms was doubled to facilitate marking of the segment boundaries. Since all comparisons of interest were across sentences within speakers, the doubling of amplitude for a few speakers allowed for a more reliable segment measuring procedure without introducing experiment bias.

7. Recall that Chomsky predicts a difference in clause boundaries between the infinitival complements of "expect" and "persuade," whereas Rosenbaum and Postal do not (see table 5.7, surface predictions). Assuming that the typical duration of /swedəd/ is longer than that of /spɛktəd/ on purely phonetic grounds (an assumption that is plausible but has not yet been tested), the finding of longer durations for /spɛktəd/ must be accounted for on syntactic grounds and would provide a strong point in favor of a performance analog of Chomsky's analysis, since on his account /spɛctəd/ is clause-final, whereas /swedəd/ is not. The difference in verb durations between /spɛktəd/ and /swedəd/ for simple sentences, however, cannot be readily attributed to a syntactic influence.

8. The only difference found for the noun "Kate" in experiment 1 that is not easily accounted for by the phonetic factor demonstrated in experiment 3 was the significant difference between EXPECT-THAT and EX-PECT-SIMPLE, for which the duration of "kate" was 13.0 msec longer before "at" than before "would." In experiment 3, a difference for "skate" before /a/ versus /w/ ("at" versus "with") in the same direction was observed, averaging 8.0 msec, but this difference failed to reach statistical significance with the relatively small $n = 10$.

9. Clark (1973) has suggested the use of variance statistics like *min F'*, where $min\ F'(i,j) = F_1 F_2 / (F_1 + F_2)$, for testing the generality of an effect across different sentence materials and different speakers using a design similar to that of experiment 3. However, because of the lack of a large data base in this experiment, it was decided to limit the analysis to computing the average durations across speakers for the sentences of each verb.

10. Since a major clause boundary existed in the complement sentences of EXPECT-type 2, an account of the single-clause lengthening for "believed" and "understood" must include some reference to a non-syntactic factor (for example, focus) whose effectiveness overrides the syntactic clause effect. Although some study of the relation between sentence stress and focus has been conducted within a transformational framework (see Akmajian and Jackendoff, 1970; Bresnan, 1971), work on

this general topic has not proceeded far enough to provide hints about the precise account of the present cases of single-clause lengthening.

6. Blocking of Phonological Rules

1. According to Bolinger (1976), this rule may be stated not as a shortening rule in the environment of a following unstressed syllable but rather as a lengthening rule in the environment of a following stressed syllable. For our purposes, the direction of the rule is irrelevant. Harris and Umeda (1974) found that the shortening effect was negligible in connected text, but this negative result may be attributed to lack of control for a number of factors.

2. The /t/ in "Clinton" was spoken as a glottal stop by some speakers. However, this cannot account for differences obtained for "Clint"-"Clinton" in the duration of the key segment /klɪn/. In experiments 1 and 2, different results are obtained for the same word pair, which can be accounted for only in terms of the structure of the syntactic boundary.

3. The possibility that blocking is only partial for a given utterance is at odds with the formulation of blocking presented in the Introduction, according to which blocking, when it occurs, should be complete because of the prohibiting of look-ahead. Thus, "partial" blocking in the present context and hereafter is assumed to represent an averaging of complete blocking and no-blocking instances for individual utterance tokens. It is also assumed that, for a given speaker and across speakers, the occurrence of blocking will depend in part on extrasyntactic factors such as speaking rate. For very fast rates, for example, it is assumed that the speaker utilizes the broadest possible syntactic domains for applying phonological rules, so that some blocking effects would be eliminated.

4. Although the data obtained with palatalization provide support for the notion that syntactic boundaries block phonological rules, it is not yet possible to determine whether the boundaries block such rules directly (by acting as junctures of processing that predict look-ahead) or whether blocking is produced by the mediating influence of a pause that often accompanies the major syntactic boundary. This issue will be tested in study 2 of this chapter.

5. Note that Selkirk's traditional formulation of juncture in terms of word boundaries, permitting two levels of boundary strength (# and # #), cannot account for the data in our study, providing impetus for the possibility that a speaker's syntactic code exerts a direct influence on the blocking of phonological rules.

6. As is shown in table 6.1, the palatalization contexts that included the proper noun "Wade" in gapped sentences (16b) and (21b) produced results very similar to results with other gapped sentences in which no proper noun accompanied the palatalization site. If sentence groups (16) and (21) are omitted from the data analysis, the same pattern of results holds.

7. Palatalization was chosen for this study over some other phonological rules because in nearly all cases its occurrence could be unequivo-

cally determined by listening. This point is confirmed below in a comparison of perceptual and acoustic analyses.

8. An analysis by speakers showed that none of the ten speakers exhibited more palatalization in the gapped sentences. Seven of the speakers showed more palatalization in the nongapped sentences, and the remaining three speakers showed no difference between the two sentence types. Two speakers from the latter group failed to palatalize any of the utterances in the experiment. Similar individual differences were observed in the other experiments of this study.

9. As noted previously, optional pausing is not the only speech wave attribute that may distinguish gapped from nongapped sentences. A small amount of segmental lengthening (see chapter 4) and an exaggerated fall in fundamental frequency (Cooper and Sorensen, 1980) also accompany the /d/-word in gapped sentences. However, evidence from experiments 4–7 suggests that phonetic manipulation of the /d/-word (including major differences in stress) produces a negligible reduction in palatalization. Phonetic manipulation of the /y/-word produces a substantial reduction, but the consistent use of unstressed pronominal adjective "your" in both gapped and nongapped sentences militates against a stress-related account of the differences observed in experiment 1.

10. The use of a pronominal /y/-word is believed to facilitate palatalization generally. This belief is in accord with the general observation that pronominals receive reduced stress and act as clitics (see, for example, Selkirk, 1972) and with the finding in experiment 2 that palatalization is reduced by emphatic stress. Our choice of /y/-words in experiment 1 and in other experiments was heavily influenced by this consideration. In addition, some possible experiments, particularly those involving other deletion sites, were excluded because the presence versus absence of a deletion was necessarily confounded with a difference in pronominal versus nonpronominal /y/-words.

The general facilitation of palatalization with "you" runs counter to the possibility, noted by Victor Zue, that palatalization is blocked when the palatalized output could be misperceived as a different word, as in the case of "you" → "Jew" (or "aid → "age"). It remains possible that such an output constraint exerts a small influence on the probability of palatalization, however.

11. It appears that the stress conditions on flapping can be relaxed when the rule applies across word boundaries.

12. Sentence (42b) may be more awkward than (42a) since the verb "bet" in (42b) is typically accompanied by a direct object. Note, however, that the (a) and (b) versions of other sentence pairs are closely matched for naturalness. The comparable results for all sentence pairs, as shown below, indicate that the blocking effects observed here cannot be attributed to greater awkwardness of (42b).

7. Theory and Further Experimentation

1. Although we use the familiar terms *serial* and *parallel* throughout this discussion, our test applies to only one of two possible types of se-

rial-parallel distinction, in which the serial model includes the condition that the output of one stage provides the input to the next (dependent model) and the parallel model includes the condition that the two stages do not interact (independent model). The serial-dependent versus parallel-independent models appear to be the most plausible processes of applying segmental lengthening in speech production (for further discussion of these general models, see Townsend, 1972).

2. Note that the same result would be obtained by applying the two stages of lengthening in the opposite serial order; that is, bottom-up. Thus, in principle our test can distinguish between serial and parallel models but not between the particular top-down and bottom-up versions of a serial model. However, top-down application is the more justifiable of the two on linguistic grounds, based on the system of rewrite rules discussed earlier.

3. We conducted an experiment to determine the relative magnitudes of segmental lengthening in utterance-final versus clause-final positions, as in sentences such as the following:

(a) Jeff will work for Paul and John will work for *Clark.*
(b) Jeff will work for *Clark* and John will work for Paul.

The data for ten speakers showed no significant differences in the duration of the key word in each of four sentence pairs ($p > 0.10$, t values ranging from 0.60 to 1.49, $df = 9$). In each case the word in utterance-final position was slightly longer, by amounts averaging from 3 to 12 percent for the four sentence pairs. The absence of significant differences between lengthening in utterance-final and in clause-final positions was replicated in another experiment using similar sentence pairs.

4. It is logically possible that any effects produced by varying the complexity of X are due to preplanning rather than to execution. According to the preplanning alternative, speakers would plan speech timing effects for the X-final segment at or before the initiation of the utterance. However, this account runs counter to the characteristics of planning observed in subsequent experiments. In particular, the duration of the X-final segment is influenced by the structural complexity of constituent X but by the general length of constituent Y. The effects observed for the influence of constituent Y must be attributed to planning on logical grounds (this constituent has not yet been spoken at the time that the key word is uttered), and since these effects are produced by variations in general length but not structural complexity, the effects of structural complexity to be described for the influence of constituent X seem to represent execution.

5. While it seems that performance factors such as planning and execution are required to provide an explanation of the direction of many of the present effects (for example, lengthening rather than shortening, blocking rather than cross-word conditioning), it is conceivable that these performance factors have become "fossilized" in modern-day speech (perhaps especially so in practiced oral reading) and that the re-

sults of our experiments actually reflect characteristics of the speaker's linguistic competence rather than performance (Chomsky, 1965). This possibility, pointed out by W. Francis Ganong (personal communication, January and November 1979), can be distinguished from the possibility that the present effects represent modern-day performance factors by conducting further studies in which nonsyntactic factors, such as constituent length and speaking rate, are systematically studied in relation to syntactic structures and possible roles of planning and execution. The preliminary results of such work favor a performance-based account.

8. Ramifications

1. We wish to thank the following researchers for their correspondence on parallels between speech and birdsong: Joan Hall-Craggs, R. E. Lemon, Peter Marler, and Keith Nelson.

References

AKMAJIAN, A., and F. HENY. 1975. *An introduction to the principles of transformational syntax.* Cambridge, Mass.: MIT Press.

AKMAJIAN, A., and R. S. JACKENDOFF, 1970. Coreferentiality and stress. *Linguistic Inquiry* 1:124–126.

ALBERT, M., R. W. SPARKS, and N. A. HELM. 1973. Melodic intonation therapy for aphasia. *Archives of Neurology* 29:130–131.

ALLEN, G. D. 1973. Segmental timing control in speech production. *Journal of Phonetics* 1:219–237.

ANDERSON, J. R. 1978. Arguments concerning representations for mental imagery. *Psychological Review* 85:249–277.

ANDERSON, S. R. 1968. Pro-sentential forms and their implications for English sentence structure. In S. Kuno, ed., *Mathematical linguistics and automatic translation.* Report NSF-24, Harvard Computation Laboratory.

ATKINSON, J. E. 1973. Aspects of intonation in speech: implications from an experimental study of fundamental frequency. Ph.D. dissertation, University of Connecticut, Storrs.

BACH, E. 1977. Review of P. M. Postal's *On Raising. Language* 53:621–654.

BAILEY, C.-J. N., and R. W. Shuy, eds. 1973. *New ways of analyzing variation in English.* Washington, D.C.: Georgetown University Press.

BAKER, C. L. 1971. Stress level and auxiliary behavior in English. *Linguistic Inquiry* 2:167–181.

BAKER, C. L., and M. K. BRAME. 1972. Global rules: a rejoinder. *Language* 48:51–75.

BARNWELL, T. P. 1971. *An algorithm for segment durations in a reading machine context.* Technological Report No. 479, Research Laboratory of Electronics, Massachusetts Institute of Technology.

BELL, A. G. 1916. *The Mechanisms of Speech.* New York: Funk and Wagnalls.

BEVER, T. G., and R. R. HURTIG. 1975. Detection of a nonlinguistic stimulus is poorest at the end of a clause. *Journal of Psycholinguistic Research* 4:1–7.

BEVER, T. G., and D. J. TOWNSEND. 1979. Perceptual mechanisms and formal properties of main and subordinate clauses. In W. E. Cooper and E. C. T. Walker, eds., *Sentence processing: psycholinguistic studies presented to Merrill Garrett.* Hillsdale, N.J.: Lawrence Erlbaum Associates, pp. 159–226.

BIERWISCH, M. 1966. Regeln für die Intonation deutscher Sätze. *Studia Grammatica* 7:99–201.

BLUMSTEIN, S. E., W. E. COOPER, H. GOODGLASS, S. STATLENDER, and J. GOTTLIEB. 1980. Production deficits in aphasia: a voice-onset time analysis. *Brain and Language* 9:153–170.

BOLINGER, D. 1964. Intonation as a universal. In *Proceedings of Linguistics IX.* The Hague: Mouton, pp. 833–844.

———. 1976. Length, vowel, juncture. *Bilingual Review* 3:43–61.

BOOMER, D. S. 1965. Hesitation and grammatical encoding. *Language and Speech* 8:148–158.

BOONE, D. R. 1966. Modification of the voices of deaf children. *Volta Review* 68:686–694.

BOOTHROYD, A., and M. DECKER. 1972. Control of voice pitch by the deaf. An experiment using a visible pitch device. *Audiology* 11: 343–353.

BORKIN, A. 1973. To be and not to be. In C. Corum, T. C. Smith-Stark, and A. Weiser, eds., *Papers from the Ninth Regional Meeting of the Chicago Linguistic Society,* pp. 44–56.

BRESNAN, J. W. 1971. Sentence stress and syntactic transformation. *Language* 47:257–281.

———. 1972. The theory of complementation in English syntax. Ph.D. dissertation, Massachusetts Institute of Technology.

———. 1976. Non-arguments for raising. *Linguistic Inquiry* 7:485–501.

BROWN, R. W. 1973. *A first language: the early stages.* Cambridge, Mass.: Harvard University Press.

BROWN, R., and U. BELLUGI. 1964. Three processes in the child's acquisition of syntax. *Harvard Educational Review* 34:138–140.

BUSNEL, R.-G. 1963. *Acoustic behavior of animals.* Amsterdam: Elsevier.

CALVERT, D., and R. SILVERMAN. 1976. *Speech and deafness.* Washington, D.C.: A. G. Dell Association.

CAPRANICA, R. R. 1965. *The evoked vocal response of the bullfrog.* Cambridge, Mass.: MIT Press.

CARLSON, R., Y. ERIKSON, B. GRANSTROM, B. LINDBLOM, and K. RAPP. 1975. Neutral and emphatic stress patterns in Swedish. In G. Fant, ed., *Proceedings of the Speech Communication Seminar.* Stockholm: Almquist & Wiksell, 2:209–218.

CARROLL, J. S., and J. W. PAYNE. 1976. *Cognition and social behavior.* Hillsdale, N.J.: Lawrence Erlbaum Associates.

CARROLL, J. M., and M. K. TANENHAUS. 1978. Functional clauses and sentence segmentation. *Journal of Speech and Hearing Research* 21:793–808.

CEDERGREN, H. J., and D. SANKOFF. 1974. Variable rules: performance as a statistical reflection of competence. *Language* 50:333–355.

CHOMSKY, C. 1969. *The acquisition of syntax in children from 5 to 10.* Cambridge, Mass.: MIT Press.

CHOMSKY, N. 1957. *Syntactic structures.* The Hague: Mouton.

———. 1965. *Aspects of the theory of syntax.* Cambridge, Mass.: MIT Press.

———. 1970. Remarks on nominalization. In R. Jacobs and P. S. Rosenbaum, eds., *Readings in English transformational grammar.* Waltham, Mass.: Ginn.

———. 1973. Conditions on transformations. In S. R. Anderson and P. Kiparsky, eds., *A Festschrift for Morris Halle.* New York: Holt, Rinehart and Winston, pp. 232–285.

———. 1977. On wh-movement. In A. Akmajian, P. Culicover, and T. Wasow, eds., *Formal syntax.* New York: Academic Press.

CHOMSKY, N., and M. HALLE. 1968. *The sound pattern of English.* New York: Harper and Row.

CHOPPY, C. 1978. Prosodic features connected to punctuations: some cases with commas. *Journal of the Acoustical Society of America* 63:585.

CLARK, H. H. 1973. The language-as-fixed-effect fallacy: a critique of language statistics in psychological research. *Journal of Verbal Learning and Verbal Behavior* 12:335–359.

CLARK, H. H., and E. V. CLARK. 1977. *Psychology and language: an introduction to psycholinguistics.* New York: Harcourt Brace Jovanovich.

CLAY, M. M., and R. H. IMLACH. 1971. Juncture, pitch, and stress as reading behavior variables. *Journal of Verbal Learning and Verbal Behavior* 10:133–139.

CLEMENTS, G. W. 1977. Tone and syntax and ewe. In D. J. Napoli, ed., *Tone, stress, and intonation.* Washington, D.C.: Georgetown University Press.

COHEN, A., and J. 't HART. 1967. On the anatomy of intonation. *Lingua* 19:177–192.

COKER, C. H., N. UMEDA, and C. P. BROWMAN. 1973. Automatic synthesis from ordinary English text. *IEEE Transactions on Audio and Electroacoustics,* AU-21, 293–297.

COLE, R. A. 1973. Listening for mispronunciations: a measure of what we hear during speech. *Perception and Psychophysics* 14:153–156.

COLE, R. A., J. JAKIMIK, and W. E. COOPER. 1978. Perceptibility of phonetic features in fluent speech. *Journal of the Acoustical Society of America* 64:44–56.

———. 1980. Segmenting speech into words. *Journal of the Acoustical Society of America* 67:1323–1332.

COOPER, G. W., and L. B. MEYER, 1960. *The rhythmic structure of music.* Chicago: University of Chicago Press.

COOPER, W. E. 1976a. Syntactic control of timing in speech production. Ph.D. dissertation, Massachusetts Institute of Technology.

———. 1976b. Inclusions. *Lingua* 40:203–222.

———. 1977. The development of speech timing. In S. J. Segalowitz and F. A. Gruber, eds., *Language development and neurological theory.* New York: Academic Press, pp. 357–373.

———. 1979 *Speech perception and production: studies in selective adaptation.* Norwood, N.J.: Ablex Publishing Corporation.

———. 1980. Syntactic-to-phonetic coding. In B. Butterworth, ed., *Language production,* volume 1: *Speech and talk.* New York: Academic Press, pp. 297–333.

COOPER, W. E., and J. PACCIA-COOPER. 1978. Unpublished data.

COOPER, W. E., M. DANLY, and S. HAMBY. 1979. Fundamental frequency (F_0) attributes in the speech of Wernicke's aphasics. In J. J. Wolf and D. H. Klatt, eds., *Speech communication papers presented at the 97th meeting of the Acoustical Society of America*. New York: Acoustical Society of America, pp. 265–270.

COOPER, W. E., C. EGIDO, and J. M. PACCIA. 1978. Grammatical control of a phonological rule: palatalization. *Journal of Experimental Psychology: Human Perception and Performance* 4:264–272.

COOPER, W. E., S. G. LAPOINTE, and J. M. PACCIA. 1977. Syntactic blocking of phonological rules in speech production. *Journal of the Acoustical Society of America* 61:1314–20.

COOPER, W. E., J. M. PACCIA, and S. G. LAPOINTE. 1978. Hierarchical coding in speech timing. *Cognitive Psychology* 10:154–177.

COOPER, W. E., and J. R. ROSS. 1975. World order. In R. E. Grossman, L. J. San, and T. J. Vance, eds., *Papers from the parasession on functionalism*. Chicago: Chicago Linguistic Society, pp. 63–111.

COOPER, W. E., and J. M. SORENSEN. 1977. Fundamental frequency contours at syntactic boundaries. *Journal of the Acoustical Society of America* 62:683–692.

———. 1980, in press. *Fundamental frequency in sentence production*. New York: Springer-Verlag.

COOPER, W. E., J. M. SORENSEN, and J. M. PACCIA. 1977. Correlations of duration for non-adjacent segments in speech: aspects of grammatical coding. *Journal of the Acoustical Society of America* 61:1046–50.

CUTLER, A. 1976. Phoneme-monitoring reaction time as a function of preceding intonation contour. *Perception and Psychophysics* 20:55–60.

DALE, P. S. 1972. *Language development: structure and function*. New York: Holt, Rinehart and Winston.

DANLY, M. 1978. A proposal for studying the encoding of syntax in the speech of children. Unpublished manuscript, Harvard University.

———. 1980. The *wh*-movement transformation and speech timing. Manuscript in preparation.

DANLY, M., and W. E. COOPER. 1978. Unpublished data.

———. 1979, in press. Sentence production: closure vs. initiation of constituents. *Linguistics*.

———. Forthcoming. Segmental and temporal aspects of phrase-final lengthening. *Phonetica*.

DANLY, M., J. G. DE VILLIERS, and W. E. COOPER. 1979. Control of speech prosody in Broca's aphasia. In J. J. Wolf and D. H. Klatt, eds., *Speech communication papers presented at the 97th meeting of the Acoustical Society of America*. New York: Acoustical Society of America, pp. 265–270.

DELATTRE, P. 1966. A comparison of syllable length conditioning among languages. *International Review of Applied Linguistics*, 4:183–198.

DOUGHERTY, R. 1970. A grammar of coordinate conjoined structures. *Foundations of Language* 46:850–898.

DOWNING, B. T. 1970. Syntactic structures and phonological phrasing in English. Ph.D. dissertation, University of Texas, Austin.

————. 1973. Parenthesization rules and obligatory pausing. *Papers in Linguistics* 6:108–128.

DuMORTIER, B. 1963. The physical characteristics of sound emissions in arthropoda. In R. G. Busnel, ed., *Acoustic behavior of animals*. Amsterdam: Elsevier, pp. 346–373.

EGIDO, C., and W. E. COOPER. 1979, in press. Syntactic blocking of alveolar flapping in speech production: the role of syntactic boundaries and deletion sites. *Journal of Phonetics*.

EGUCHI, S., and I. J. HIRSH. 1969. Development of speech sounds in children. *Acta Otolaryngolica*, supplement no. 257.

EMONDS, J. E. 1970. Root and structure-preserving transformations. Ph.D. dissertation, Massachusetts Institute of Technology.

————. 1976. *A transformational approach to English syntax: root structure-preserving, and local transformations*. New York: Academic Press.

FAY, D. 1977. Transformational errors. Unpublished manuscript prepared for the working group on "Slips of the Tongue and Ear," 12th International Congress of Linguistics, August 31–September 2, 1977, Vienna, Austria.

————. 1980. Performing transformations. In R. A. Cole, ed., *Perception and production of fluent speech*. Hillsdale, N.J.: Lawrence Erlbaum Associates, pp. 441–468.

FODOR, J. D. 1977. *Semantics: theories of meaning in generative grammar*. New York: Thomas Y. Crowell.

FODOR, J. A., T. G. BEVER, and M. F. GARRETT. 1974. *The psychology of language: an introduction to psycholinguistics and generative grammar*. New York: McGraw-Hill.

FODOR, J. A., J. D. FODOR, M. F. GARRETT, and J. R. LACKNER. 1974. Effects of surface and underlying clausal structure on click location. Unpublished manuscript.

FOLKINS, J. W., C. J. MILLER, and F. D. MINIFIE. 1975. Rhythm and syllable timing in phrase level stress patterning. *Journal of Speech and Hearing Research* 18:739–753.

FONAGY, I., and K. MAGDICS. 1960. Speed of utterance in phrases of different lengths. *Language and Speech* 3:179–192.

FORD, M. 1978. Planning units and syntax in sentence production. Ph.D. dissertation, University of Melbourne.

FORD, M., and V. M. HOLMES. 1978. Planning units and syntax in sentence production. *Cognition* 6:35–53.

FORNER, L. L., and T. J. HIXON. 1977. Respiratory kinematics in profoundly hearing-impaired speakers. *Journal of Speech and Hearing Research* 20:373–408.

FORSTER, K. I. 1966. Left to right processes in the construction of sentences. *Journal of Verbal Learning and Verbal Behavior* 5:285–291.

————. 1967. Sentence completion latencies as a function of constituent structure. *Journal of Verbal Learning and Verbal Behavior* 6:878–883.

FOSS, D. J. 1969. Decision processes during sentence comprehension: effects of lexical item difficulty and position upon decision times. *Journal of Verbal Learning and Verbal Behavior* 8:457–462.

FOWLER, C. A. 1977. Timing control in speech production. Ph.D. dissertation, University of Connecticut, Storrs. Also available from Indiana Linguistics Club.

FRASER, J. B. 1970. A reply to "On declarative sentences." In S. Kuno, ed., *Mathematical linguistics and automatic translation*. Report NSF-24, Harvard Computation Laboratory.

FROMKIN, V. A. 1971. The non-anomalous nature of anomalous utterances. *Language* 47:27–52.

FRY, D. B. 1957. Duration and intensity as physical correlates of linguistic stress. *Journal of the Acoustical Society of America* 27:765–768.

FUGISAKI, H., and T. OMURA. 1971. Characteristics of duration of pauses and speech segments in connected speech. *Annual Report, Engineering Research Institute*, Faculty of Engineering, Univeristy of Tokyo, 30:69–74.

GARRETT, M. F. 1975. The analysis of sentence production. In G. Bower, ed., *Advances in learning theory and motivation*, vol. 9. New York: Academic Press, pp. 133–177.

GEERS, A. E. 1978. Intonation contour and syntactic structure as predictions of apparent segmentation. *Journal of Experimental Psychology: Human Perception and Performance* 4:273–283.

GOLD, B. 1977. Digital speech networks. *Proceedings of the Institute of Electronics and Electrical Engineering* 65:1636–58.

GOLDMAN-EISLER, F. 1968. *Psycholinguistics: experiments in spontaneous speech*. New York: Academic Press.

———. 1972. Pauses, clauses, and sentences. *Language and Speech* 15:103–113.

GOODGLASS, H., and N. GESCHWIND. 1976. Language disorders (aphasia). In E. C. Carterette and M. P. Friedman, eds., *Handbook of perception: VIII, language and speech*. New York: Academic Press, pp. 389–428.

GOODGLASS, H., and J. HUNT. 1958. Grammatical complexity and aphasic speech. *Word* 14:197–207.

GREGORY, J. 1979. Some proposed studies investigating the speech and reading of the hearing-impaired. Unpublished manuscript, Harvard University.

GRINDER, J. 1971. Chains of coreference. *Linguistic Inquiry* 2:183–202.

GROSJEAN, F. 1979. A study of timing in a manual and a spoken language: American Sign Language and English. *Journal of Psycholinguistic Research* 8:379–405.

GROSJEAN, F., and M. COLLINS. 1979. Breathing, pausing, and reading. *Phonetica* 36:98–114.

GROSJEAN, F., and A. DESCHAMPS. 1975. Analyse contrastive des variables temporelles de l'anglais et du français: vitesse de parole et variables composantes, phenomènes d'hésitation. *Phonetica* 31:144–184.

GROSJEAN, F., L. GROSJEAN, and H. LANE. 1979. The patterns of silence: performance structures in sentence production. *Cognitive Psychology* 11:58–81.

GROSJEAN, F., and H. LANE. 1977. Pauses and syntax in American Sign Language. *Cognition* 5:101–117.

HALL-CRAGGS, J. 1962. The development of song in the blackbird (*turdus merula*). *Ibis* 104:277–300.

HANKAMER, J. 1971. Constraints on deletion in syntax. Ph.D. dissertation, Yale University.

HANKAMER, J., and I. SAG. 1976. Deep and surface anaphora. *Linguistic Inquiry* 7:391–426.

HARNETT, D. L. 1975. *Introduction to statistical methods*, 2d ed. Reading, Mass.: Addison-Wesley.

HARRIS, M. S., and N. UMEDA. 1974. Effect of speaking mode on temporal factors in speech: vowel duration. *Journal of the Acoustical Society of America* 56:1016–18.

HAYCOCK, G. S. 1933. *The teaching of speech.* Washington, D.C.: Volta Bureau.

HENDERSON, A., F. GOLDMAN-EISLER, and A. SKARBEK. 1965. The common value of pausing time in spontaneous speech. *Quarterly Journal of Experimental Psychology* 17:343–345.

HOOD, R. B. 1966. Some physical concomitants of the perception of speech rhythm of the deaf. Ph.D. dissertation, Stanford University.

HOUDE, R. A. 1973. Instantaneous visual feedback in speech training for the deaf. Paper presented at Convention of American Speech and Hearing Association, October 1973.

HOUSE, A. 1961. On vowel duration in English. *Journal of the Acoustical Society of America* 33:1174–78.

HUDGINS, C. V., and F. C. NUMBERS. 1942. An investigation of the intelligibility of the speech of the deaf. *Genetic Psychology Monographs* 25:289–392.

HUDSON, R. A. 1976. Conjunction reduction, gapping, and right-node raising. *Language* 52:535–562.

HUGGINS, A. W. F. 1969. A facility for studying perception of timing in natural speech. *Quarterly Progress Report of the M.I.T. Research Laboratory of Electronics* 95:81–83.

———. 1972. Just-noticeable difference for segment duration in natural speech. *Journal of the Acoustical Society of America* 51:1270–78.

———. 1974. An effect of syntax on syllable timing. *Quarterly Progress Report of the M.I.T. Research Laboratory of Electronics*, 114:179–185.

———. 1975. On isochrony and syntax. In G. Fant and M. A. A. Tathan, eds., *Auditory analysis and perception of speech.* New York: Academic Press, pp. 455–464.

———. 1978. Speech timing and intelligibility. In J. Requin, ed., *Attention and performance VII.* Hillsdale, N.J.: Lawrence Erlbaum Associates, pp. 279–297.

HYMAN, L. M. 1975. *Phonology: theory and analysis.* New York: Holt, Rinehart and Winston.

INGRISANO, D., and C. WEISMER. 1979. s duration: methodological influences and linguistic variables. *Phonetica* 36:32–43.

JACKENDOFF, R. S. 1971. Gapping and related rules. *Linguistic Inquiry* 2:21–35.

————. 1972. *Semantic interpretation in generative grammar.* Cambridge, Mass.: MIT Press.

————. 1973. The base rules for prepositional phrases. In S. R. Anderson and P. Kiparsky, eds., *A Festschrift for Morris Halle.* New York: Holt, Rinehart and Winston, pp. 345–356.

————. 1974. *An introduction to $\bar{X}$ notation.* Indiana University Linguistic Club Papers.

————. 1977. $\bar{X}$ *syntax: a study of phrase structure.* Cambridge, Mass.: MIT Press.

JOHN, J. E. J., and J. N. HOWARTH. 1965. The effect of time distortions on the intelligibility of deaf children's speech. *Language and Speech* 8:127–134.

KATZ, J. J. 1974. *Semantic theory.* New York: Harper & Row.

KENT, R. D. 1976. Anatomical and neuromuscular maturation of the speech mechanism: evidence from acoustic studies. *Journal of Speech and Hearing Research* 19:421–447.

KEYSER, S. J., and P. M. POSTAL. 1976. *Beginning English Grammar.* New York: Harper and Row.

KING, H. V. 1970. On blocking the rules for contraction in English. *Linguistic Inquiry* 1:134–136.

KLATT, D. H. 1975. Vowel lengthening is syntactically determined in a connected discourse. *Journal of Phonetics* 3:129–140.

————. 1976. Structure of a phonological rule component for a synthesis by rule program. *IEEE Transactions on Acoustics, Speech, and Signal Processing* 24:391–398.

————. 1977. Review of the ARPA speech understanding project. *Journal of the Acoustical Society of America* 62:1345–66.

KLATT, D. H., and W. E. COOPER. 1975. Perception of segment duration in sentence contexts. In A. Cohen and S. G. Nooteboom, eds., *Structure and process in speech perception.* Heidelberg: Springer-Verlag, pp. 69–89.

KLIMA, E. S., and U. BELLUGI. 1979. *The signs of language.* Cambridge, Mass.: Harvard University Press.

KLOKER, D. 1975. Vowel and sonorant lengthening as cues to phonological phrase boundaries. *Journal of the Acoustical Society of America* 57:S33 (abstract).

KOOIJ, J. G. 1971. *Ambiguity in natural language.* Amsterdam: North-Holland.

KOUTSOUDAS, A. 1971. Gapping, conjunction reduction, and coordinate deletion. *Foundations of Language* 7:337–386.

KOZHEVNIKOV, V. A., and L. A. CHISTOVICH, 1965. *Speech: articulation and perception.* Washington, D.C.: Joint Publications Research Service 30, 543, U.S. Dept. of Commerce.

KUČERA, H., and W. N. FRANCIS. 1967. *Computational analysis of present-day American English.* Providence, R.I.: Brown University Press.

KUNO, S. 1975. Three perspectives in the functional approach to syntax. In R. E. Grossman, L. J. San, and T. J. Vance, eds., *Papers from the parasession on functionalism.* Chicago: Chicago Linguistic Society, pp. 276–336.

LABOV, W. 1969. Contraction deletion and inherent variability of the English copula. *Language* 45:715–762.

LAFERRIERE, M., and V. ZUE. 1977. The flapping rule in American English: an acoustic study. *Journal of the Acoustical Society of America* 61:S31 (abstract).

LAKOFF, G. 1970. Global rules. *Language* 46:627–639.

LANGACKER, R. W. 1974. Movement rules in functional perspective. *Language* 50:630–664.

LANGENDOEN, D. T. 1976. Finite-state parsing of phrase-structure languages and the status of readjustment rules in grammar. *Linguistic Inquiry* 6:533–554.

LASNIK, H. 1972. Analyses of negation in English. Ph.D. dissertation, Massachusetts Institute of Technology.

LEA, W. A. 1973. An approach to syntactic recognition without phonemics. *IEEE Transactions on Audio and Electroacoustics*, AU-21, 249–258.

LEHISTE, I., ed. 1967. *Readings in acoustic phonetics.* Cambridge, Mass.: MIT Press.

LEHISTE, I. 1970. *Suprasegmentals.* Cambridge, Mass.: MIT Press.

———. 1972. Timing of utterances and linguistic boundaries. *Journal of the Acoustical Society of America* 51:2018–24.

———. 1973. Phonetic disambiguation of syntactic ambiguity. *Glossa* 7:107–122.

———. 1977. Isochrony reconsidered. *Journal of Phonetics* 5:253–263.

LEHISTE, I., J. P. OLIVE, and L. A. STREETER. 1976. Role of duration in disambiguating syntactically ambiguous sentences. *Journal of the Acoustical Society of America* 60:1199–1202.

LERDAHL, F., and R. JACKENDOFF. 1977. Toward a formal theory of tonal music. *Journal of Music Theory*, Spring 1977, 111–171.

LEVELT, W. J. M., W. ZWANENBURG, and G. R. E. OUWENEEL. 1970. Ambiguous surface structure and phonetic form in French. *Foundations of Language* 6:260–273.

LIBERMAN, M. 1975. The intonational system of English. Ph.D. dissertation, Massachusetts Institute of Technology.

LIBERMAN, M. Y., and L. STREETER. 1976. Use of nonsense syllable mimicry in the study of prosodic phenomena. *Journal of the Acoustical Society of America* 60:S27 (abstract).

LIEBERMAN, P. 1963. Some effects of semantic and grammatical context on the production and perception of speech. *Language and Speech,* 6:172–187.

———. 1967. *Intonation, perception, and language.* Cambridge, Mass.: MIT Press.

LIGHTFOOT, M. J. 1970. Accent and time in descriptive prosody. *Word* 26:47–64.

LILLY, J. C. 1963. Distress call of the bottlenose dolphin: stimuli and evoked behavioral responses. *Science* 139:116–118.

———. 1965. Vocal mimicry in *Tursiops:* ability to match number and durations of human vocal bursts. *Science* 147:300–301.

LINDBLOM, B. 1964. A note on segment duration in Swedish polysyllables.

Quarterly Progress Status Report, Speech Transmission Laboratory, K.T.H. Stockholm, 1.

————. 1978. Final lengthening in speech and music. Paper read at a symposium on the prosody of the Nordic language, Lund, June 1978.

LINDBLOM, B., and K. RAPP. 1973. Some temporal regularities of spoken Swedish. *Papers from the Institute of Linguistics,* University of Stockholm, Publication 21.

LING, D. 1976. *Speech and the hearing-impaired child: theory and practice.* Washington, D.C.: A. G. Bell Association.

LISKER, L., and A. S. ABRAMSON. 1967. Some effects of context on voice onset time in English stops. *Language and Speech* 10:1–28.

LOUNSBURY, F. G. 1954. Transitional probability, linguistic structure, and systems of habit-family hierarchies. In C. E. Osgood and T. A. Sebeok, eds., *Psycholinguistics: a survey of theory and research problems.* Bloomington: Indiana University Press.

LYBERG, B. 1979. Final lengthening—partly a consequence of restrictions on the speed of fundamental frequency change? *Journal of Phonetics* 7:187–196.

MACCLAY, H., and C. E. OSGOOD. 1959. Hesitation phenomena in spontaneous English speech. *Word* 1:19–44.

MCALLISTER, R. 1971. Predicting physical aspects of English stress. *Quarterly Progress Report,* Speech Transmission Laboratory, Royal Institute of Technology, Stockholm, 1:20–29.

MCCAWLEY, J. D. 1968. The role of semantics in grammar. In E. Bach and R. Harms, eds., *Universals in Linguistic Theory.* New York: Holt, Rinehart and Winston, pp. 125–169.

MCNEILL, D. 1979. *The conceptual basis of language.* Hillsdale, N.J.: Lawrence Erlbaum Associates.

MAEDA, S. 1976. A characterization of American English intonation. Ph.D. dissertation, Massachusetts Institute of Technology.

MARCUS, M. P. 1980. *A theory of syntactic recognition for natural language.* Cambridge, Mass.: MIT Press.

MARSLEN-WILSON, W. D. 1975. Sentence processing as an interactive process. *Science* 189:226–228.

MARSLEN-WILSON, W. D., and A. WELSH. 1978. Processing interactions and lexical access during word recognition in continuous speech. *Cognitive Psychology* 10:29–63.

MARTIN, J. E. 1969. Semantic determinants of preferred adjective order. *Journal of Verbal Learning and Verbal Behavior* 8:697–704.

MARTIN, J. E., B. KOLODZIEJ, and J. GENAY. 1971. Segmentation of sentences into phonological phrases as a function of constituent length. *Journal of Verbal Learning and Verbal Behavior* 10:226–233.

MARTIN, J. G. 1967. Hesitations in the speaker's production and listener's reproduction of utterances. *Journal of Verbal Learning and Verbal Behavior* 6:903–909.

————. 1970. On judging pauses in spontaneous speech. *Journal of Verbal Learning and Verbal Behavior* 9:75–78.

————. 1971. Some acoustic and grammatical features of spontaneous speech. In D. J. Horton and J. J. Jenkins, eds., *The perception of language.* Columbus, Ohio: C. E. Merrill.

———. 1972. Rhythmic (hierarchical) versus serial structure in speech and other behaviors. *Psychological Review* 79:487–509.

MATTHEI, E. M. 1978. The acquisition and ordering of prenominal modifiers: a preliminary report. Paper presented at the April 1978 Language Acquisition Workshop, University of Massachusetts, Amherst.

MATTINGLY, I. G. 1968. Synthesis by rule of general American English. Ph.D. dissertation. University of Connecticut, Storrs.

MELTZER, R. H., J. G. MARTIN, C. B. MILLS, D. L. IMHOFF, and D. ZOHAR. 1976. Reaction time to temporally-displaced phoneme targets in continuous speech. *Journal of Experimental Psychology: Human Perception and Performance* 2:277–290.

NAPOLI, D. J., and M. NESPOR. 1979. The syntax of word-initial consonant gemination in Italian. *Language* 55:812–841.

NASH, R. 1970. John likes Mary more than Bill. *Phonetica* 22:170–188.

NICKERSON, R. S., K. N. STEVENS, A. BOOTHROYD, and A. ROLLINS. 1974. *Some observations on timing in the speech of deaf and hearing speakers.* Bolt Baranek and Newman, Inc., Report No. 2905.

NOOTEBOOM, S. G. 1973. The perceptual reality of some prosodic durations. *Journal of Phonetics* 1:25–45.

NOOTEBOOM S. G., and DOODEMAN, J. N. 1980. Production and perception of vowel length in spoken sentences. *Journal of the Acoustical Society of America* 67:276–287.

NOTTEBOHM, F. 1970. Ontogeny of bird song. *Science* 167:950–956.

OHALA, J. J. 1975. The temporal regulation of speech. In G. Fant and M. A. A. Tatham, eds., *Auditory analysis and perception of speech.* New York: Academic Press, pp. 431–453.

OLLER, D. K., and B. L. SMITH. 1977. Effect of final-syllable position on vowel duration in infant babbling. *Journal of the Acoustical Society of America* 62:994–997.

OSBERGER, M. J. 1977. Correction of deviant timing patterns in deaf children's speech using computer techniques. *Journal of the Acoustical Society of America* 61:S8 (abstract).

———. 1978. The effect of timing errors on the intelligibility of deaf children's speech. *Journal of the Acoustical Society of America* 63:534.

O'SHAUGHNESSY, D. 1976. Modelling fundamental frequency, and its relationship to syntax, semantics, and phonetics. Ph.D. dissertation, Massachusetts Institute of Technology.

OSHIKA, B. T., V. W. ZUE, R. V. WEEKS, H. NEU, and J. AURBACH. 1975. The role of phonological rules in speech understanding research. *IEEE Transactions on Acoustics, Speech, and Signal Processing* 23:104–112.

PACCIA-COOPER, J., and W. E. COOPER. 1980, in press. The processing of phrase structures in speech production. In P. D. Eimas and J. L. Miller, eds., *Perspectives on the study of speech.* Hillsdale, N.J.: Lawrence Erlbaum Associates.

PETERSON, G. E., and I. LEHISTE. 1960. Duration of syllabic nuclei in English. *Journal of the Acoustical Society of America* 32:693–703.

PIERREHUMBERT, J. 1979. Intonation synthesis based on metrical grids. In J. J. Wolf and D. H. Klatt, eds., *Speech communication papers presented to the 97th meeting of the Acoustical Society of America.* New York: Acoustical Society of America, pp. 523–526.

PINKER, S., and D. BIRDSONG. 1979. Speaker's sensitivity to rules of frozen word order. *Journal of Verbal Learning and Verbal Behavior* 18:497–508.

POLLACK, D. 1970. *Educational audiology for the hearing-impaired infant.* Springfield, Ill.: C. C. Thomas.

POSNER, M. I. 1973. *Cognition: an introduction.* Glenview, Ill.: Scott, Foresman and Company.

POSTAL, P. M. 1974. *On raising: one rule of English grammar and its theoretical implications.* Cambridge, Mass.: MIT Press.

REDDY, D. R., ed. 1974. *Speech understanding systems.* New York: Academic Press.

REIS, M. 1973. Is there a rule of subject-to-object raising in German? In C. Coru, T. C. Smith-Stark, and A. Weiser, eds., *Papers from the Ninth Regional Meeting of the Chicago Linguistic Society.* Chicago: Chicago Linguistic Society.

ROBINSON, J. J. 1973. Predicting phonological phrases. Unpublished manuscript, University of Michigan, Ann Arbor.

————. 1975. Performance grammars. In D. R. Reddy, ed., *Speech recognition: invited papers presented at the 1974 IEEE Symposium.* New York: Academic Press.

ROEPER, T. 1978. A lexical approach to language acquisition. Paper presented at the April 1978 Language Acquisition workshop, University of Massachusetts, Amherst.

ROSENBAUM, P. S. 1967. *The grammar of English Predicate Complement Constructions.* Cambridge, Mass.: MIT Press.

ROSENBERG, S. 1977. *Sentence production: developments in research and theory.* Hillsdale, N.J.: Lawrence Erlbaum Associates.

ROSS, J. R. 1967. Constraints on variables in syntax. Ph.D. dissertation, Massachusetts Institute of Technology.

————. 1969. A proposed rule of tree-pruning. In D. Riebel and S. Schene, eds., *Modern studies in English: readings in transformational grammar.* Englewood Cliffs, N.J.: Prentice-Hall, pp. 288–299.

————. 1970. Gapping and the order of constituents. In M. Bierwisch and K. Heidolph, eds., *Progress in linguistics.* The Hague: Mouton.

ROSS, J. R., and W. E. COOPER. 1979. *Like* syntax. In W. E. Cooper and E. C. T. Walker, eds., *Sentence processing: psycholinguistic studies presented to Merrill Garrett.* Hillsdale, N.J.: Lawrence Erlbaum Associates, pp. 343–418.

ROTENBERG, J. 1975. French liaison, phrase structure, and semicyclical rules. Unpublished manuscript, Massachusetts Institute of Technology.

SAG, I. 1976. Deletion and logical form. Ph.D. dissertation, Massachusetts Institute of Technology.

SAMPSON, G. 1972. A proposal for constraining deletion. *Lingua* 29:23–29.

SCHERER, K. R., H. London, and J. J. Wolf. 1973. The voice of confidence:

paralinguistic cues and audience evaluation. *Journal of Research in Personality* 7:31–44.

SCHLESINGER, I. M. 1977. *Production and comprehension of utterances.* Hillsdale, N.J.: Lawrence Erlbaum Associates.

SCHOLES, R. J. 1971. *Acoustic cues for constituent structure.* The Hague: Mouton.

SELKIRK, E. O. 1972. The phrase phonology of English and French. Ph.D. dissertation, Massachusetts Institute of Technology.

———. 1974. French liaison and the X̄ notation. *Linguistic Inquiry* 5:573–590.

SHATTUCK-HUFNAGEL, S. 1979. Sentence production: a model based on speech errors patterns. In W. E. Cooper and E. C. T. Walker, eds., *Sentence processing: psycholinguistic studies presented to Merrill Garrett.* Hillsdale, N.J.: Lawrence Erlbaum Associates, pp. 295–342.

SMITH, B. L. 1978. Temporal aspects of English speech production: a developmental perspective. *Journal of Phonetics* 6:37–67.

SORENSEN, J. M., and W. E. COOPER. 1980. Syntactic coding of fundamental frequency in speech production. In R. A. Cole, ed., *Perception and production of fluent speech.* Hillsdale, N.J.: Lawrence Erlbaum Associates, pp. 399–440.

SORENSEN, J. M., W. E. COOPER, and J. M. PACCIA. 1978. Speech timing of grammatical categories. *Cognition* 6:135–153.

SPARKS, R., N. HELM, and M. ALBERT. 1974. Aphasia rehabilitation resulting from melodic intonation therapy. *Cortex* 10:303–316.

SPARKS, R. W., and A. L. HOLLAND. 1976. Method: Melodic intonation therapy for aphasia. *Journal of Speech and Hearing Disorders* 41:287–297.

STANLEY, R. 1969. The phonology of the Navaho verb. Ph.D. dissertation, Massachusetts Institute of Technology.

———. 1973. Boundaries in phonology. In S. R. Anderson and P. Kiparsky, eds., *A Festschrift for Morris Halle.* New York: Holt, Rinehart and Winston.

STELMACH, G. E., ed. 1976. *Motor control: issues and trends.* New York: Academic Press.

STERNBERG, S., S. MONSELL, R. L. KNOLL, and C. E. WRIGHT. 1978. The latency and duration of rapid movement sequences: Comparisons of speech and typewriting. In G. Stelmach, ed., *Information processing in motor control and learning.* New York: Academic Press, pp. 117–152.

STILLINGS, J. T. 1975. The formulation of gapping in English as evidence for variable types in syntactic transformations. *Linguistic Analysis* 1:247–273.

STOCKWELL, R. P. 1972. The role of intonation: reconsiderations and other considerations. In D. Bolinger, ed., *Intonation.* London: Penguin Books, pp. 87–109.

STRATTON, W. D. 1973. Intonation feedback for the deaf through the tactile senses. Ph.D. dissertation, Massachusetts Institute of Technology.

SUCI, G. J. 1967. The validity of pause as an index of units in language. *Journal of Verbal Learning and Verbal Behavior* 6:26–32.

SUMMERFIELD, A. Q., and M. P. HAGGARD. 1972. Speech rate effects in the perception of voicing. *Speech Synthesis and Perception: Research on Speech Synthesis and Speech Perception in the Department of Psychology,* Cambridge University, 6:1–12.

't HART, J., and A. COHEN. 1973. Intonation by rule: a perceptual quest. *Journal of Phonetics* 1:309–327.

TAVAKOLIAN, S. 1978. The conjoined clause analysis of relative clauses and other structures. In H. Goodluck and L. Solan, eds., *Papers in the structure and development of child language.* University of Massachusetts Occasional Papers, vol. 4.

THOMPSON, S. A. 1968. Relative clauses and conjunctions. *The Ohio State University Working Papers in Linguistics,* 1:80–99.

THORPE, W. H. 1961. *Bird-song.* Cambridge: Cambridge University Press.

TINGLEY, B. M., and G. D. ALLEN. 1975. Development of speech timing control in children. *Child Development* 46:186–194.

TOWNSEND, J. T. 1972. Some results on the identifiability of parallel and serial processes. *British Journal of Mathematical and Statistical Psychology* 25:168–199.

TRAGER, G. L., and H. L. SMITH. 1951. *Outline of English structure.* Studies in Linguistics, no. 3. Norman, Okla.: Battenburg.

UMEDA, N. 1977. Consonant duration in American English. *Journal of the Acoustical Society of America* 61:846–858.

VENDLER, Z. 1968. *Adjectives and Nominalizations.* The Hague: Mouton.

WALES, R., and H. TONER. 1979. Intonation and ambiguity. In W. E. Cooper and E. C. T. Walker, eds., *Sentence processing: psycholinguistic studies presented to Merrill Garrett.* Hillsdale, N.J.: Lawrence Erlbaum Associates, pp. 135–158.

WASOW, T. 1972. Anaphoric relations in English. Ph.D. dissertation, Massachusetts Institute of Technology.

WEBB, R., F. WILLIAMS, and F. MINIFIE. 1967. Effects of verbal decision behavior upon respiration during speech production. *Journal of Verbal Learning and Verbal Behavior* 10:49–56.

WEISMER, G., and D. INGRISANO. 1979. Phrase-level timing patterns in English: effects of emphatic stress location and speaking rate. Unpublished manuscript.

WELFORD, A. T. 1976. *Skilled performance: perceptual and motor skills.* Glenview, Ill.: Scott Foresman and Company.

WILBUR, R. B. 1979. *American Sign Language and Sign Systems.* Baltimore, Md.: University Park Press.

WILLIAMS, C. E., and K. N. STEVENS. 1972. Emotions and speech: some acoustical correlates. *Journal of the Acoustical Society of America* 52:1238–50.

WILLIAMS, E. S. 1975. Small clauses in English. In J. Kimball, ed., *Syntax and semantics,* vol. 4. New York: Academic Press.

WINGFIELD, A. 1975. The intonation-syntax interaction: prosodic features in perceptual processing of sentences. In A. Cohen and S. G. Nooteboom, eds., *Structure and process in speech perception.* New York: Springer-Verlag, pp. 146–156.

WINGFIELD, A., and J. F. KLEIN. 1971. Syntactic structure and acoustic pattern in speech perception. *Perception and Psychophysics* 9:23–25.

WINTER, P., D. PLOOG, and J. LATTA. 1966. Vocal repertoire of the squirrel monkey (*saimiri sciureus*). *Experimental Brain Research* 1:359–384.

WOLF, J. J., and W. A. WOODS. 1976. The HWIM speech understanding system—overview and performance. *Journal of the Acoustical Society of America* 60:S11 (abstract).

YNGVE, V. 1960. A model and a hypothesis for language structure. *Proceedings of the American Philosophical Society* 104:444–466.

ZUE, V. W. and M. LAFERRIERE. 1979. Acoustic study of medial /t,d/ in American English. *Journal of the Acoustical Society of America* 66:1039–1050.

ZURIF, E. B., and S. E. BLUMSTEIN. 1978. Language and the brain. In M. Halle, J. Bresnan, and G. A. Miller, eds., *Linguistic theory and psychological reality*. Cambridge, Mass.: MIT Press, pp. 229–245.

ZURIF, E. B., and A. CARAMAZZA. Psycholinguistic structures in aphasia: studies in syntax and semantics. In H. Whitaker and H. Whitaker, eds., *Studies in neurolinguistics*, vol. 1. New York: Academic Press, pp. 261–292.

ZWICKY, A. M. 1970. Auxiliary reduction in English. *Linguistic Inquiry* 1:323–336.

Index

Abramson, A. S., 218
Acoustic methods: for alveolar flapping, 151–152; for palatalization, 142–143; for speech timing, 19, 20–22
Adjectives, 54, 62–65, 79; ambiguous sentences and, 26, 28; conjoined, 86, 163–164; in foreign languages, 67; processing of, by children, 232–233; speech synthesis and, 223; stress and, 146–147
Adverbial: clauses, 134–135; preposed phrases, 97–99
Adverbs, 54, 62–65; ambiguous sentences and, 29–32; speech perception and, 217
Akmajian, A., 4, 34, 51, 153, 245
Albert, M., 230
Algorithm for determining boundary strength, 180. See also Comprehensive algorithm for prosodic effects
Allen, G. D., 6, 222, 231
Alveolar flapping: speech synthesis and, 223; syntactic boundary strength and, 150–155, 176–177; verb gapping and, 155–157
Ambiguous sentences: fundamental frequency in, 52; perceptual processing of, 214, 216–217, 218; phonological rules in, 159–160; preposing in, 46, 97–99; timing effects in, 26–49, 62
American Sign Language, 225–226
Anderson, J. R., 16
Anderson, S. R., 51
Animal communication, 227–229

Aphasia, 68, 229–231
Atkinson, J. E., 52
Auxiliary reduction, 156, 158

Babbling, 231
Bach, E., 106
Backing rules, 100–105, 126, 201
Bailey, C.-J. N., 149
Baker, C. L., 15, 145, 158, 160
Barnwell, T. P., 118, 129, 131
Bell, A. G., 234
Bellugi, U., 68, 226
Bever, T. G., 4, 17, 69, 215, 218, 222, 242
Bierwisch, M., 6, 138, 182, 190
Birdsong, D., 236
Birdsong. See Animal communication
Bisection, 184–185, 187–189
Blocking: in nonspeech behaviors, 229; of fundamental frequency in perception, 219–220; of phoneme perception, 218–219
Blocking of phonological rules, 15, 128–160, 171, 181, 186–187; alveolar flapping, 150–157, 176–177, 223; dialect differences and, 236; French liaison, 15, 140; speech planning and, 167; speaking rate and, 157, 182, 186, 190; speech synthesis and, 223; stress and, 15, 145–147
Blumstein, S. E., 229
Bolinger, D., 205, 211, 246
Boomer, D. S., 6
Boone, D. R., 234
Boothroyd, A., 234
Borkin, A., 111, 121

Boundary markers, 153, 158, 169
Brame, M. K., 15, 145, 158, 160
Branching depth hypothesis, 138–140, 151, 170–174
Breathing: clause boundaries and, 167. *See also* Pausing, for breath
Bresnan, J. W., 4, 106, 121, 122, 245
Browman, C. P., 53, 54, 224
Brown, R. W., 68, 231
Busnel, R.-G., 228

Calvert, D., 234
Canonical word order, 57, 91, 105, 165. *See also* Root transformations
Capranica, R. R., 228
Caramazza, A., 229
Carlson, R., 224
Carroll, J. M., 164
Carroll, J. S., 236
Catalexis, 226
Cedergren, H. J., 149
Chistovich, L. A., 6
Chomsky, C., 231
Chomsky, N., 3, 4, 8, 13, 15, 16, 17, 25, 49, 57, 65, 106, 107, 109, 115, 117, 120, 125, 132, 135, 140, 153, 159, 169, 179, 243, 245, 249
Chomsky-adjunction, 179
Choppy, C., 224
Clark, E., 199, 208
Clark, H. H., 22, 199, 208, 245
Clauses, 7–12, 23, 167–168; adverbial, 134–135; complement, 71–75, 100–102, 106–117, 120–124, 134–135, 172; conditional, 106, 115, 164–165, 204; fundamental frequency and, 212; indirect question, 38–39; perceptual processing of, 215; relative, 10, 11, 38–39, 81–85, 103–104, 106, 134–135, 204, 232; speech planning and, 201–204, 206
Clay, M. M., 233
Clements, G. W., 236
Click detection studies, 115, 215–216, 222
Cohen, A., 211, 224
Coker, C. H., 53, 54, 224
Cole, R. A., 149, 215, 216, 218
Collapsing convention, 175–178
Collins, M., 94, 96, 152
Combination convention, 175–178
Communications engineering: speech

recognition, 18, 224–225; speech synthesis, 18, 19, 53, 62, 210, 211, 222–224. *See also* Comprehensive algorithm for prosodic effects
Complement clauses, 71–75, 100–102, 106–117, 120–124, 134–135, 172
Comprehensive algorithm for prosodic effects, 182–193, 200
Conditional clauses, 106, 115, 164–165, 204
Conjunctions, 54, 86, 163–164, 171; deletion of, 12, 163–164, 225
Consonant clusters, 147–149, 208
Constituent-final lengthening, 7–12, 26, 60, 99, 126–127; ambiguous sentences and, 26–49, 62; in foreign languages, 236; as a perceptual cue, 80, 163, 200, 213–221; in spontaneous speech, 23. *See also* Phrase-final lengthening; Utterance-final lengthening
Constituent length, 182, 186, 207–208; fundamental frequency and, 205–206; pausing and, 6, 94–97, 189–190, 201–203; reaction time and, 227; segmental lengthening and, 189–190, 201–203; speaking rate and, 188; speech planning and, 190, 201–204, 227
Constituent type. *See* Phrase type
Content words. *See* Major grammatical category words
Controversial nodes, 178–180
Cooper, G. W., 226
Cooper, W. E., 5, 7, 21, 28, 47, 48, 49, 52, 80, 84, 90, 91, 96, 97, 109, 115, 149, 158, 166, 167, 175, 178, 179, 181, 191, 199, 200, 205, 206, 211, 212, 213, 214, 216, 218, 220, 229, 230, 231, 236, 242, 243, 245, 247
Cross-word phonetic conditioning effects. *See* Phonological rules
Cumulative phrase-final lengthening, 27, 46–47, 49–50, 194–197, 201
Cutler, A., 215

Dale, P. S., 231
Danly, M., 159, 167, 175, 178, 179, 181, 191, 229, 230, 232
DeVilliers, J. G., 229, 230
Deafness. *See* Hearing impairment
Decker, M., 234
Delattre, P., 118

Deletion transformations, 17, 69–89, 141–145, 215; auxiliary reduction and, 156; conjunction deletion, 12, 163–164, 225; direct object deletion, 57–62; fundamental frequency and, 212; noun phrase deletion, 17, 64, 110; object deletion, 57–62; phonological rule application and, 155–158; relative clause reduction, 83–85; subject deletion, 80–81; "to be" deletion, 110–112, 121; whiz deletion, 82–83. *See also* Gapping

Deschamps, A., 7

Determiner, 54

Development of speech, 231–233

Dialect differences, 236

Disambiguation, 43, 46, 52, 97–99

Domains of processing, 23, 46–47, 128–129, 150, 168; in aphasia, 229–230; deletions and, 145; fundamental frequency and, 211–212; in music, 226; in perception, 218–219; phonological rule application and, 14–15, 157–158; speaking rate and, 190

Dominance relations. *See* Hierarchical coding

Doodeman, J. N., 213

Dougherty, R., 13, 17

Downing, B. T., 11, 172, 241

Egido, C., 67

Eguchi, S., 231

Emonds, J. E., 11, 12, 46, 51, 91, 100, 102, 103, 131, 132, 241

Equi-NP deletion, 110

Erasure principle, 169

Errors in spontaneous speech, 18, 68, 124–126, 168

Extraposition from noun phrase, 103–105

Fay, D., 18, 124, 125, 126

Flanking nodes, 171, 174–175

Fodor, J. A., 4, 17, 69, 115, 215, 218, 222

Fodor, J. D., 16, 115, 163

Folkins, J. W., 188

Fonagy, I., 188, 202

Ford, M., 163, 206, 207

Foreign languages, 66–67, 205, 224, 236

Forner, L. L., 234

Forster, K. I., 198

Foss, D. J., 215

Fowler, C. A., 6

Francis, W. N., 147

Fraser, J. B., 51

Free deletions, 70, 81–86

French liaison, 15, 140

Frequency of word usage: palatalization and, 147–149

Fromkin, V. A., 18

Fronting rules. *See* Preposing

Frozen word order, 226–227, 236–237

Fry, D. B., 53

Fujisaki, H., 236

Function words. *See* Minor grammatical category words

Functional completeness, 164–165

Fundamental frequency, 5, 158, 180–181, 199, 211–213; in ambiguous sentences, 52; in aphasia, 229–230; constituent length and, 205–206; declination of, 205–206, 211–212, 223, 230; fall-rise patterns, 212; functional completeness and, 164; in hearing-impaired speech, 234; perceptual processing of, 5, 204, 219–220; preposing and, 96–97; resetting, 190, 211–212; segmental lengthening and, 166, 200; speech planning and, 204–206; speech recognition by machine and, 224–225; speech synthesis and, 223; stress and, 5, 53; topline rule, 212, 230

Ganong, W. F., 249

Gapping, 85–89; noun gapping, 70–71, 75–80, 87, 89; verb gapping, 13, 70–75, 87, 89, 141–145, 155–157, 215

Garrett, M. F., 4, 17, 18, 68, 69, 115, 126, 168, 215, 218, 222

Geers, A. E., 221

Genay, J., 190

Geschwind, N., 230

Glottal stop insertion, 223

Gold, B., 232

Goldman-Eisler, F., 6, 7, 162, 167, 188

Goodglass, H., 68, 230

Grammatical categories, 53–68, 169, 178, 181, 184, 189

Grammatical rules, 106. *See also* Phrase structure rules; Transformational rules

Grass, R., 242
Gregory, J., 235
Grimes, C., 205
Grinder, J., 57
Grosjean, F., 6, 7, 94, 96, 152, 182, 184, 185, 189, 225, 226
Grosjean, L., 6, 182

Haggard, M. P., 218
Hall-Craggs, J., 228, 249
Halle, M., 8, 65, 153, 169, 243
Hamby, S., 230
Hankamer, J., 70, 71, 81, 84, 112, 244
Harnett, D. L., 22
Harris, M. S., 246
Haycock, G. S., 234
Hearing impairment: American Sign Language, 225–226; lipreading, 221–222; speech abnormalities and, 234; speech training and, 233–235
Heavy NP shift, 132–133
Helm, N., 230
Henderson, A., 167
Heny, F., 4, 34, 51, 153
Hierarchical coding, 24–49, 124, 167, 168; left-to-right processing and, 3, 24, 198–199; top-down processing and, 3, 24, 46–47, 194–198
Hirsh, I. J., 231
Hixon, T. J., 234
Holmes, V. M., 206, 207
Hood, R. B., 234
Houde, R. A., 234
House, A., 118
Howarth, J. N., 234
Hudgins, C. V., 234
Hudson, R. A., 13
Huggins, A. W. F., 20, 129, 131, 136, 143, 152, 213, 214, 235
Hunt, J., 68
Hurtig, T. G., 215
Hyman, L. M., 145

Idea formation, 2–3, 23, 162–163, 213
Indirect questions, 38–39
Identity deletions, 70–81, 85–86. *See also* Gapping
Imitation paradigm, 231–232
Imlach, R. H., 233
Inclusion constraint, 109
Infinitival complements, 107–110, 112–117, 120–124

Information flow models. *See* Models of speech information flow
Information load, 68; deletion transformations and, 88; grammatical category and, 64–65; lexical class and, 54; word duration and, 54; word frequency and, 147–149. *See also* Memory load; Processing load
Ingrisano, D., 188, 241
Insect chirps, 228
Inherent phonetic segment duration, 67–68, 191
Intensity, 53. *See also* Stress
Intonation. *See* Fundamental frequency
Isochrony, 88–89, 214

Jackendoff, R. S., 3, 13, 15, 16, 17, 25, 29, 51, 70, 71, 131, 226, 245
Jakimik, J., 149, 216, 218
John, J. E. J., 234

Katz, J. J., 163
Kent, R. D., 231
Keyser, S. J., 49, 50, 51
King, H. V., 15, 156, 158
Klatt, D. H., 6, 7, 18, 89, 136, 166, 191, 213, 214, 220, 223, 224
Klein, J. F., 222
Klima, E. S., 226
Kloker, D., 7, 18, 22, 136
Kolodziej, B., 190
Koutsoudas, A., 13
Kooij, J. G., 46
Kozhevnikov, V. A., 6
Kučera, H., 147
Kuno, S., 71, 242

Labov, W., 149
Lackner, J. R., 115
Laferriere, M., 152
Lakoff, G., 16, 158, 159, 160
Lane, H., 6, 182, 225
Langacker, R. W., 90, 91, 100
Langendoen, D. T., 8, 10
Lapointe, S. G., 28, 47, 242
Lasnik, H. 39
Latta, J., 228
Laver, J. D. M., 6
Lea, W. A., 224, 225
Left-branching structures, 26, 28, 47, 64
Left dislocation, 11, 91, 94–97

Left-to-right syntactic processing, 3, 24, 198–199

Lehiste, I., 1, 5, 6, 26, 52, 89, 118, 131, 214, 218

Lemon, R. E., 249

Lerdahl, F., 226

Levelt, W. J. M., 52

Lexical access, 163, 164

Lexical insertion, 3, 68

Liberman, M. Y., 19, 46, 205

Lieberman, P., 7, 8, 46, 94

Lightfoot, M. J., 54

Lilly, J. C., 228

Lindblom, B., 7, 19, 129, 224, 226, 236

Linear additivity, 195, 197

Linear coding, 47–48

Ling, D., 234

Lipreading, 221–222

Lisker, L., 218

Logical attributes, 163, 165

Lounsbury, F. G., 87

Lyberg, B., 166

McAllister, R., 205

McCawley, J. D., 16

MacClay, H., 6, 87

McNeill, D., 5, 207, 208

Maeda, S., 205

Magdics, K., 188, 202

Major grammatical category words, 53–54, 67–68; bisection principle and, 184, 189; boundary markers and, 169; syntactic boundary strength and, 181

Marcus, M. P., 222–223

Marler, P., 249

Marslen-Wilson, W. D., 215, 218

Martin, J. E., 6, 86, 190

Martin, J. G., 6, 7

Matthei, E. M., 232

Mattingly, I. G., 223

Melodic intonation therapy, 230

Meltzer, R. H., 219

Memory load, 207. *See also* Information load; Processing load

Method of one-sided variation, 166, 200–203, 208

Meyer, L. B., 226

Miller, C. J., 188

Minifie, F., 167, 188

Minor grammatical category words, 53–54, 65–66, 68, 181

Mispronunciations: perception of, 149, 215–216. *See also* Errors in spontaneous speech

Models of speech information flow, 2–6, 9, 161–167, 194. *See also* Comprehensive algorithm for prosodic effects

Morphological boundaries, 153

Motor program of articulation, 5

Movement transformations, 46, 132–133; backing rules, 100–105, 126, 201; passive transformation, 91, 106, 109, 164; raising, 105–124, 201. *See also* Preposing; WH fronting

Music, 226–227

Napoli, D. J., 236

Nash, R., 52

Negation, 163–164; scope of, 39–43

Nelson, K., 249

Nespor, M., 236

Nickerson, R. S., 234

Node height principle, 47, 170–174

Node type. *See* Phrase type

Nonflanking nodes, 171, 174–175

Nooteboom, S. G., 213

Nottebohm, F., 227, 228

Noun gapping, 70–71, 75–80, 87, 89

Noun phrases: controversial NP nodes, 179–180; deletion of, 17, 64, 110; duplication of, in speech errors, 125; modifying relations involving, 26, 34–39; movement transformations involving, 100–102, 103–105; processing of, 50, 167–168, 203–204

Nouns, 53–59, 65

Numbers, F. C., 234

Object deletion, 57–62

Ohala, J. J., 6

Olive, J. P., 52, 214, 218

Oller, D. K., 231

Omura, R., 236

Osberger, M. J., 234, 235

Osgood, C. E., 6, 87

O'Shaughnessy, D., 46, 52, 205

Oshika, B. T., 137

Ouweneel, G. R. E., 52

Paccia, J. M., 21, 28, 47, 242

Paccia-Cooper, J., 49

Palatalization, 128, 137, 140–141; acoustic analysis of, 142–143; non-

syntactic influences on, 145–149;
perceptual judgment of, 142; verb
gapping and, 141–145
Paragraph contexts for ambiguous
sentences, 43–45, 217
Parallel processing, 166, 194–197
Paraphasia, 230
Parentheticals, 11, 223–224
Parser: in speech synthesis, 222–223
Passive transformation, 91, 106, 109,
164
Pausing: acoustic analysis of, 19,
20–22; algorithm for, 182–193; in
ambiguous sentences, 26–49; in
American Sign Language, 225; for
breath, 94, 96, 152; conjoined adjectives and, 12, 86; conjoined clauses
and, 11, 174; constituent length
and, 6, 94–97, 189–190, 201–203;
deletion transformations and,
12–14, 71–80; dialect differences
and, 236; in hearing-impaired
speech, 234, 235; hesitation,
162–163; as a perceptual cue, 88,
163, 200, 213–221; perceptual judgments of, 7–14; speaking rate and,
6, 144, 182, 186, 188, 190; speech
processing and, 199–204; in spontaneous speech, 87; in typewriting,
227; verbal learning and, 220–221
Payne, J. W., 236
Perception, 8, 52, 149, 210, 213–221
Perceptual segmentation, 100, 105,
127, 164; in lipreading, 222
Peterson, G. E., 118
Phoneme monitoring, 215
Phonemes: perception of, 218–219
Phonemic reduction, 65–66, 128, 156,
158–160
Phonetic conditioning effects. *See* Phonetic influences on segment duration; Phonological rules
Phonetic influences on segment duration, 117–120
Phonological rule blocking. *See* Block-
ing of phonological rules
Phonological rules, 14–15; alveolar
flapping, 150–157, 176–177, 223;
French liaison, 15, 140; palatalization, 128, 137, 140–149; phonemic
reduction, 65–66, 128, 156, 158–160;
speech recognition by machine and,

225; trochaic shortening, 129–140,
171, 181, 201
Phrase-final lengthening, 54, 56–59,
60–65, 90; in ambiguous sentences,
26–49, 62; in animal communication, 227–229; blocking of trochaic
shortening and, 136–137; in children's speech, 231–233; in frozen
conjuncts, 236–237; grammatical
category type and, 66–68; cf. music,
226–227; noun gapping and, 79–80;
as a perceptual cue, 88, 163, 200,
213–221; phrase type and, 136–137;
reading ability and, 233; speech
processing and, 199–204; speech
synthesis and, 223; in spontaneous
speech, 136
Phrase structure rules, 3, 24–25, 53,
138, 194
Phrase type, 136–137, 153–158, 178,
204
Pierrehumbert, J., 219
Pinker, S., 236
Pitch, 5, 204, 219–220
Planning speech, 6, 68, 100, 124, 127,
166; cf. American Sign Language,
225–226; in aphasia, 229; clauses
versus phrases, 203–204; constituent length and, 190, 201–204, 227;
fundamental frequency and,
204–206; left-to-right processing,
198–199; method of one-sided
variation, 200–203; phonological
rule application and, 167; in spontaneous speech, 206–208; top-down
processing, 194–197; cf. typewriting, 227
Ploog, D., 228
Pollack, D., 234
Posner, M. I., 163
Postal, P. M., 48, 49, 50, 51, 106, 108,
109, 117, 244, 245
Postposing. *See* Backing rules
Prefabricated routines in spontaneous
speech, 209
Preposing, 11–12, 90–100, 124, 127;
ambiguous sentences and, 46,
97–99; clause, 134–135; constituent
length and, 203; fundamental frequency and, 96–97; heavy NP shift,
132–133; prepositional phrase,
91–99, 132–133; speech planning
and, 201; vocative, 97–99

Prepositional phrase preposing, 91–99, 132–133
Prepositions: speech perception and, 217
Processing load, 198. *See also* Information load; Memory load
Pronouns: stress and, 146–147
Propositions: speech planning and, 207
Proximity index, 184–185, 188

Questions: indirect, 38–39; WH, 126, 159–160

Raising, 105–124; speech planning and, 201
Rapp, K., 7, 19, 224, 236
Reaction time, 206–207, 215–218, 227
Reading ability, 233
Reading machine for the blind, 222
Recursive structures: processing of by children, 232–233
Reddy, D. R., 224
Reis, M., 81, 112, 244
Relative clauses, 10, 38–39, 106, 179; nonrestrictive, 11; processing of by children, 232; restrictive, 134–135; speech planning and, 204; transformations involving, 81–85, 103–104
Rewrite rules. *See* Phrase structure rules
Right dislocation, 12, 100–102
Robinson, J. J., 138, 149, 182
Roeper, T., 231
Root transformations, 11, 12, 91–99, 100–103, 126, 132–133
Rosenbaum, P. S., 102, 106, 107, 108, 117, 244, 245
Rosenberg, S., 208
Ross, J. R., 12, 13, 16, 51, 52, 70, 71, 81, 82, 91, 100, 102, 112, 125, 132, 236, 244
Rotenberg, J., 15, 236

Sag, I., 70, 71
Sampson, G., 57, 70
Sankoff, D., 149
Scherer, K. R., 236
Schlesinger, I. M., 208
Scholes, R. J., 52, 54
Scope of negation, 39–43
Segmental lengthening: acoustic analysis of, 19, 20–22; algorithm for,

182–193; in ambiguous sentences, 26–49, 62; cf. American Sign Language, 225; in aphasia, 229–230; constituent length and, 94–97, 189–190, 201–203; dialect differences and, 236; fundamental frequency and, 200; in hearing-impaired speech, 234; information load and, 54; as a perceptual cue, 88, 163, 200, 213–221; phonetic environment and, 117–120; speaking rate and, 6, 157, 182, 186, 188, 190; stress and, 53
Selkirk, E. O., 15, 129, 140, 158, 169, 236, 246, 247
Semantics, 16–17, 48–49, 69, 123, 163–165
Serial processing, 166, 194–197
Shattuck-Hufnagel, S., 18, 126
Short-term memory, 199, 207
Shuy, R. W., 149
Silverman, R., 234
Skarbek, A., 167
Smith, B. L., 7, 231, 232
Social-personal influences on prosody, 235–236
Sorensen, J. M., 5, 21, 80, 96, 97, 158, 166, 199, 200, 205, 206, 211, 212, 220, 243, 247
Sparks, R. W., 230
Speaking rate: constituent length and, 188; domains of processing and, 190; in hearing-impaired speech, 234; perception of, 218–219; perceptual blocking and, 218–219, 220; phonological rule application and, 157, 182, 186, 190; speech timing and, 6, 144, 157, 182, 186, 188, 190
Speech recognition by machine, 18, 224–225
Speech shadowing, 215–216
Speech synthesis, 18, 19, 53, 62, 210, 211, 222–224. *See also* Comprehensive algorithm for prosodic effects
Spontaneous speech, 5, 18, 136; fundamental frequency declination, 205, 206; cf. practiced reading, 22–23, 43; processing in, 206–208, 209
Stanley, R., 129, 153
Stelmach, G. E., 227
Sternberg, S., 227
Stevens, K. N., 96, 236

Stillings, J. T., 13, 71
Stockwell, R. P., 241
Stratton, W. D., 234
Streeter, L., 19, 52, 214, 218
Stress, 4, 6, 13, 19, 80, 164; acoustic components of, 5; fundamental frequency and, 5, 53; grammatical category and, 53, 146–147; isochrony, 88–89, 214; phonological rule application and, 15, 145–147; preposing and, 96–97; segmental duration and, 53; speaking rate and, 188; speech synthesis and, 224. *See also* Trochaic shortening
Strict subcategorization, 135
Structure-preserving transformations, 91, 102–104, 106, 109, 164
Subject deletion, 80–81
Suci, G. J., 220
Summerfield, A. Q., 218
Syntactic boundary strength, 169, 170–174, 182–184; algorithm for calculating, 180; alveolar flapping and, 150–155, 176–177; in American Sign Language, 225–226; dialect differences and, 236; fundamental frequency and, 212; phrase type and, 153–158; speaking rate and, 157; trochaic shortening and, 138–140
Syntactic boundary strength metric, 167, 168–182; algorithm, 180; branching depth, 170–174; controversial nodes, 178–180; flanking nodes, 171, 174–175; left vs. right phrases, 175–178, 180, 207; node height, 170–174; node type, 178; nonflanking nodes, 171, 174–175; starting point nodes, 169–170
Syntactic deep structure. *See* Underlying level of syntactic representation

Tanenhaus, M. K., 164
Tavakolian, S., 232
Telegraphic speech, 68
Tensed-S condition, 109–110, 112–117, 120–121
't Hart, J., 211, 224
Thompson, S. A., 11
Thorpe, W. H., 227
Tingley, B. M., 231
"To be" deletion, 110–112, 121
Toner, H., 52

Top-down syntactic processing, 3, 24, 46–47, 194–198; speech recognition by machine and, 225
Topicalization, 91–97
Topline rule, 212, 230
Townsend, J. T., 194, 218, 248
Trager, G. L., 7
Transformational rules, 4, 11–14, 25, 69. *See also* Deletion transformations; Movement transformations
Transitional accessibility hypothesis, 87–88
Tree-pruning convention, 81–85, 112
Trochaic feet, 226
Trochaic shortening, 129–140, 171, 181, 201
Typewriting, 227

Umeda, N., 53, 54, 147, 224, 246
Underlying level of syntactic representation, 14, 50–52, 153, 165–166, 207
Utterance-final lengthening: in babbling, 231; speech processing and, 199

Vendler, Z., 86
Verbs, 53–62, 121–124
Verb gapping, 13, 70–75, 87, 89; alveolar flapping and, 155–157; palatalization and, 141–145; perception and, 215
Verb phrases, 49–50, 167–168; modifying relations involving, 29–32, 34–39
Verbal learning: individual differences in, 220–221
Vocal fold vibration, 5
Vocatives, 32–34, 51–52, 97–99
Vowel length: palatalization and, 147–149

Wales, R., 52
Wasow, T., 70, 83
Webb, R., 167
Weismer, G., 188, 241
Welford, A. T., 227
Welsh, A., 218
Wilbur, R. B., 226
WH fronting, 125–126, 158–160
WH questions, 126, 159–160